CREATED BY **JOSS WHEDON**

EREMY **LAMBERT** MIRKA **ANDOLFO** CARMELO **ZAGARIA** VALENTINA **PINTI** SIYA **OUM**

Buffy the Vampire Slayer™

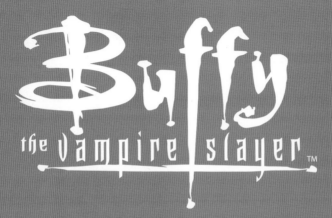

VOLUME EIGHT

A RAINBOW UPON HER HEAD

Published by
BOOM! STUDIOS

Series Designers
Madison Goyette
& Grace Park

Collection Designer
Chelsea Roberts

Assistant Editor
Gavin Gronenthal

Editor
Elizabeth Brei

Special Thanks to **Sierra Hahn**, **Jonathan Manning**,
Becca J. Sadowski, & **Nicole Spiegel**.

Ross Richie Chairman & Founder
Joy Huffman CFO
Matt Gagnon Editor-in-Chief
Filip Sablik President, Publishing & Marketing
Stephen Christy President, Development
Lance Kreiter Vice President, Licensing & Merchandising
Bryce Carlson Vice President, Editorial & Creative Strategy
Kate Henning Director, Operations
Elyse Strandberg Manager, Finance
Michelle Ankley Manager, Production Design
Sierra Hahn Executive Editor
Dafna Pleban Senior Editor
Shannon Watters Senior Editor
Eric Harburn Senior Editor
Elizabeth Brei Editor
Kathleen Wisneski Editor
Sophie Philips-Roberts Editor
Jonathan Manning Associate Editor
Allyson Gronowitz Associate Editor
Gavin Gronenthal Assistant Editor
Gwen Waller Assistant Editor
Ramiro Portnoy Assistant Editor

Kenzie Rzonca Assistant Editor
Rey Netschke Editorial Assistant
Marie Krupina Design Lead
Grace Park Design Coordinator
Chelsea Roberts Design Coordinator
Madison Goyette Production Designer
Crystal White Production Designer
Samantha Knapp Production Design Assistant
Esther Kim Marketing Lead
Breanna Sarpy Marketing Lead, Digital
Amanda Lawson Marketing Coordinator
Grecia Martinez Marketing Assistant, Digital
José Meza Consumer Sales Lead
Ashley Troub Consumer Sales Coordinator
Morgan Perry Retail Sales Lead
Harley Salbacka Sales Coordinator
Megan Christopher Operations Coordinator
Rodrigo Hernandez Operations Coordinator
Zipporah Smith Operations Coordinator
Jason Lee Senior Accountant
Sabrina Lesin Accounting Assistant
Lauren Alexander Administrative Assistant

BOOM! STUDIOS | **20th TELEVISION**

BUFFY THE VAMPIRE SLAYER Volume Eight, January 2022.
Published by BOOM! Studios, a division of Boom Entertainment,
Inc. © 2022 20th Television. Originally published in single magazine
form as BUFFY THE VAMPIRE SLAYER No. 27-28, BUFFY THE
VAMPIRE SLAYER: TEA TIME No. 1. © 2021 20th Television.
BOOM! Studios™ and the BOOM! Studios logo are trademarks of
Boom Entertainment, Inc., registered in various countries and categories.
All characters, events, and institutions depicted herein are fictional. Any
similarity between any of the names, characters, persons, events, and/or
institutions in this publication to actual names, characters, and persons,
whether living or dead, events, and/or institutions is unintended and
purely coincidental. BOOM! Studios does not read or accept unsolicited
submissions of ideas, stories, or artwork.

BOOM! Studios, 5670 Wilshire Boulevard, Suite 400, Los Angeles,
CA 90036-5679. Printed in China. First Printing.

ISBN: 978-1-68415-820-1, eISBN: 978-1-64668-453-3

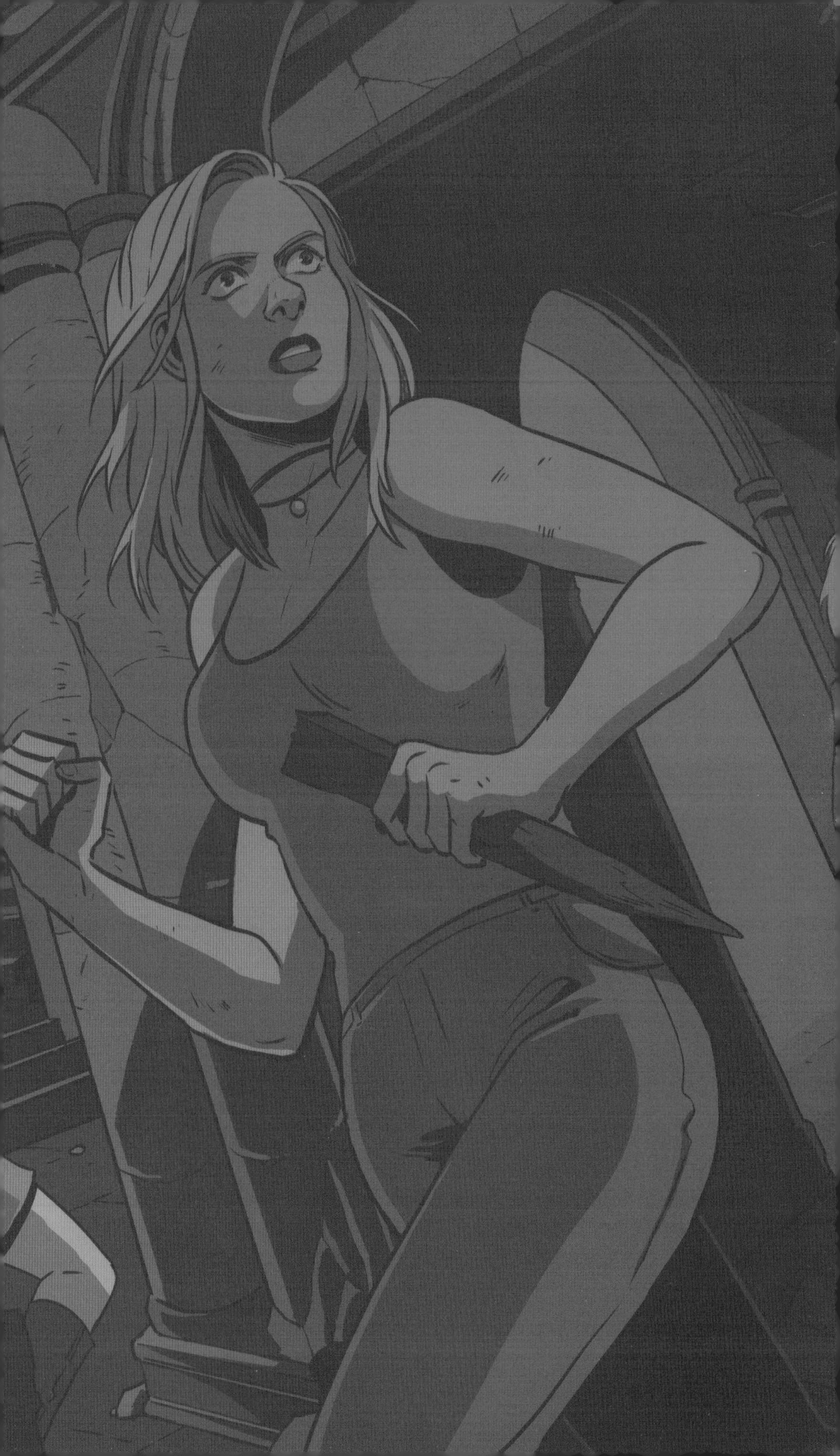

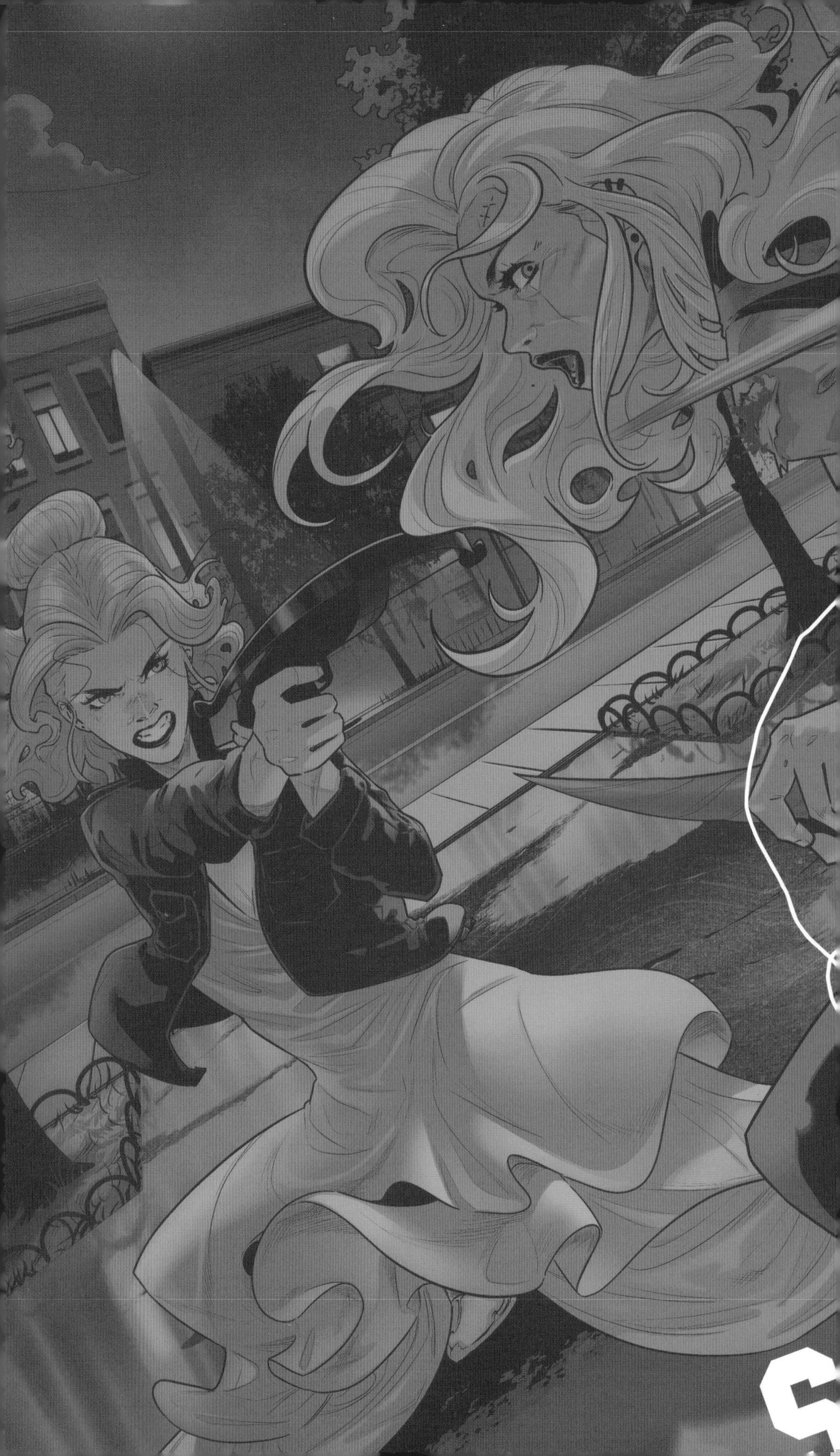

Created by
Joss Whedon

Written by
Jeremy Lambert

Illustrated by
Carmelo Zagaria (Chapter 27)
Valentina Pinti (Chapter 28)

Colored by
Raúl Angulo

INTERLUDE: TEA TIME

Written by
Mirka Andolfo

Illustrated by
Siya Oum
with inks by **Giuseppe Cafaro,
Francesca Follini, & Dario Formisani**

Colored by
Eleonora Bruni

Lettered by
Ed Dukeshire

Cover by
Frany

CHAPTER TWENTY-SEVEN

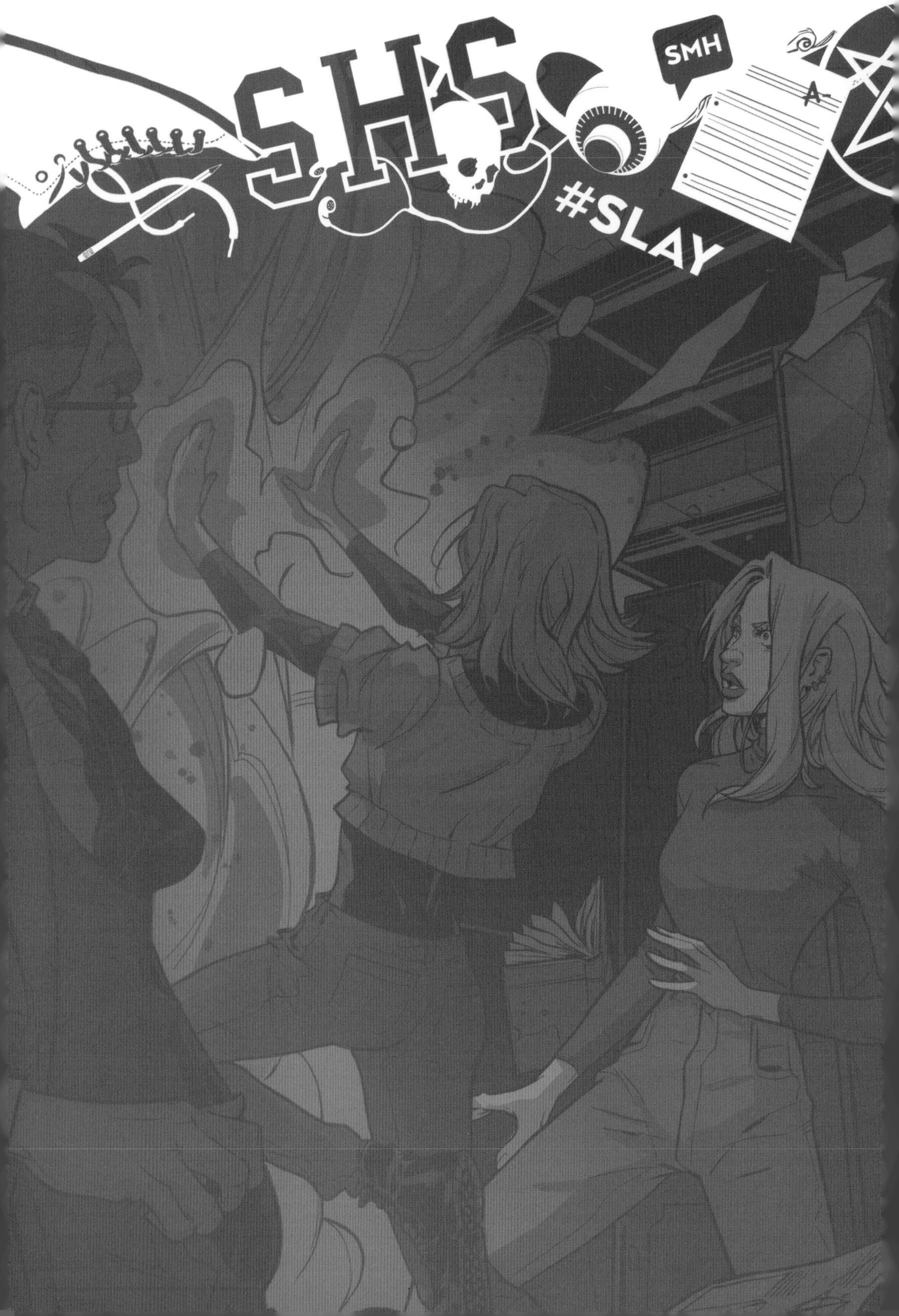

S.H.S.
SMH
#SLAY

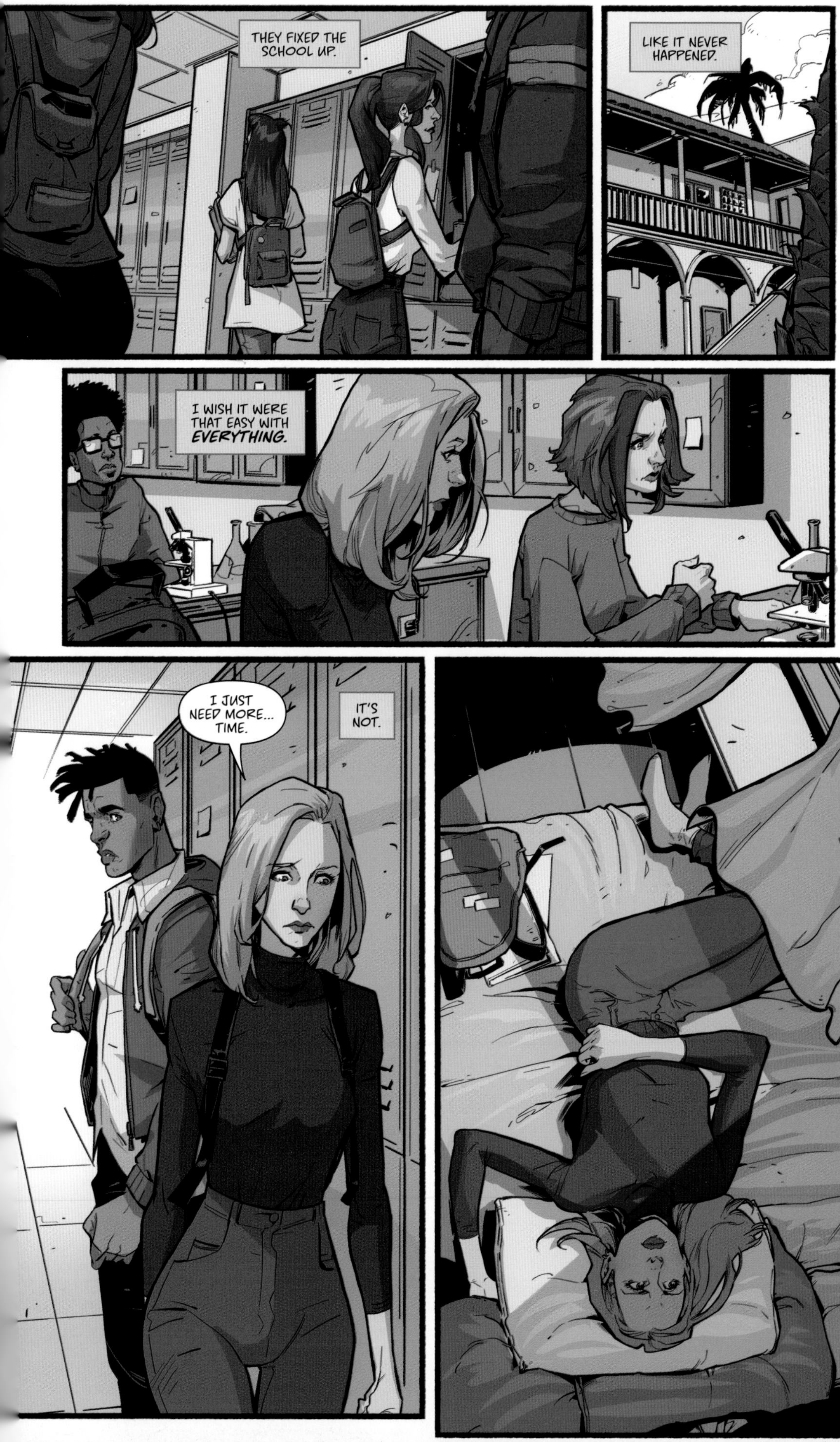
THEY FIXED THE SCHOOL UP.
LIKE IT NEVER HAPPENED.
I WISH IT WERE THAT EASY WITH ***EVERYTHING.***
I JUST NEED MORE... TIME.
IT'S NOT.

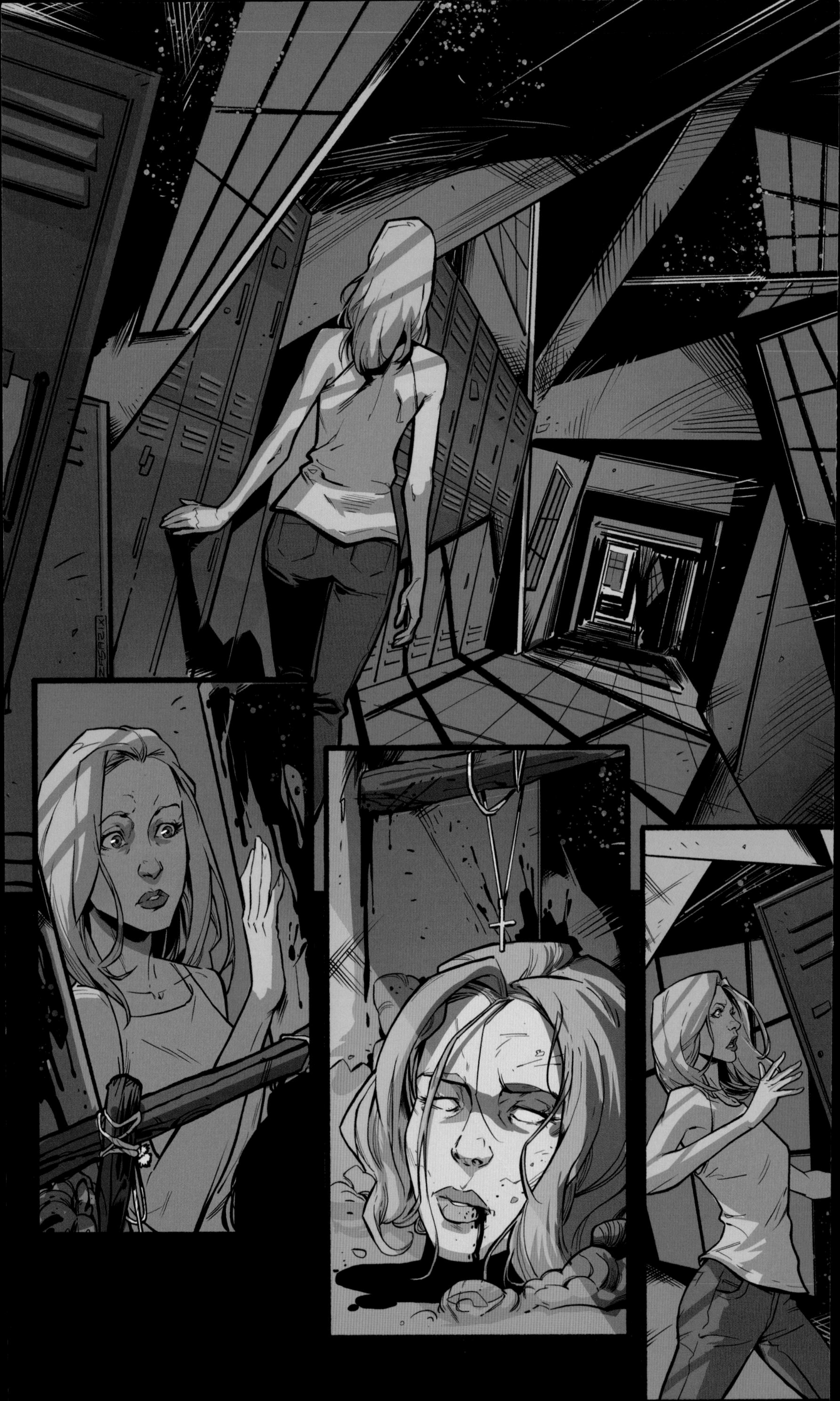

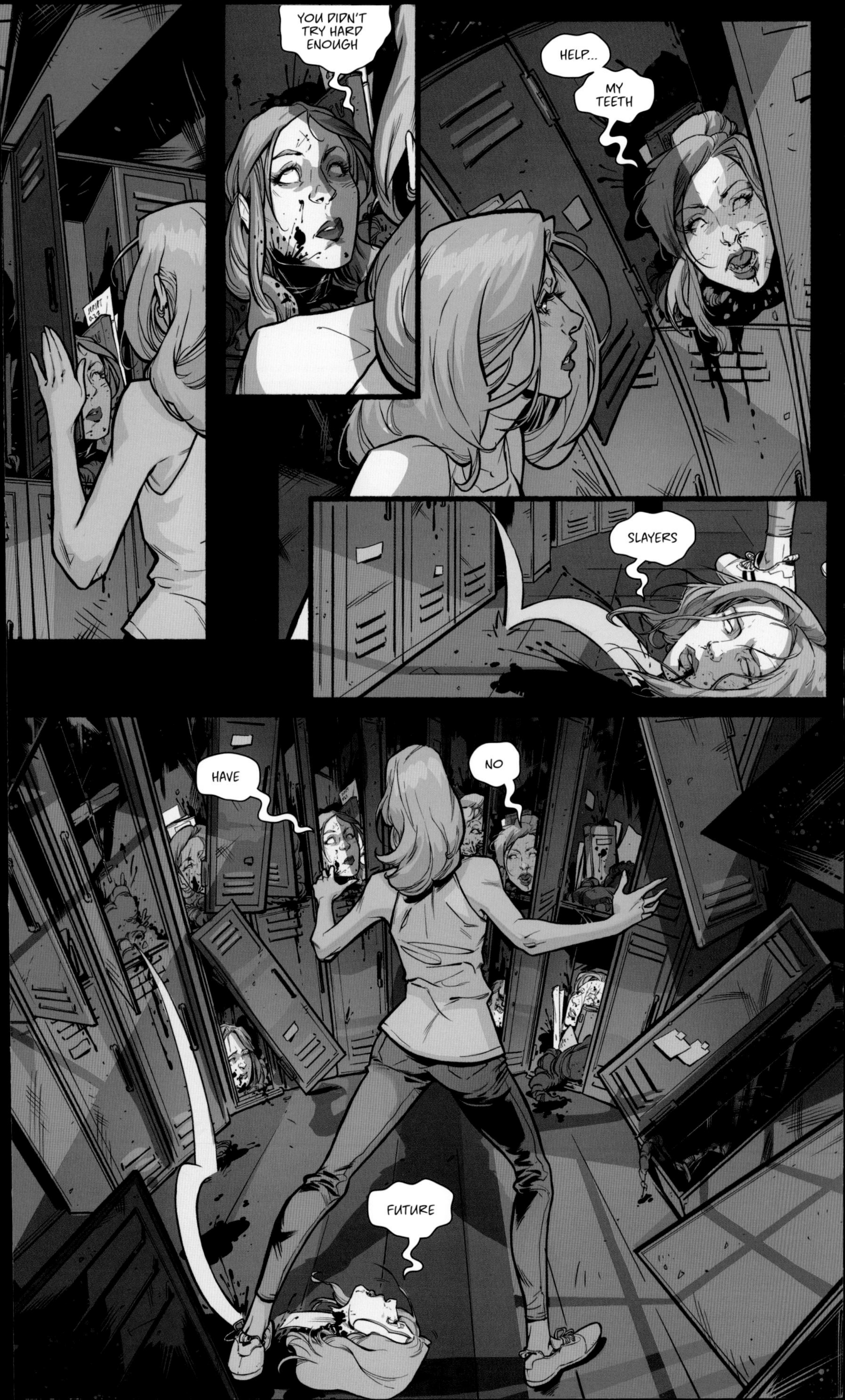
YOU DIDN'T TRY HARD ENOUGH
HELP...
MY TEETH
SLAYERS
HAVE
NO
FUTURE

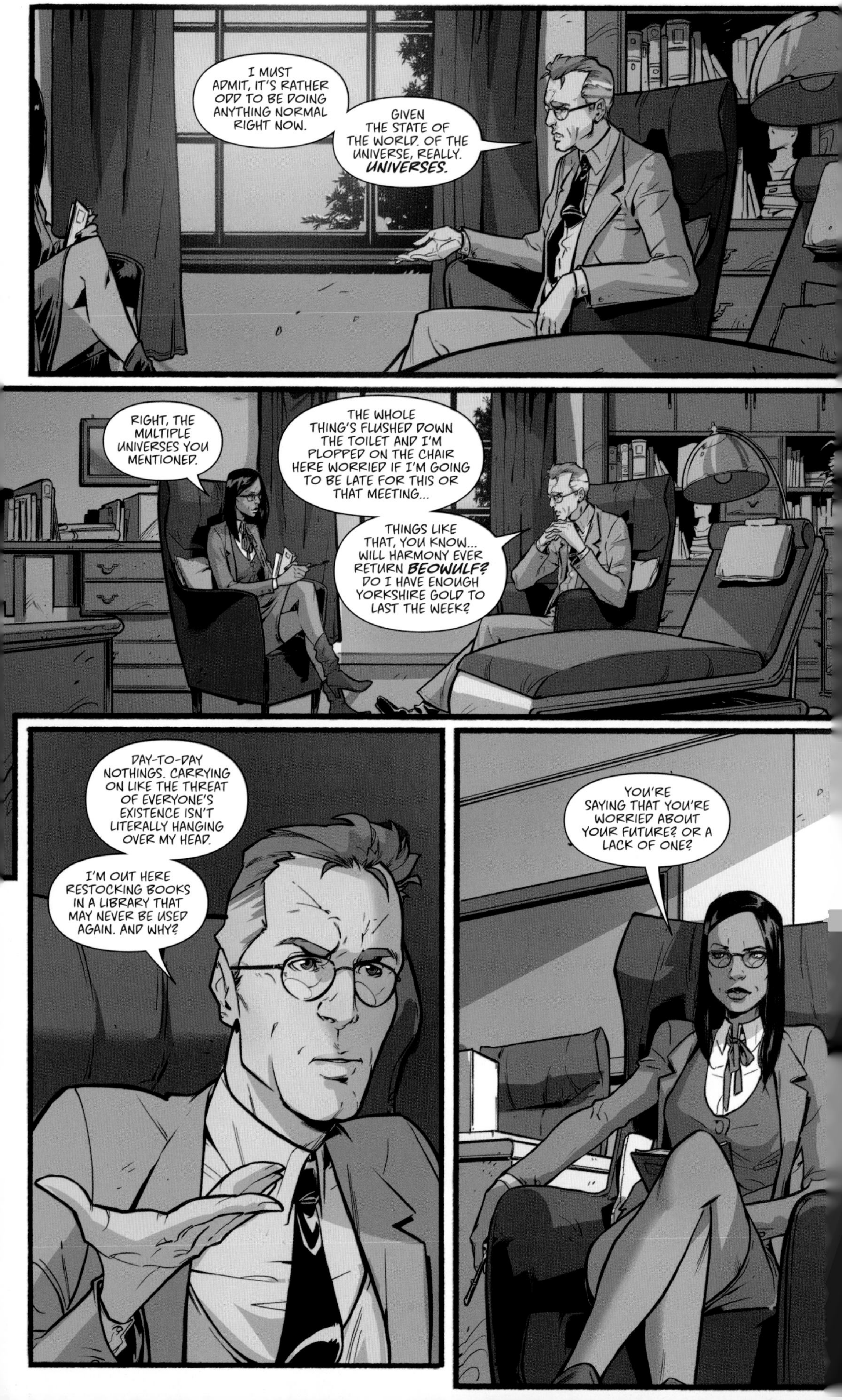
I MUST ADMIT, IT'S RATHER ODD TO BE DOING ANYTHING NORMAL RIGHT NOW.
GIVEN THE STATE OF THE WORLD. OF THE UNIVERSE, REALLY. ***UNIVERSES.***
RIGHT, THE MULTIPLE UNIVERSES YOU MENTIONED.
THE WHOLE THING'S FLUSHED DOWN THE TOILET AND I'M PLOPPED ON THE CHAIR HERE WORRIED IF I'M GOING TO BE LATE FOR THIS OR THAT MEETING...
THINGS LIKE THAT, YOU KNOW... WILL HARMONY EVER RETURN ***BEOWULF?*** DO I HAVE ENOUGH YORKSHIRE GOLD TO LAST THE WEEK?
DAY-TO-DAY NOTHINGS. CARRYING ON LIKE THE THREAT OF EVERYONE'S EXISTENCE ISN'T LITERALLY HANGING OVER MY HEAD.
I'M OUT HERE RESTOCKING BOOKS IN A LIBRARY THAT MAY NEVER BE USED AGAIN. AND WHY?
YOU'RE SAYING THAT YOU'RE WORRIED ABOUT YOUR FUTURE? OR A LACK OF ONE?

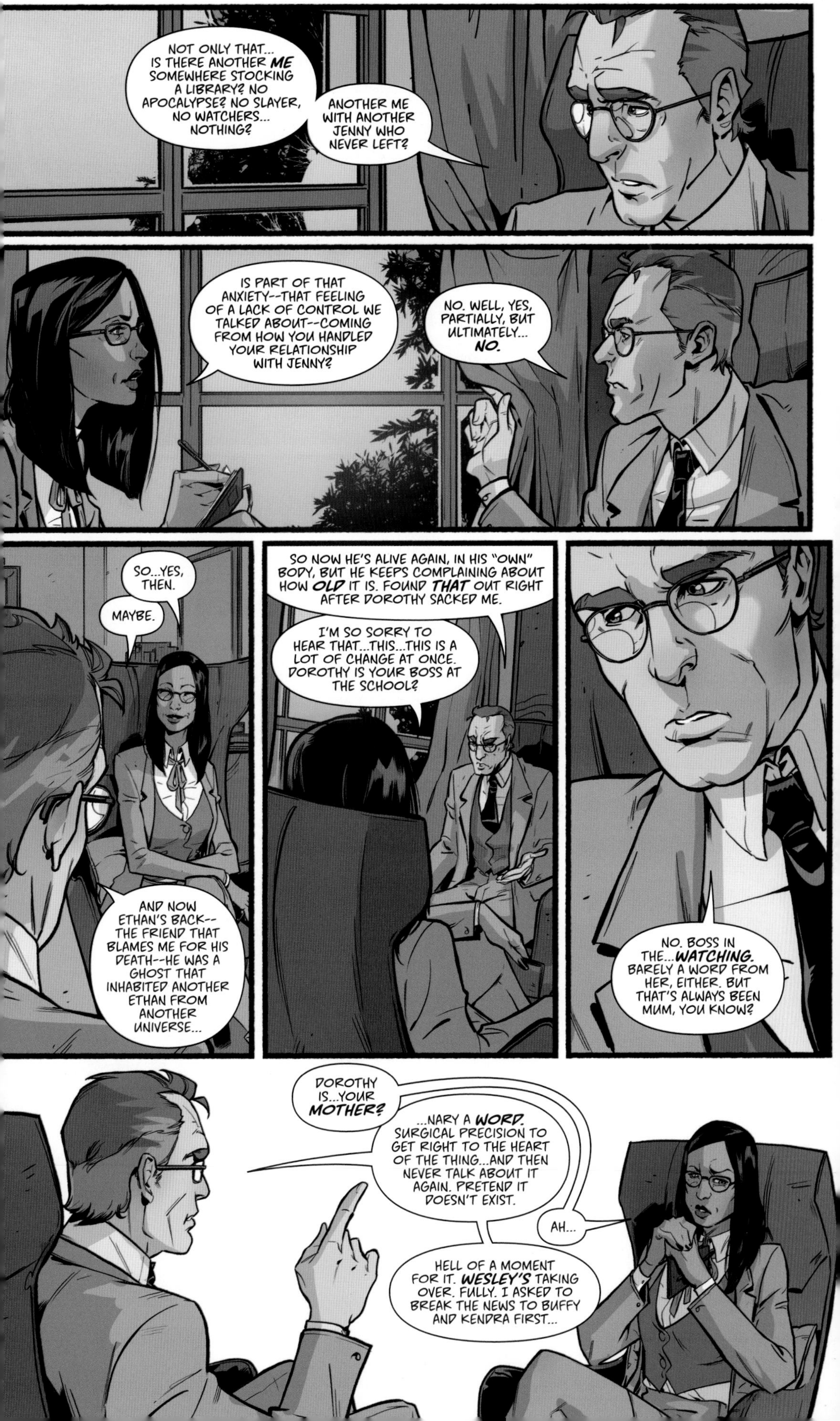
NOT ONLY THAT... IS THERE ANOTHER ***ME*** SOMEWHERE STOCKING A LIBRARY? NO APOCALYPSE? NO SLAYER, NO WATCHERS... NOTHING?
ANOTHER ME WITH ANOTHER JENNY WHO NEVER LEFT?
IS PART OF THAT ANXIETY--THAT FEELING OF A LACK OF CONTROL WE TALKED ABOUT--COMING FROM HOW YOU HANDLED YOUR RELATIONSHIP WITH JENNY?
NO. WELL, YES, PARTIALLY, BUT ULTIMATELY... ***NO.***
SO...YES, THEN.
MAYBE.
AND NOW ETHAN'S BACK--THE FRIEND THAT BLAMES ME FOR HIS DEATH--HE WAS A GHOST THAT INHABITED ANOTHER ETHAN FROM ANOTHER UNIVERSE...
SO NOW HE'S ALIVE AGAIN, IN HIS "OWN" BODY, BUT HE KEEPS COMPLAINING ABOUT HOW ***OLD*** IT IS. FOUND ***THAT*** OUT RIGHT AFTER DOROTHY SACKED ME.
I'M SO SORRY TO HEAR THAT...THIS...THIS IS A LOT OF CHANGE AT ONCE. DOROTHY IS YOUR BOSS AT THE SCHOOL?
NO. BOSS IN THE...***WATCHING.*** BARELY A WORD FROM HER, EITHER. BUT THAT'S ALWAYS BEEN MUM, YOU KNOW?
DOROTHY IS...YOUR ***MOTHER?***
...NARY A ***WORD.*** SURGICAL PRECISION TO GET RIGHT TO THE HEART OF THE THING...AND THEN NEVER TALK ABOUT IT AGAIN. PRETEND IT DOESN'T EXIST.
AH...
HELL OF A MOMENT FOR IT. ***WESLEY'S*** TAKING OVER. FULLY. I ASKED TO BREAK THE NEWS TO BUFFY AND KENDRA FIRST...

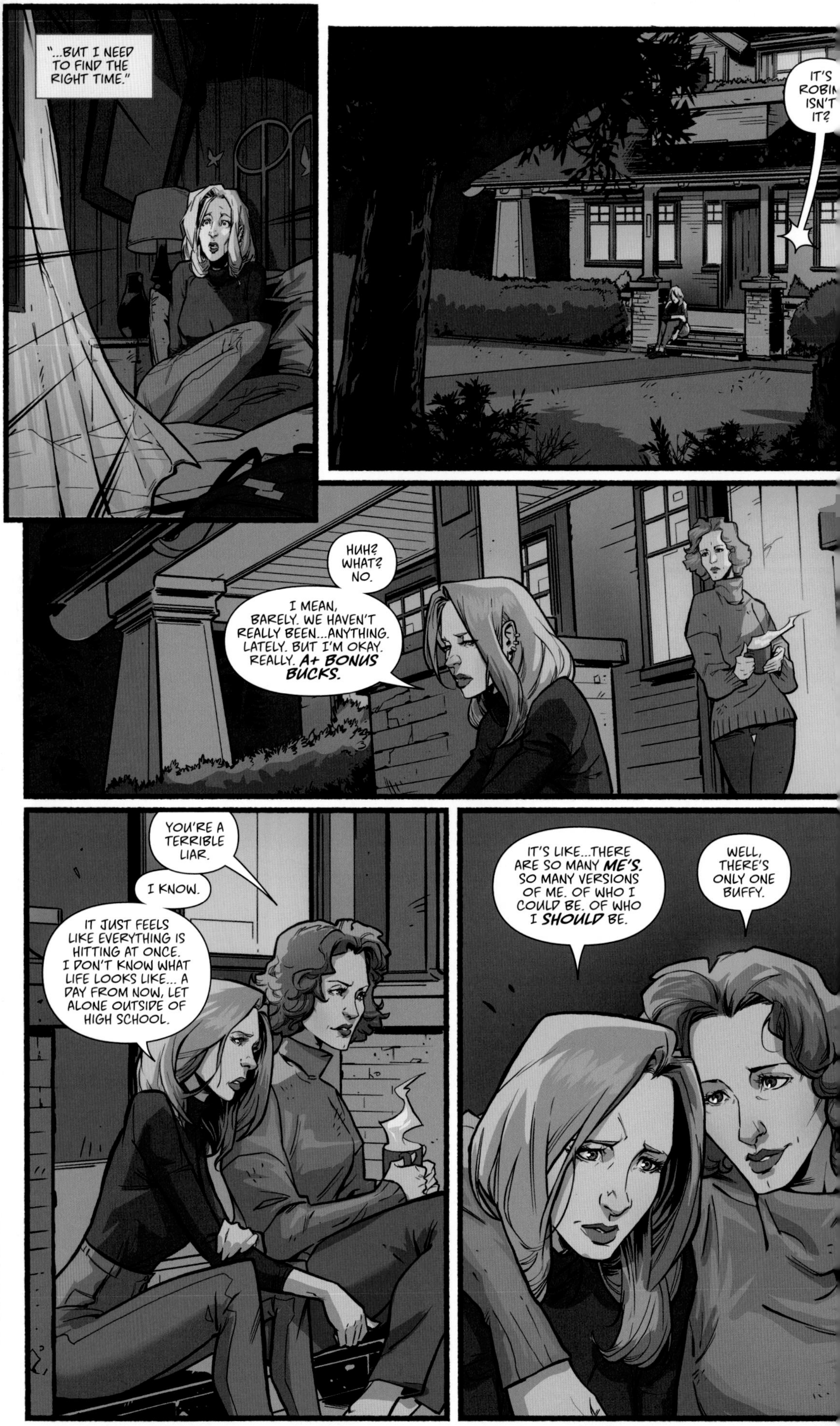
"...BUT I NEED TO FIND THE RIGHT TIME."
IT'S ROBIN ISN'T IT?
HUH? WHAT? NO.
I MEAN, BARELY. WE HAVEN'T REALLY BEEN...ANYTHING. LATELY. BUT I'M OKAY. REALLY. A+ BONUS BUCKS.
YOU'RE A TERRIBLE LIAR.
I KNOW.
IT JUST FEELS LIKE EVERYTHING IS HITTING AT ONCE. I DON'T KNOW WHAT LIFE LOOKS LIKE... A DAY FROM NOW, LET ALONE OUTSIDE OF HIGH SCHOOL.
IT'S LIKE...THERE ARE SO MANY ME'S. SO MANY VERSIONS OF ME. OF WHO I COULD BE. OF WHO I SHOULD BE.
WELL, THERE'S ONLY ONE BUFFY.

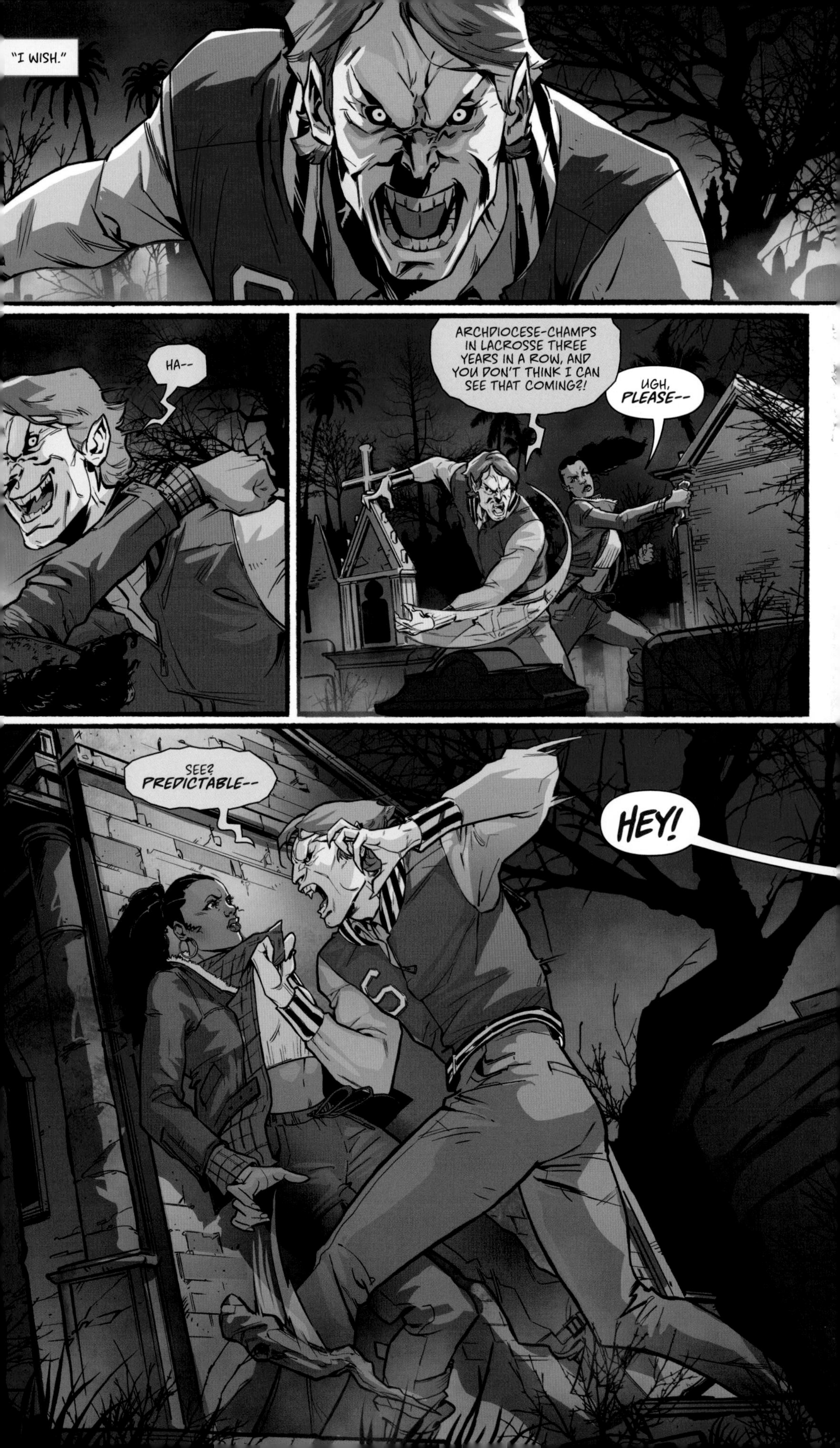
"I WISH."
HA--
ARCHDIOCESE-CHAMPS IN LACROSSE THREE YEARS IN A ROW, AND YOU DON'T THINK I CAN SEE THAT COMING?!
UGH, PLEASE--
SEE? PREDICTABLE--
HEY!

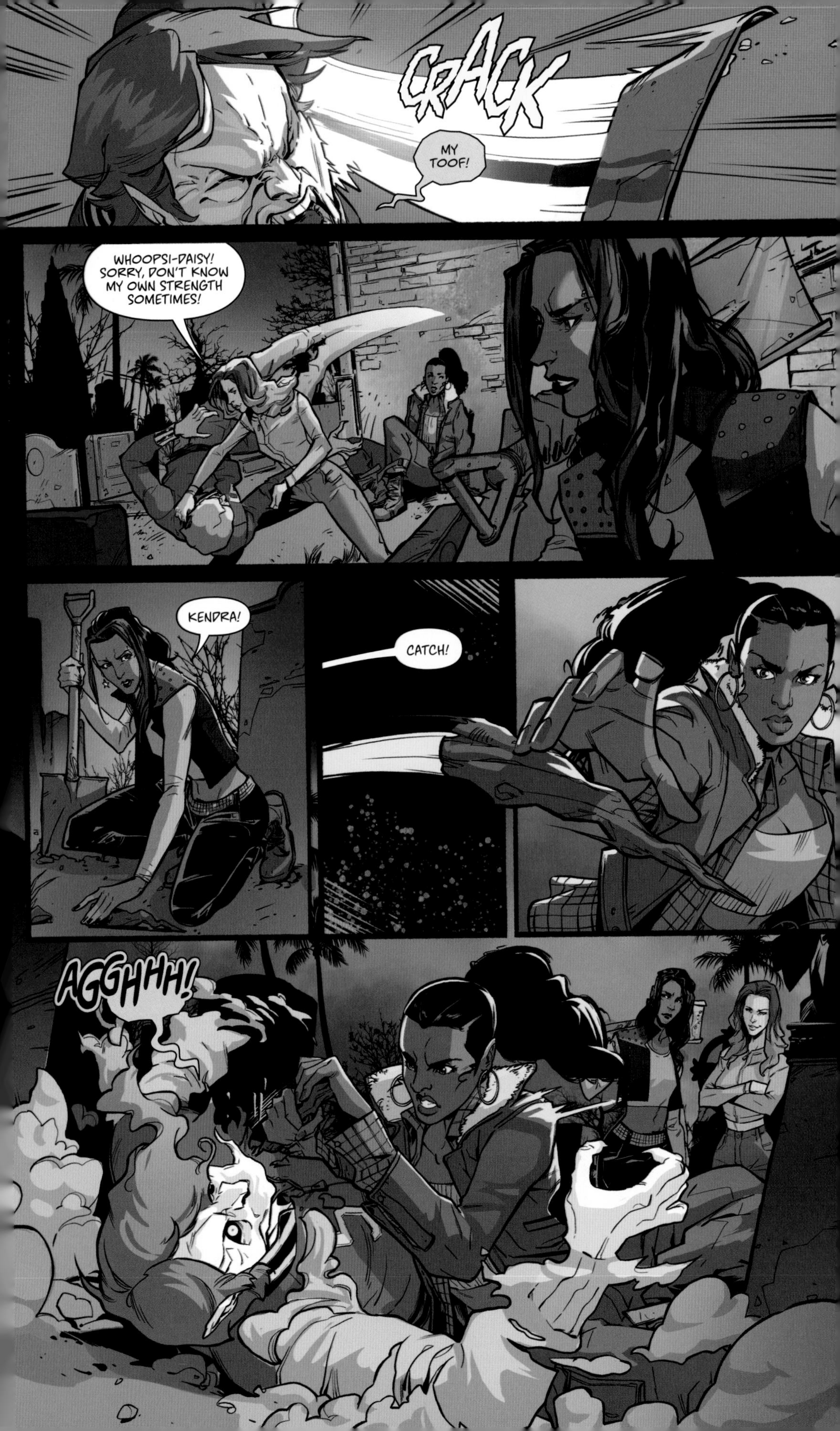
CRACK
MY TOOF!
WHOOPSI-DAISY! SORRY, DON'T KNOW MY OWN STRENGTH SOMETIMES!
KENDRA!
CATCH!
AGGHHH!

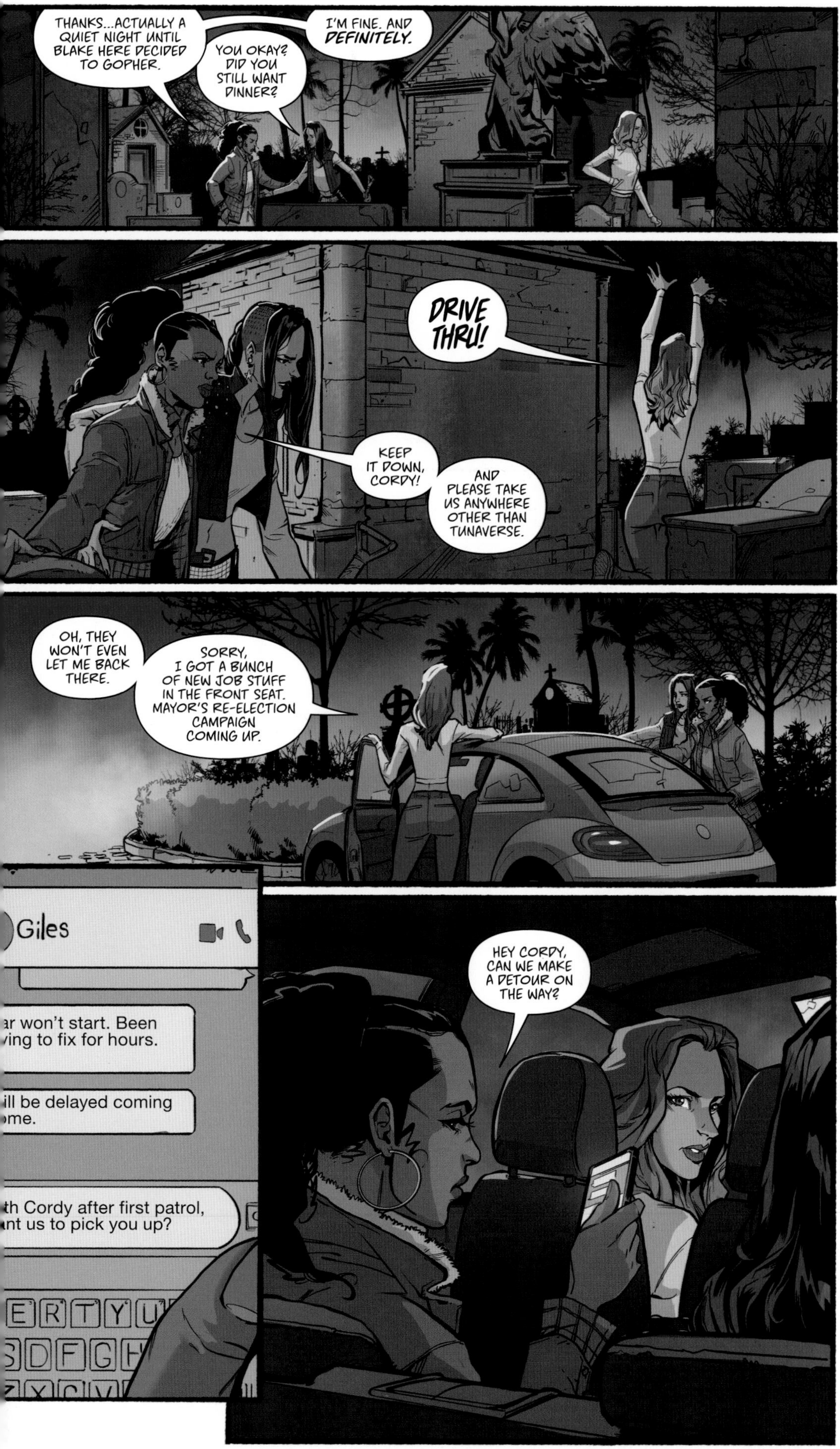
THANKS...ACTUALLY A QUIET NIGHT UNTIL BLAKE HERE DECIDED TO GOPHER.
YOU OKAY? DID YOU STILL WANT DINNER?
I'M FINE. AND *DEFINITELY.*
DRIVE THRU!
KEEP IT DOWN, CORDY!
AND PLEASE TAKE US ANYWHERE OTHER THAN TUNAVERSE.
OH, THEY WON'T EVEN LET ME BACK THERE.
SORRY, I GOT A BUNCH OF NEW JOB STUFF IN THE FRONT SEAT. MAYOR'S RE-ELECTION CAMPAIGN COMING UP.
Giles
ar won't start. Been
ving to fix for hours.
ill be delayed coming
ome.
th Cordy after first patrol,
ant us to pick you up?
HEY CORDY, CAN WE MAKE A DETOUR ON THE WAY?

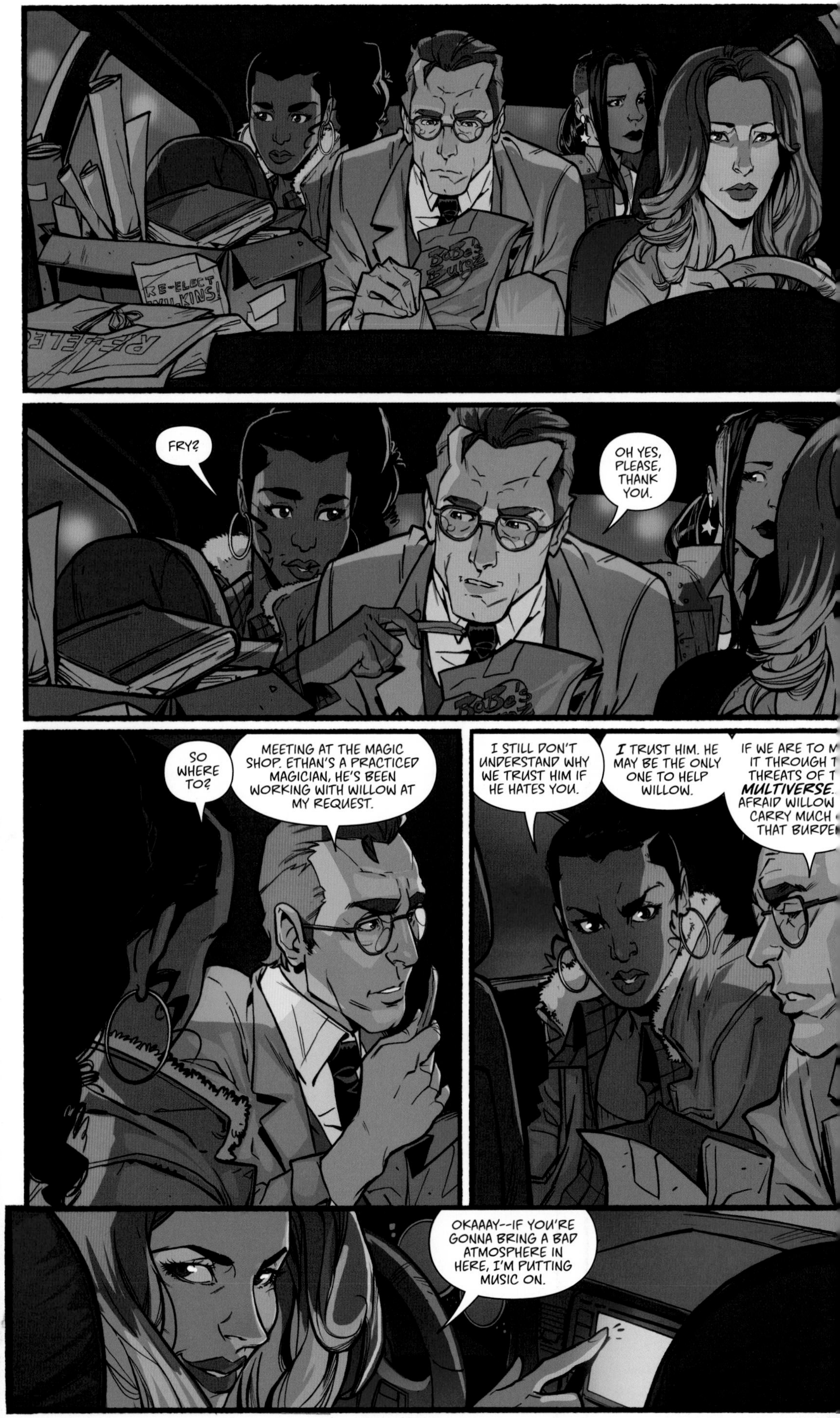
RE-ELECT WILKINS!
FRY?
OH YES, PLEASE, THANK YOU.
SO WHERE TO?
MEETING AT THE MAGIC SHOP. ETHAN'S A PRACTICED MAGICIAN, HE'S BEEN WORKING WITH WILLOW AT MY REQUEST.
I STILL DON'T UNDERSTAND WHY WE TRUST HIM IF HE HATES YOU.
I TRUST HIM. HE MAY BE THE ONLY ONE TO HELP WILLOW.
IF WE ARE TO M IT THROUGH T THREATS OF T ***MULTIVERSE***. AFRAID WILLOW CARRY MUCH THAT BURDE
OKAAAY--IF YOU'RE GONNA BRING A BAD ATMOSPHERE IN HERE, I'M PUTTING MUSIC ON.

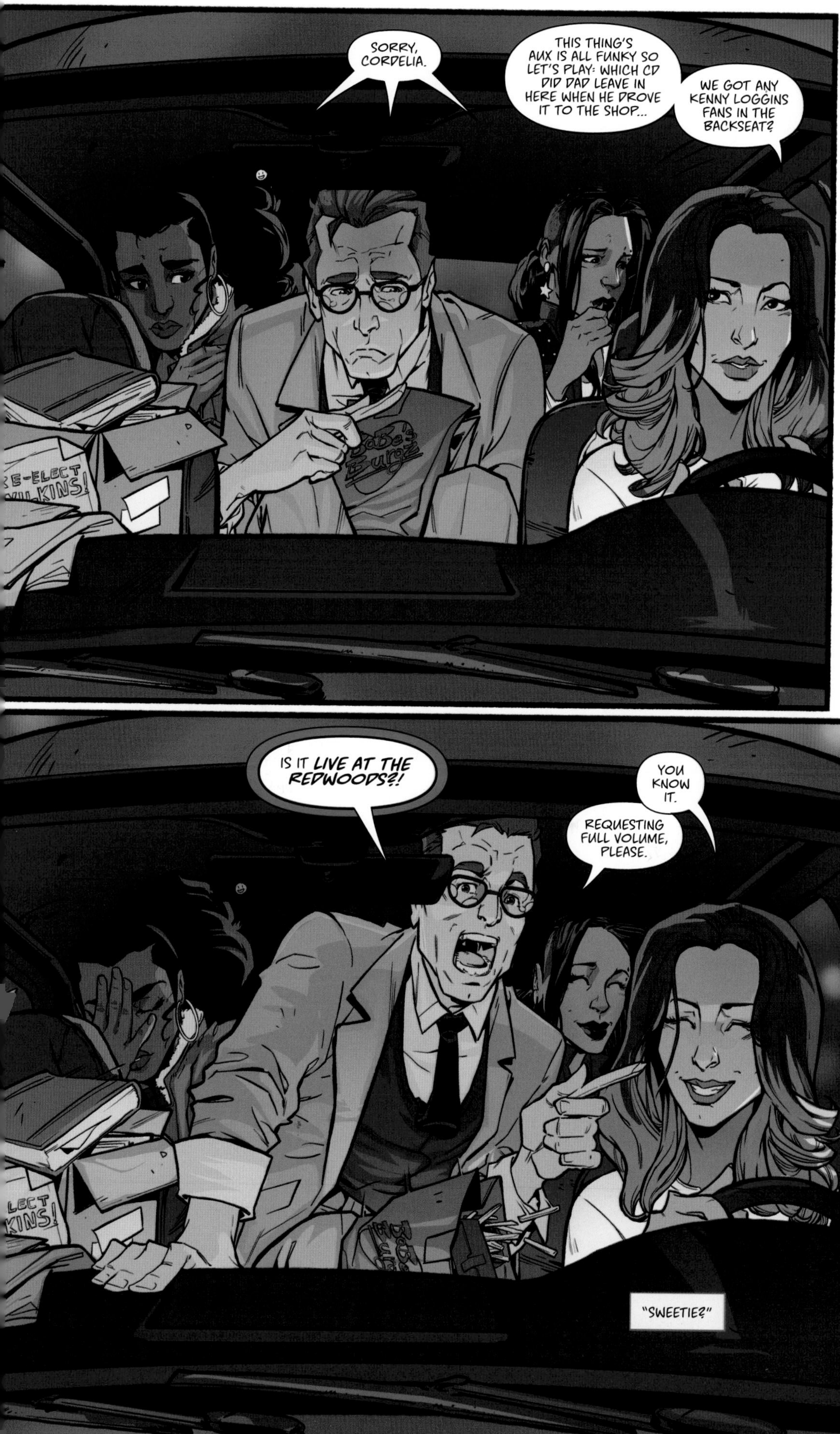
SORRY, CORDELIA.
THIS THING'S AUX IS ALL FUNKY SO LET'S PLAY: WHICH CD DID DAD LEAVE IN HERE WHEN HE DROVE IT TO THE SHOP...
WE GOT ANY KENNY LOGGINS FANS IN THE BACKSEAT?
IS IT *LIVE AT THE REDWOODS*?!
YOU KNOW IT.
REQUESTING FULL VOLUME, PLEASE.
"SWEETIE?"

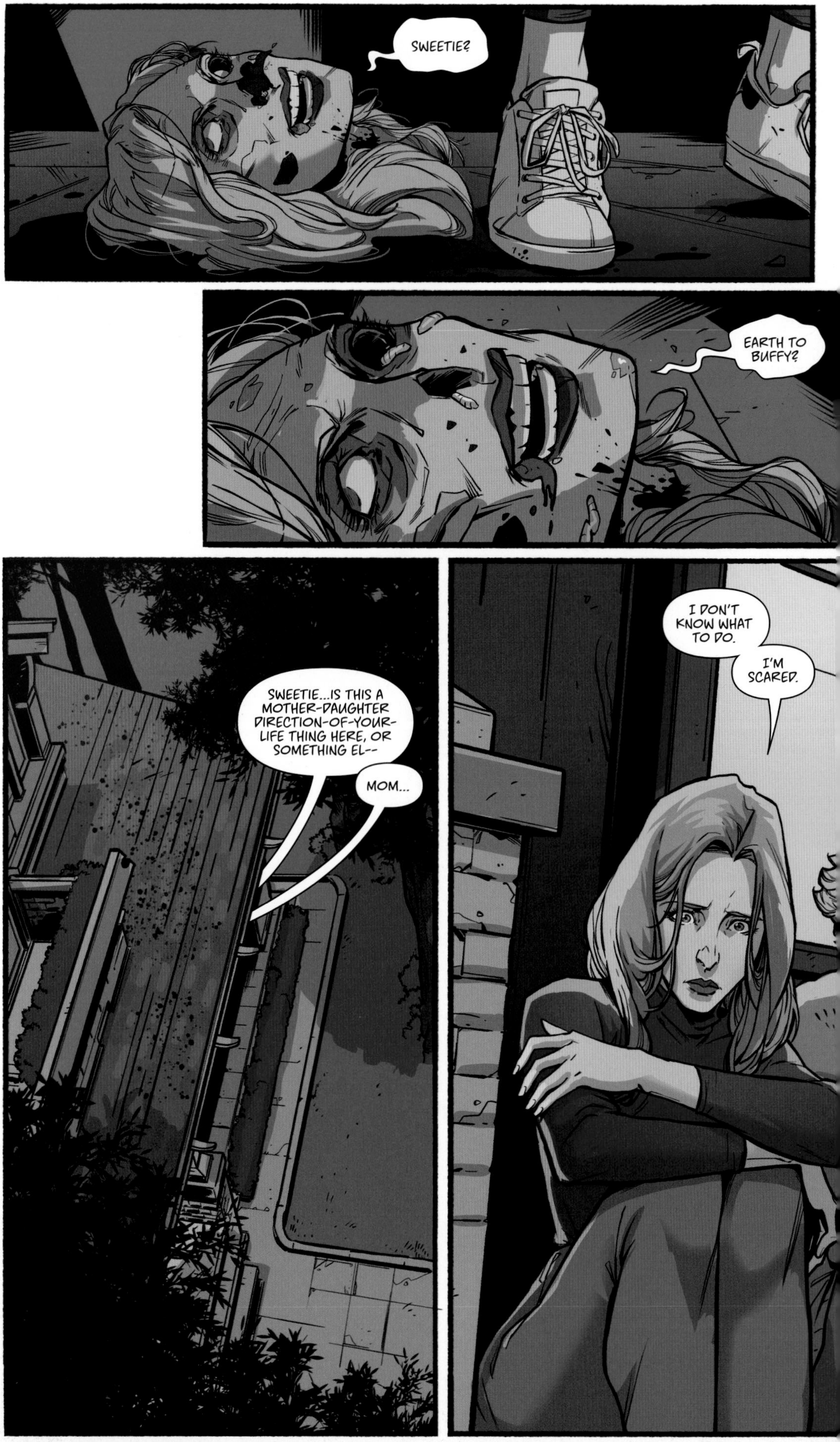
SWEETIE?
EARTH TO BUFFY?
SWEETIE...IS THIS A MOTHER-DAUGHTER DIRECTION-OF-YOUR-LIFE THING HERE, OR SOMETHING EL--
MOM...
I DON'T KNOW WHAT TO DO.
I'M SCARED.

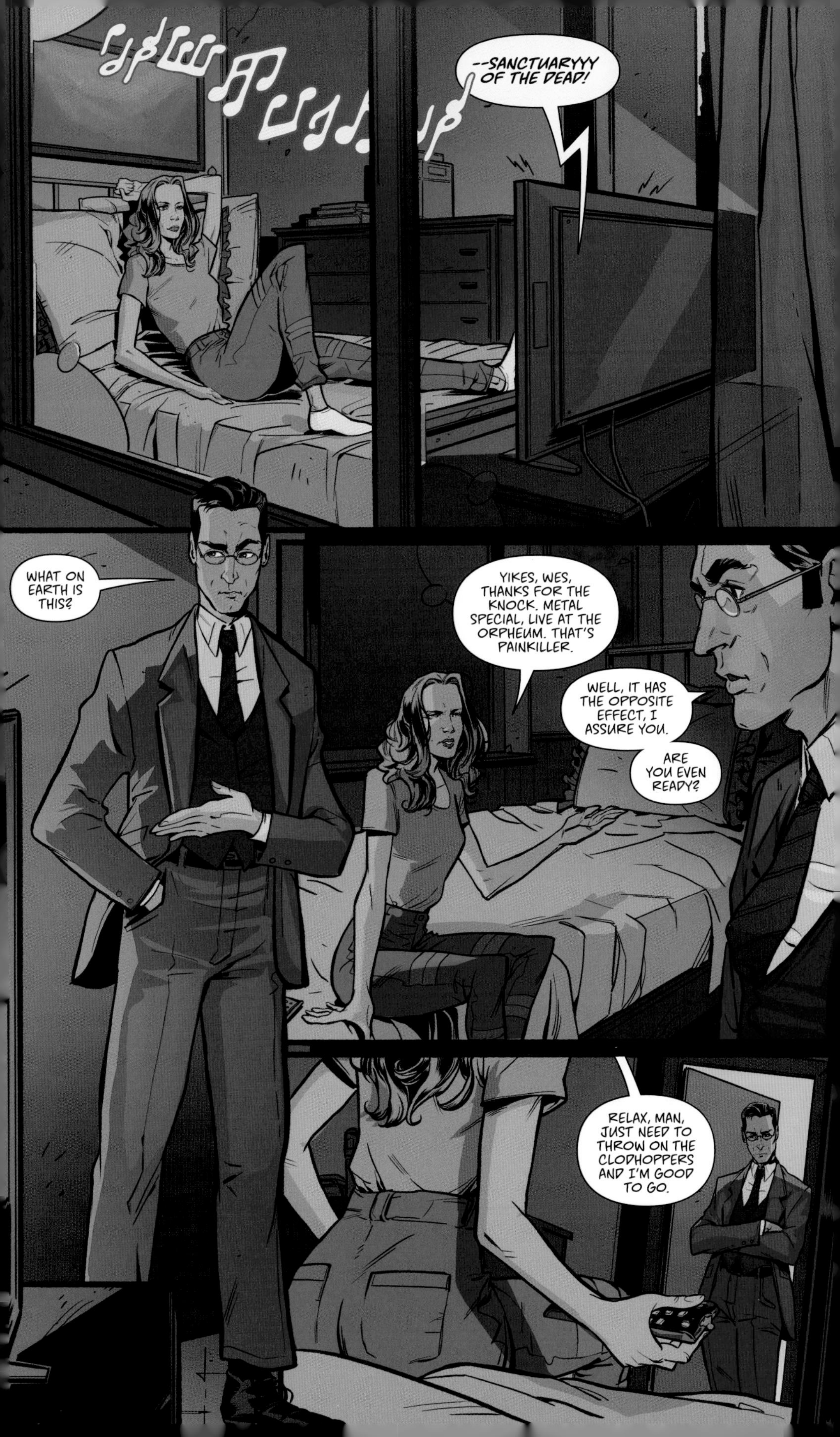

--SANCTUARYYY OF THE DEAD!
WHAT ON EARTH IS THIS?
YIKES, WES, THANKS FOR THE KNOCK. METAL SPECIAL, LIVE AT THE ORPHEUM. THAT'S PAINKILLER.
WELL, IT HAS THE OPPOSITE EFFECT, I ASSURE YOU.
ARE YOU EVEN READY?
RELAX, MAN, JUST NEED TO THROW ON THE CLODHOPPERS AND I'M GOOD TO GO.

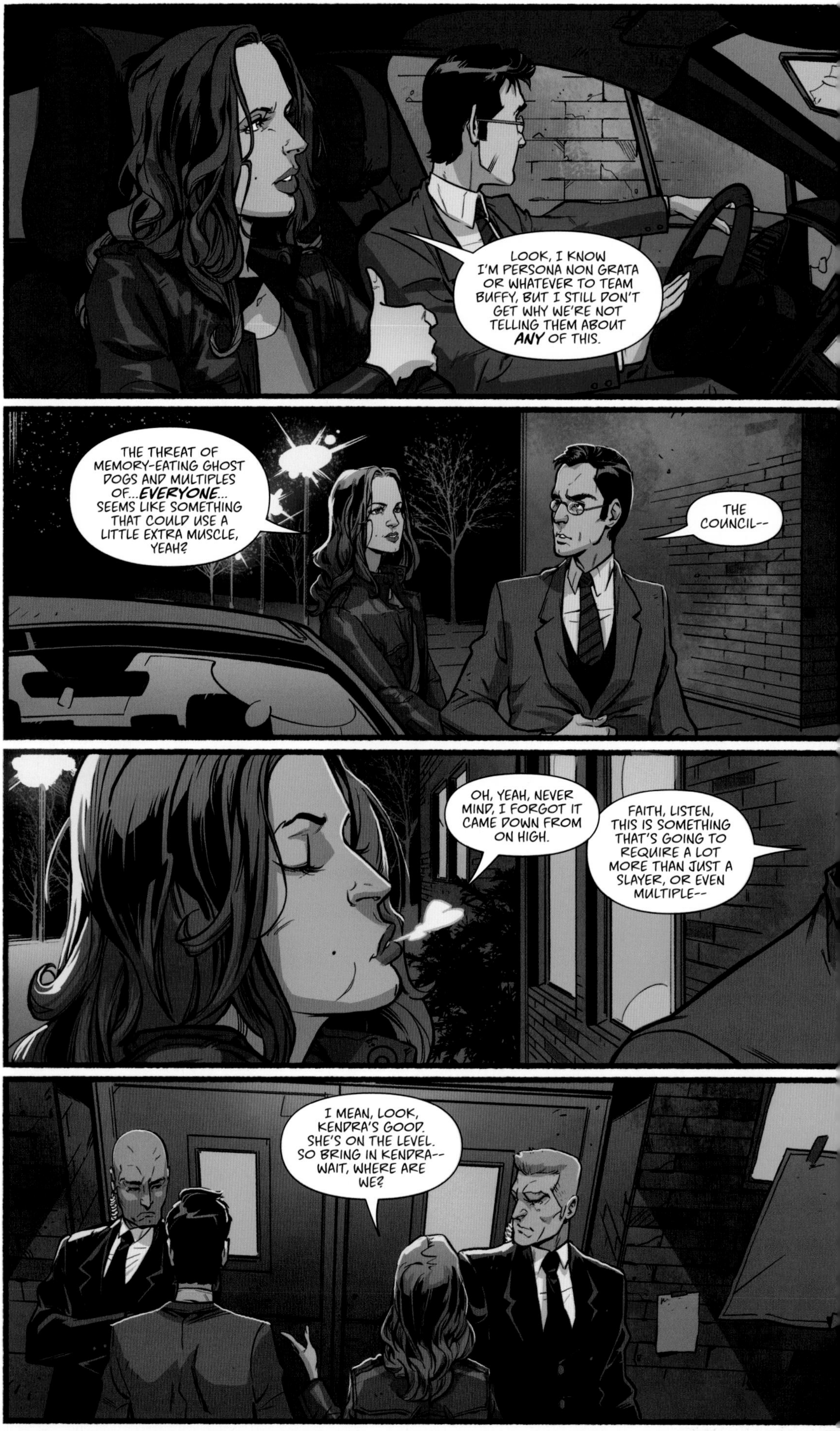
LOOK, I KNOW I'M PERSONA NON GRATA OR WHATEVER TO TEAM BUFFY, BUT I STILL DON'T GET WHY WE'RE NOT TELLING THEM ABOUT ***ANY*** OF THIS.
THE THREAT OF MEMORY-EATING GHOST DOGS AND MULTIPLES OF...***EVERYONE***... SEEMS LIKE SOMETHING THAT COULD USE A LITTLE EXTRA MUSCLE, YEAH?
THE COUNCIL--
OH, YEAH, NEVER MIND, I FORGOT IT CAME DOWN FROM ON HIGH.
FAITH, LISTEN, THIS IS SOMETHING THAT'S GOING TO REQUIRE A LOT MORE THAN JUST A SLAYER, OR EVEN MULTIPLE--
I MEAN, LOOK, KENDRA'S GOOD. SHE'S ON THE LEVEL. SO BRING IN KENDRA-- WAIT, WHERE ARE WE?

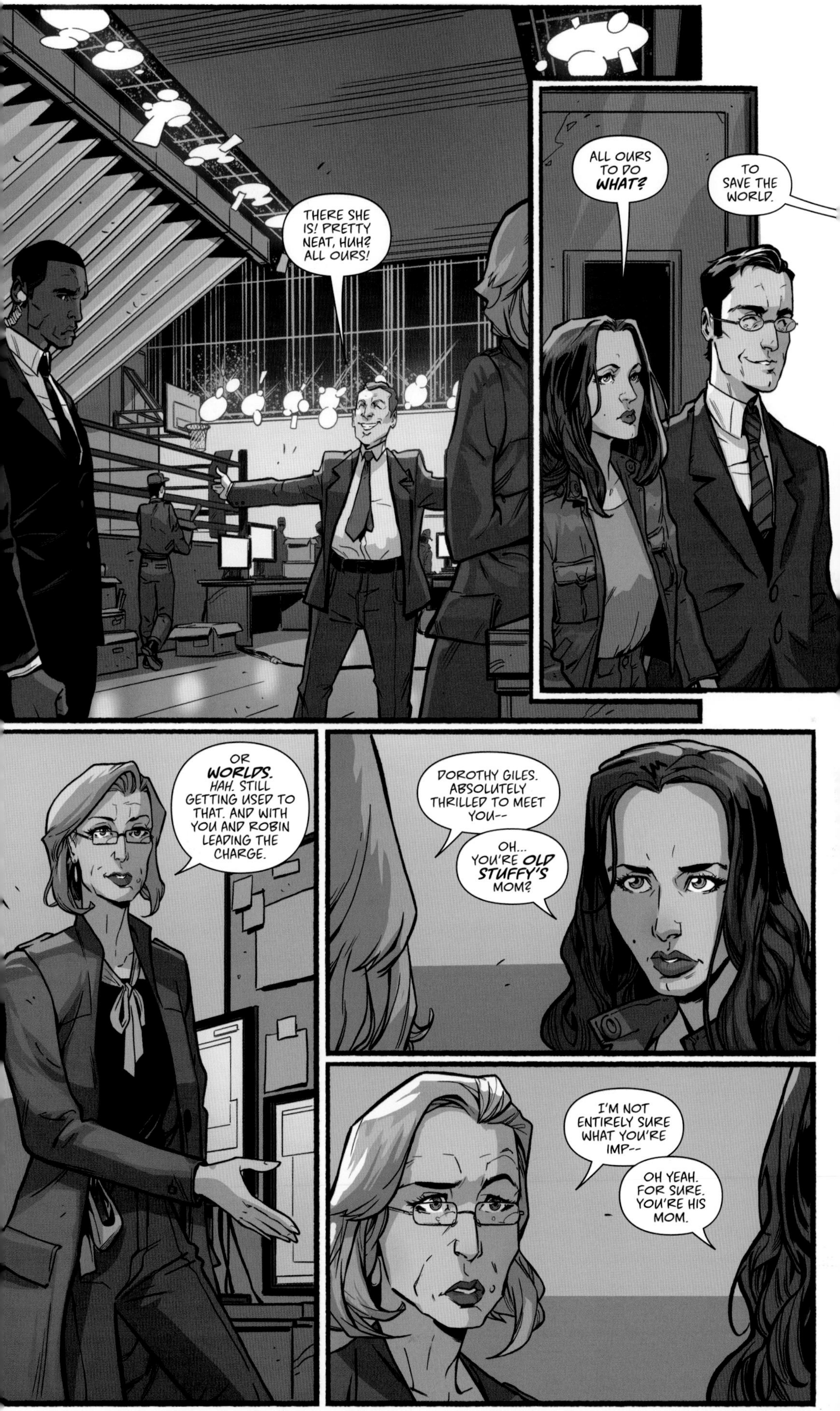
THERE SHE IS! PRETTY NEAT, HUH? ALL OURS!
ALL OURS TO DO WHAT?
TO SAVE THE WORLD.
OR WORLDS. HAH. STILL GETTING USED TO THAT. AND WITH YOU AND ROBIN LEADING THE CHARGE.
DOROTHY GILES. ABSOLUTELY THRILLED TO MEET YOU--
OH... YOU'RE OLD STUFFY'S MOM?
I'M NOT ENTIRELY SURE WHAT YOU'RE IMP--
OH YEAH. FOR SURE. YOU'RE HIS MOM.

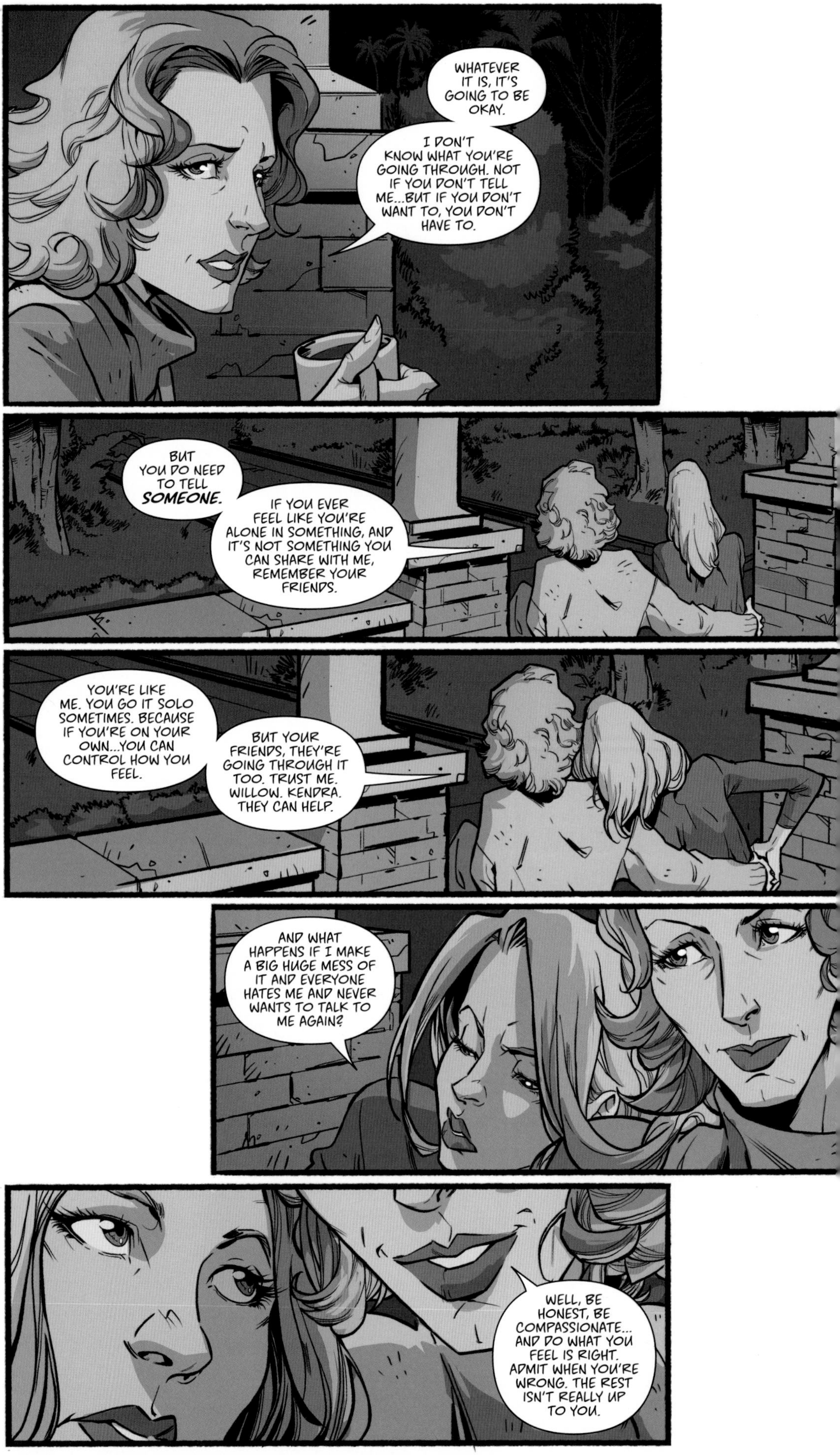
WHATEVER IT IS, IT'S GOING TO BE OKAY.
I DON'T KNOW WHAT YOU'RE GOING THROUGH. NOT IF YOU DON'T TELL ME...BUT IF YOU DON'T WANT TO, YOU DON'T HAVE TO.
BUT YOU DO NEED TO TELL ***SOMEONE.***
IF YOU EVER FEEL LIKE YOU'RE ALONE IN SOMETHING, AND IT'S NOT SOMETHING YOU CAN SHARE WITH ME, REMEMBER YOUR FRIENDS.
YOU'RE LIKE ME. YOU GO IT SOLO SOMETIMES. BECAUSE IF YOU'RE ON YOUR OWN...YOU CAN CONTROL HOW YOU FEEL.
BUT YOUR FRIENDS, THEY'RE GOING THROUGH IT TOO. TRUST ME. WILLOW. KENDRA. THEY CAN HELP.
AND WHAT HAPPENS IF I MAKE A BIG HUGE MESS OF IT AND EVERYONE HATES ME AND NEVER WANTS TO TALK TO ME AGAIN?
WELL, BE HONEST, BE COMPASSIONATE... AND DO WHAT YOU FEEL IS RIGHT. ADMIT WHEN YOU'RE WRONG. THE REST ISN'T REALLY UP TO YOU.

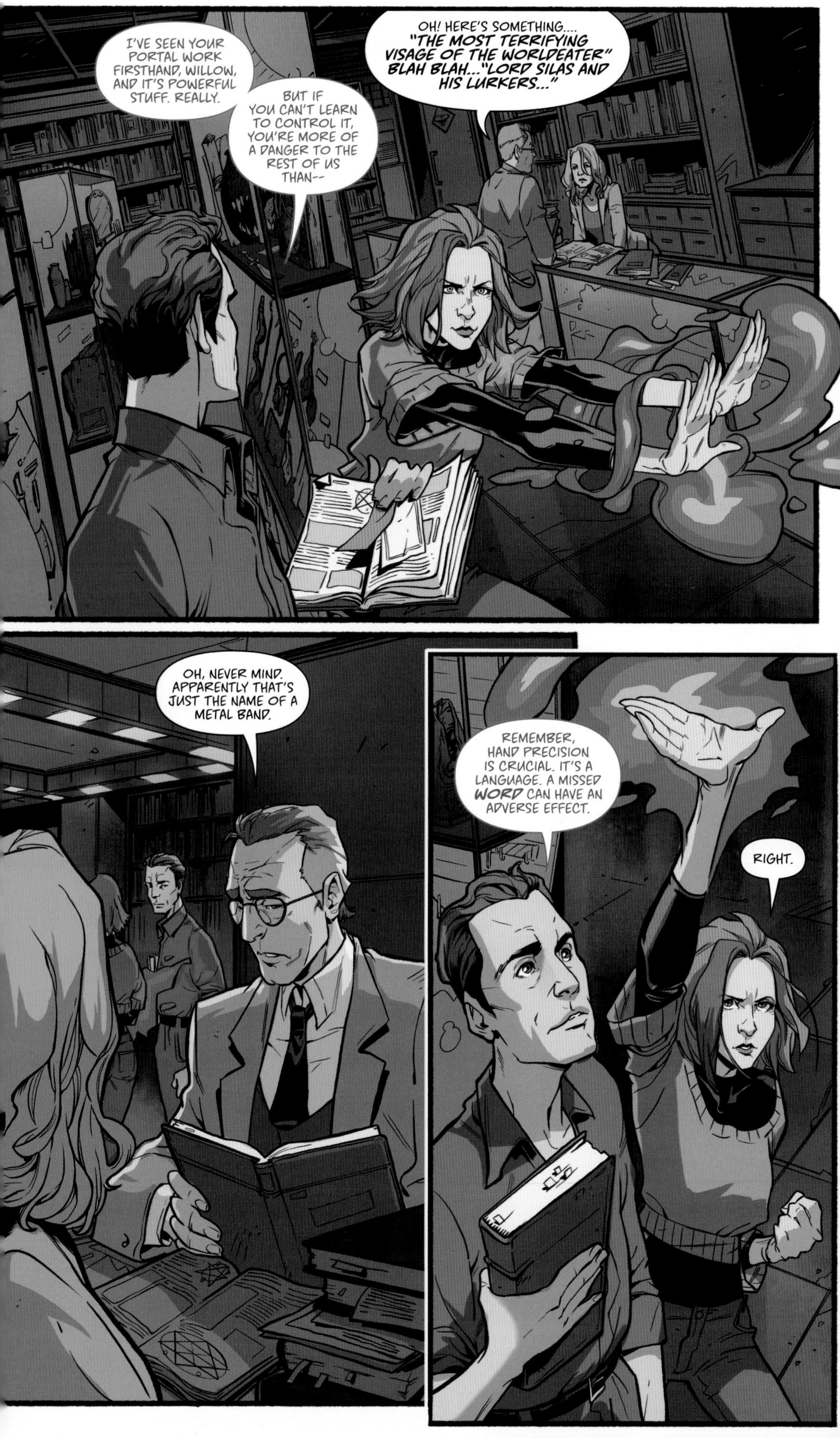
I'VE SEEN YOUR PORTAL WORK FIRSTHAND, WILLOW, AND IT'S POWERFUL STUFF. REALLY.
BUT IF YOU CAN'T LEARN TO CONTROL IT, YOU'RE MORE OF A DANGER TO THE REST OF US THAN--
OH! HERE'S SOMETHING.... "THE MOST TERRIFYING VISAGE OF THE WORLDEATER" BLAH BLAH..."LORD SILAS AND HIS LURKERS..."
OH, NEVER MIND. APPARENTLY THAT'S JUST THE NAME OF A METAL BAND.
REMEMBER, HAND PRECISION IS CRUCIAL. IT'S A LANGUAGE. A MISSED WORD CAN HAVE AN ADVERSE EFFECT.
RIGHT.

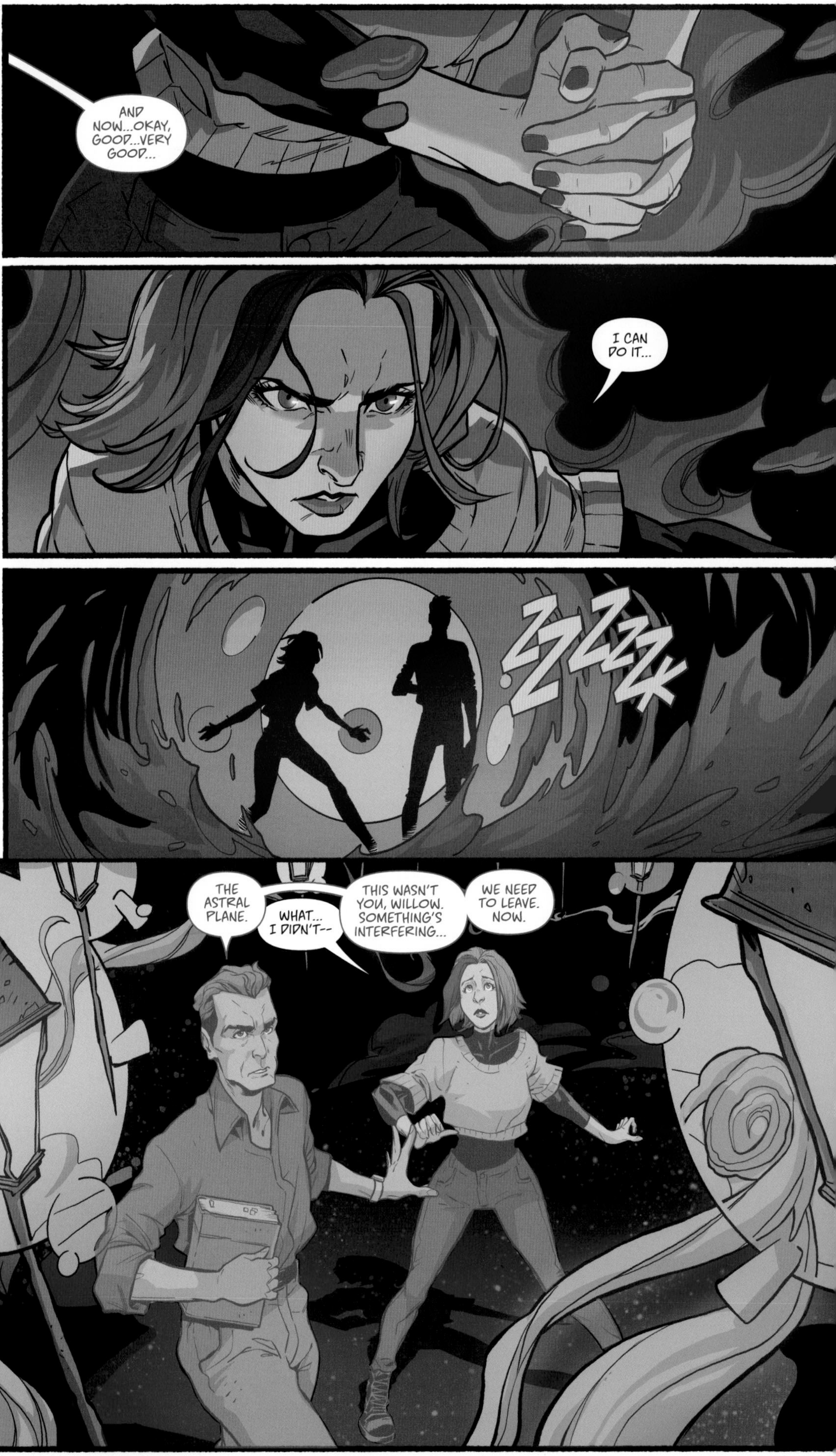
AND NOW...OKAY, GOOD...VERY GOOD...
I CAN DO IT...
ZZZZZK
THE ASTRAL PLANE.
WHAT... I DIDN'T--
THIS WASN'T YOU, WILLOW. SOMETHING'S INTERFERING...
WE NEED TO LEAVE. NOW.

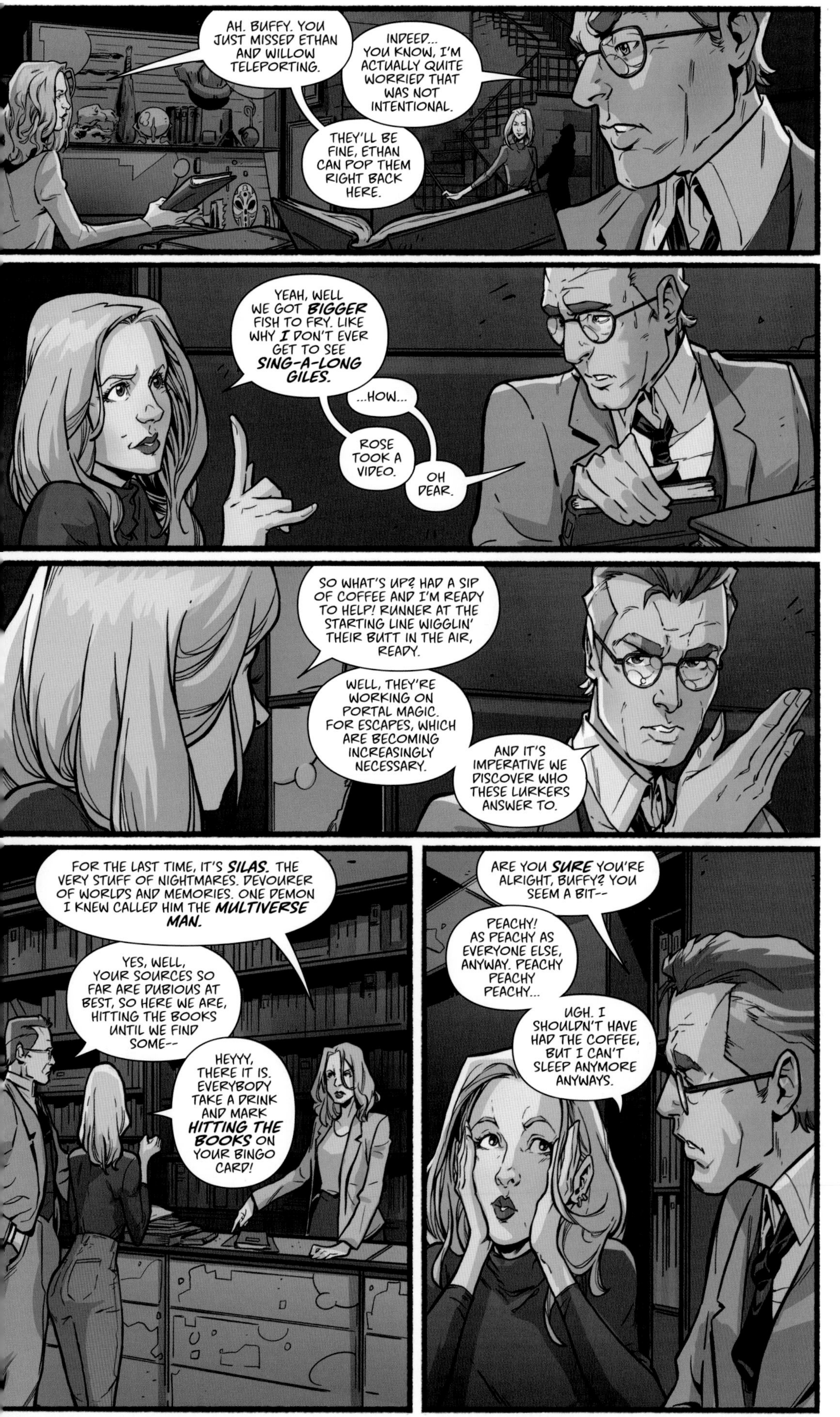
AH. BUFFY. YOU JUST MISSED ETHAN AND WILLOW TELEPORTING.
INDEED... YOU KNOW, I'M ACTUALLY QUITE WORRIED THAT WAS NOT INTENTIONAL.
THEY'LL BE FINE, ETHAN CAN POP THEM RIGHT BACK HERE.
YEAH, WELL WE GOT BIGGER FISH TO FRY. LIKE WHY I DON'T EVER GET TO SEE SING-A-LONG GILES.
...HOW...
ROSE TOOK A VIDEO.
OH DEAR.
SO WHAT'S UP? HAD A SIP OF COFFEE AND I'M READY TO HELP! RUNNER AT THE STARTING LINE WIGGLIN' THEIR BUTT IN THE AIR, READY.
WELL, THEY'RE WORKING ON PORTAL MAGIC. FOR ESCAPES, WHICH ARE BECOMING INCREASINGLY NECESSARY.
AND IT'S IMPERATIVE WE DISCOVER WHO THESE LURKERS ANSWER TO.
FOR THE LAST TIME, IT'S SILAS. THE VERY STUFF OF NIGHTMARES. DEVOURER OF WORLDS AND MEMORIES. ONE DEMON I KNEW CALLED HIM THE MULTIVERSE MAN.
YES, WELL, YOUR SOURCES SO FAR ARE DUBIOUS AT BEST, SO HERE WE ARE, HITTING THE BOOKS UNTIL WE FIND SOME--
HEYYY, THERE IT IS. EVERYBODY TAKE A DRINK AND MARK HITTING THE BOOKS ON YOUR BINGO CARD!
ARE YOU SURE YOU'RE ALRIGHT, BUFFY? YOU SEEM A BIT--
PEACHY! AS PEACHY AS EVERYONE ELSE, ANYWAY. PEACHY PEACHY PEACHY...
UGH. I SHOULDN'T HAVE HAD THE COFFEE, BUT I CAN'T SLEEP ANYMORE ANYWAYS.

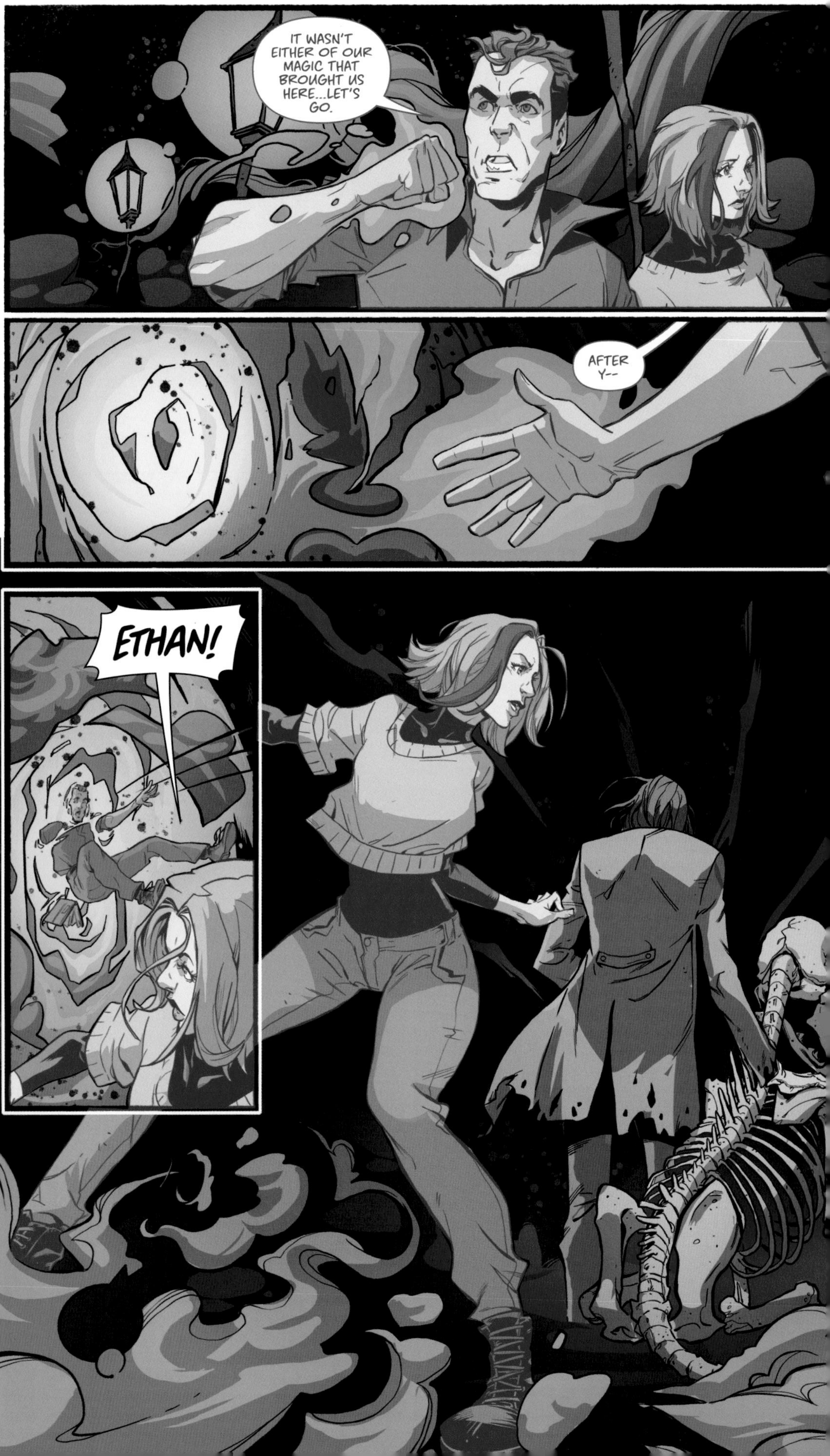
IT WASN'T EITHER OF OUR MAGIC THAT BROUGHT US HERE...LET'S GO.
AFTER Y--
ETHAN!

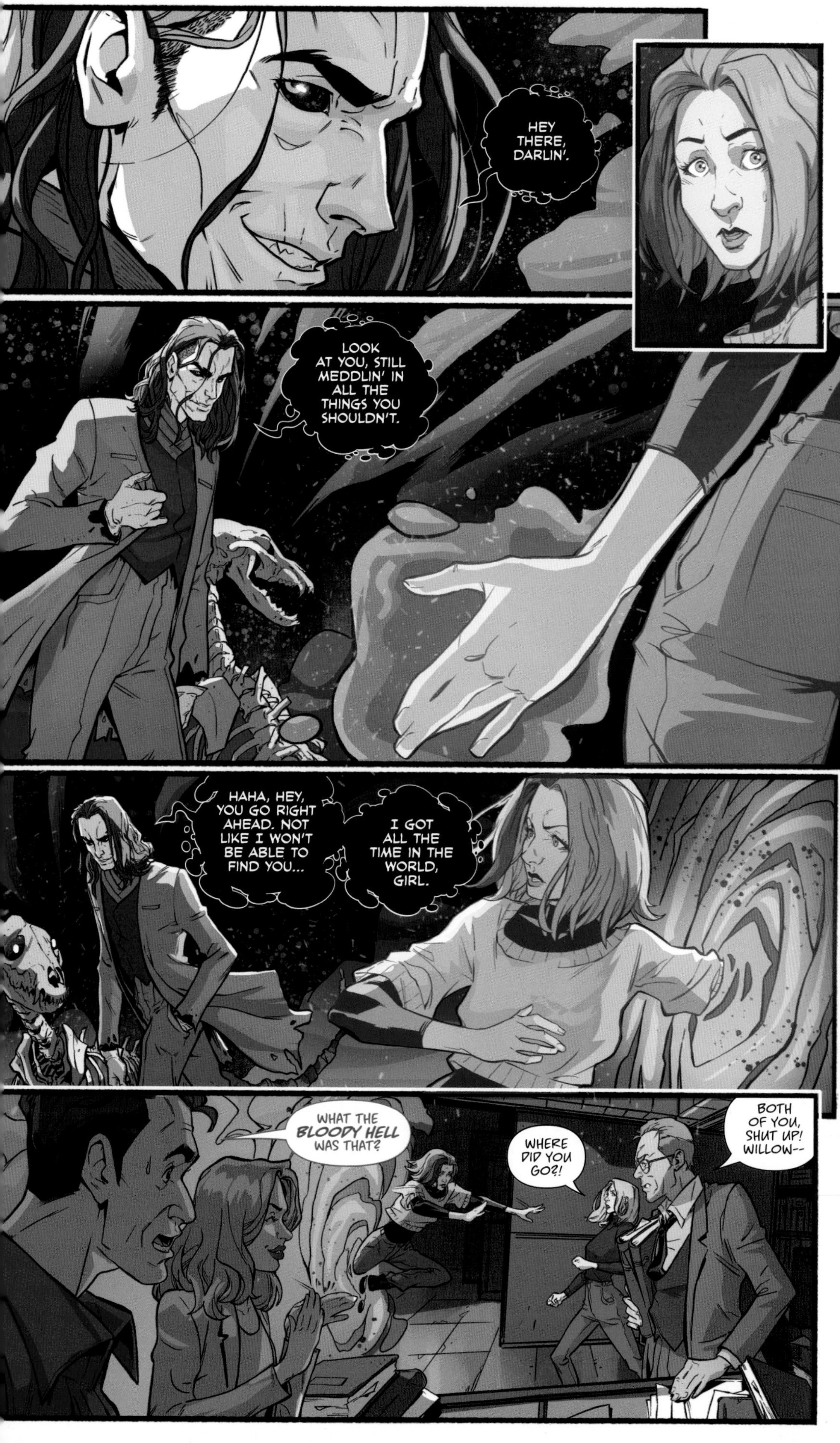
HEY THERE, DARLIN'.
LOOK AT YOU, STILL MEDDLIN' IN ALL THE THINGS YOU SHOULDN'T.
HAHA, HEY, YOU GO RIGHT AHEAD. NOT LIKE I WON'T BE ABLE TO FIND YOU...
I GOT ALL THE TIME IN THE WORLD, GIRL.
WHAT THE BLOODY HELL WAS THAT?
WHERE DID YOU GO?!
BOTH OF YOU, SHUT UP! WILLOW--

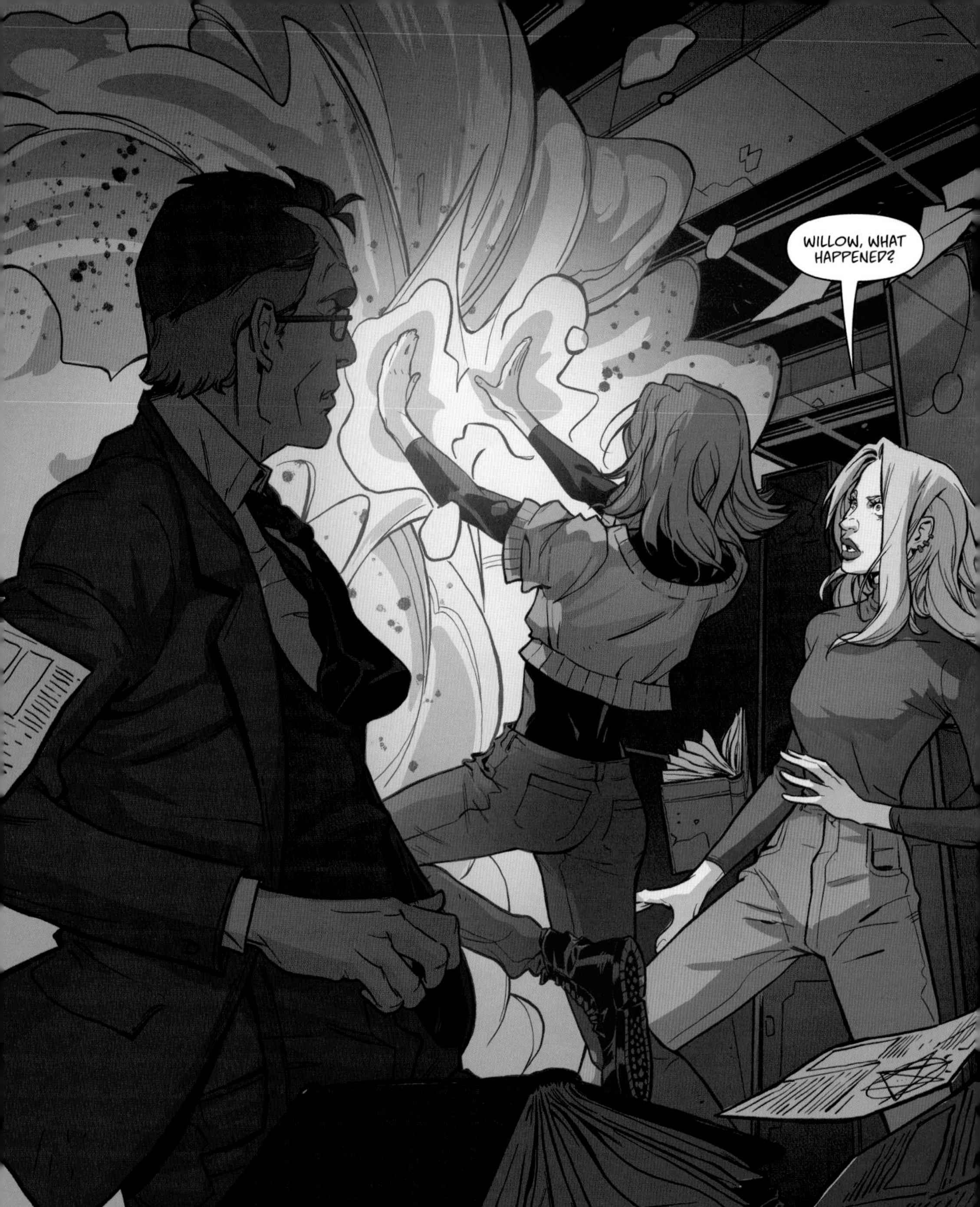
WILLOW, WHAT HAPPENED?

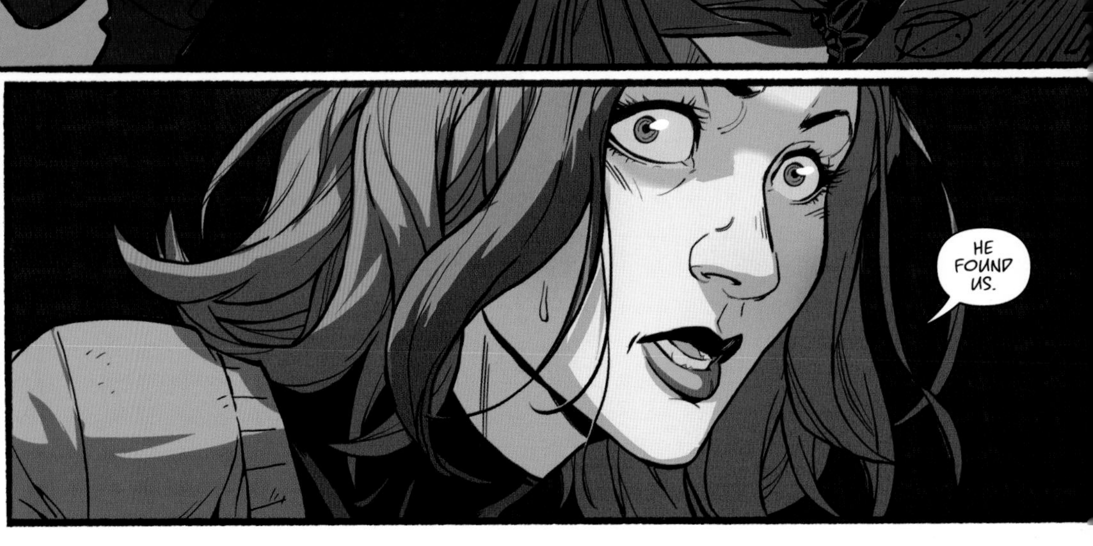
HE FOUND US.

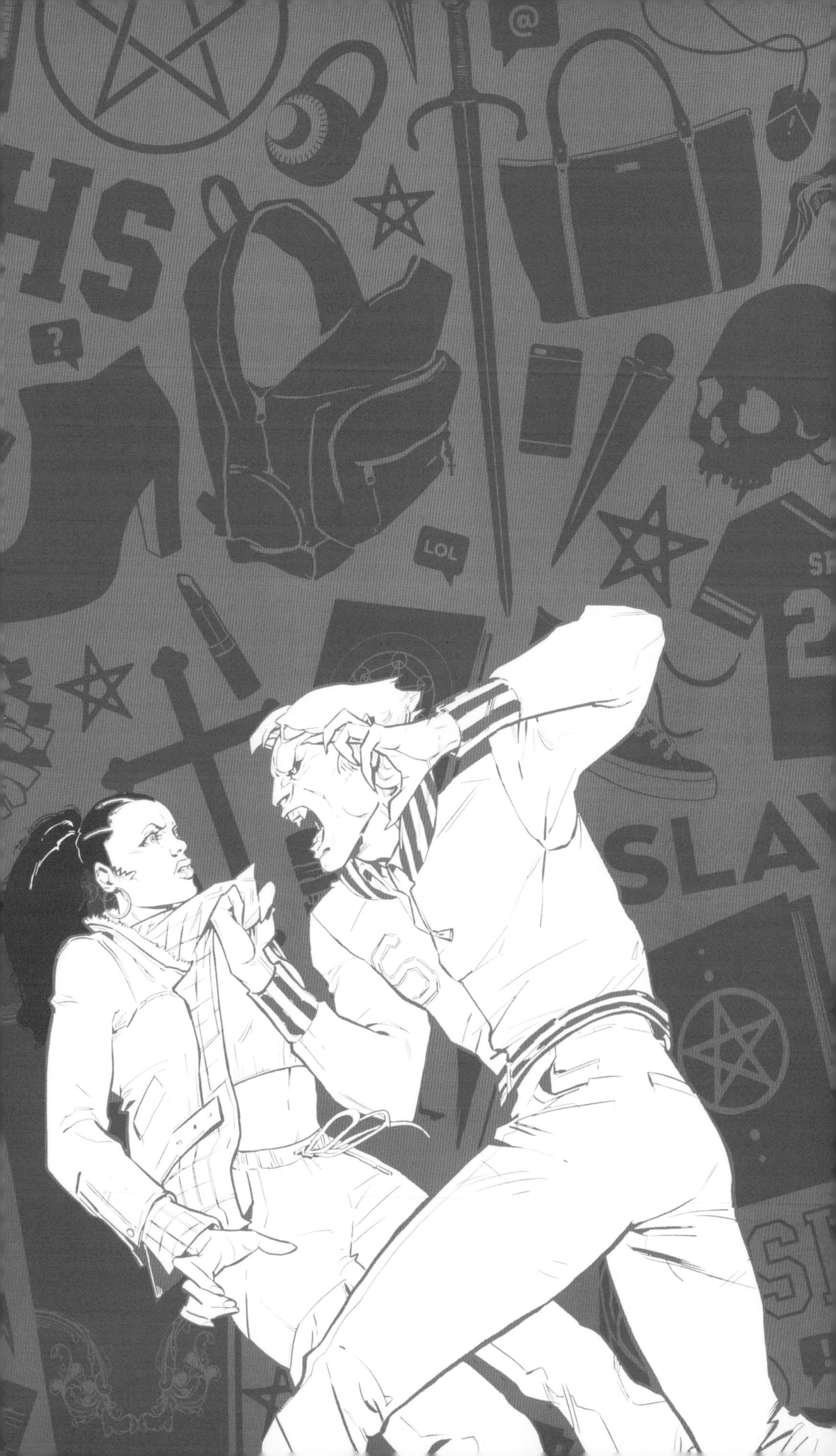
HS
LOL
SLA

CHAPTER
TWENTY-EIGHT

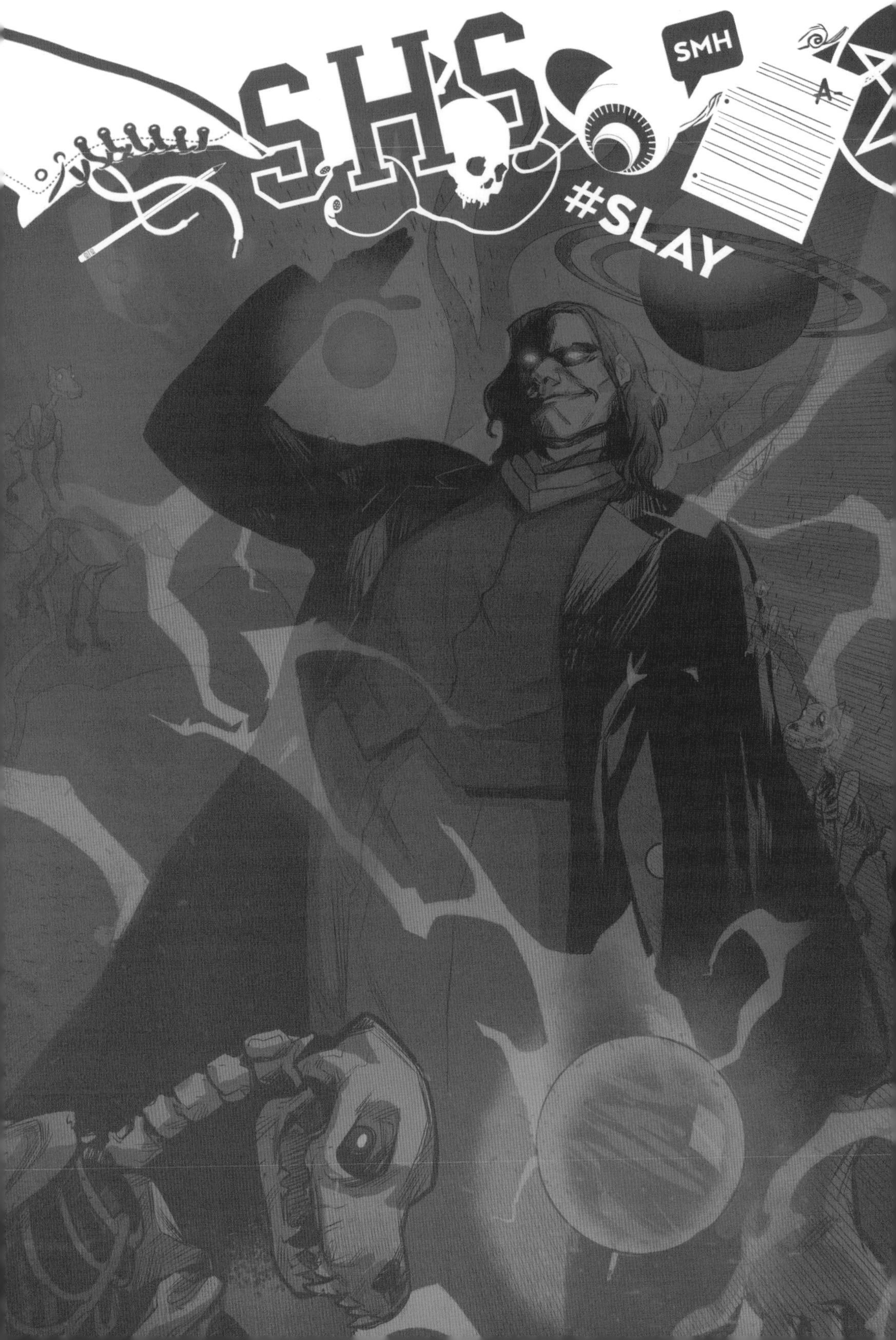
S.H.S.
SMH
#SLAY

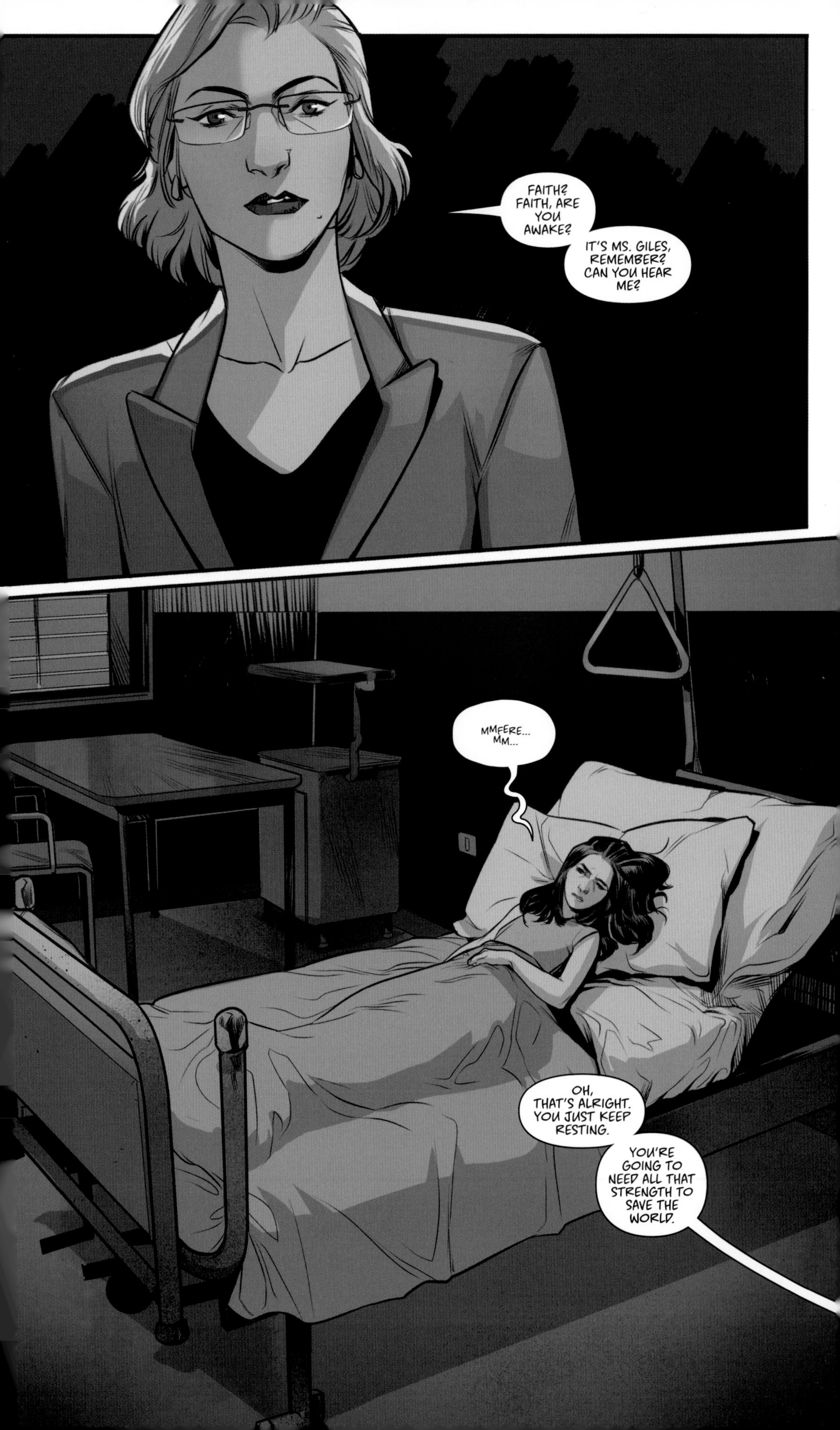
FAITH? FAITH, ARE YOU AWAKE?
IT'S MS. GILES, REMEMBER? CAN YOU HEAR ME?
MMFERE... MM...
OH, THAT'S ALRIGHT. YOU JUST KEEP RESTING.
YOU'RE GOING TO NEED ALL THAT STRENGTH TO SAVE THE WORLD.

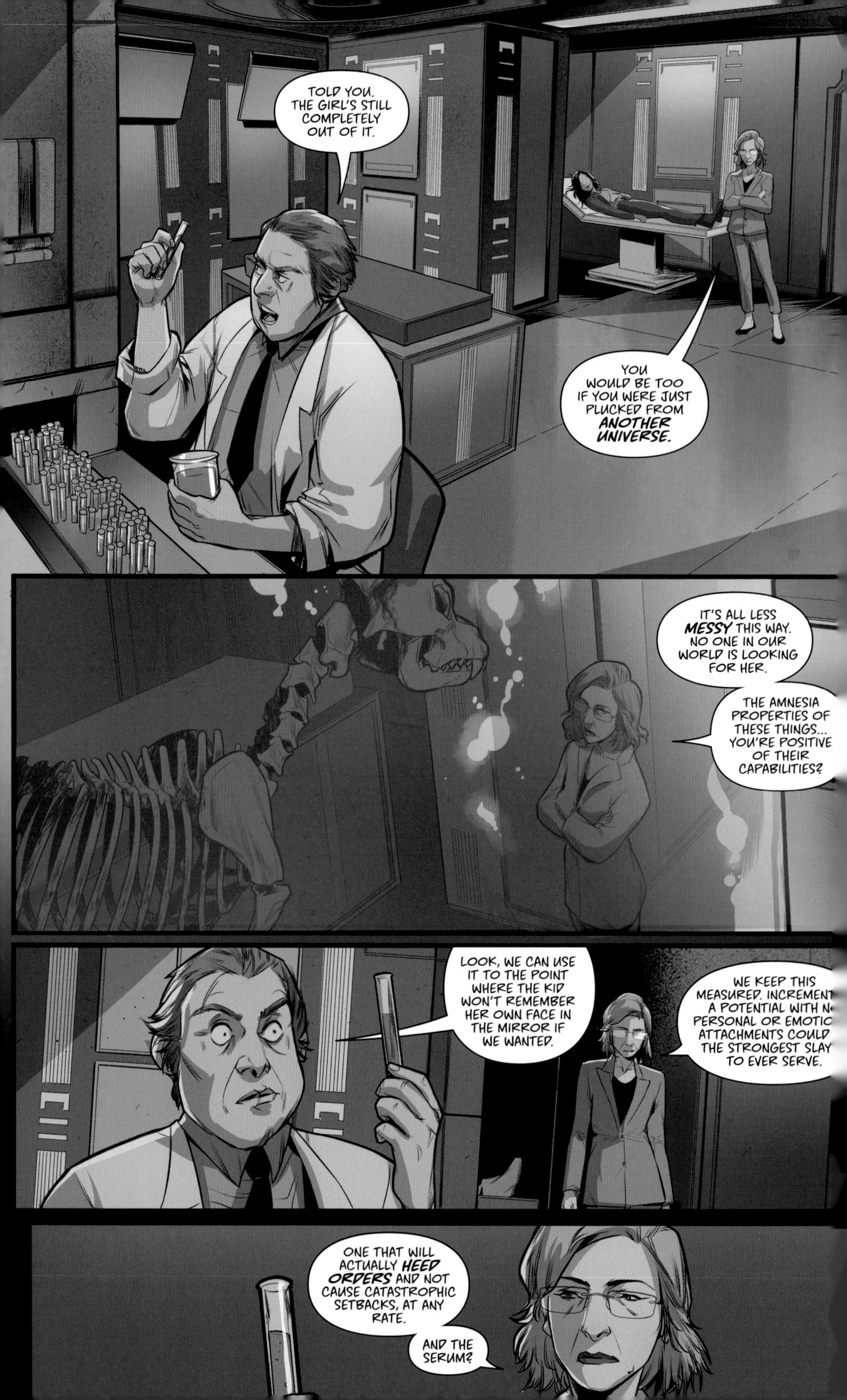
TOLD YOU. THE GIRL'S STILL COMPLETELY OUT OF IT.
YOU WOULD BE TOO IF YOU WERE JUST PLUCKED FROM **ANOTHER UNIVERSE.**
IT'S ALL LESS **MESSY** THIS WAY. NO ONE IN OUR WORLD IS LOOKING FOR HER.
THE AMNESIA PROPERTIES OF THESE THINGS... YOU'RE POSITIVE OF THEIR CAPABILITIES?
LOOK, WE CAN USE IT TO THE POINT WHERE THE KID WON'T REMEMBER HER OWN FACE IN THE MIRROR IF WE WANTED.
WE KEEP THIS MEASURED. INCREMENT A POTENTIAL WITH N PERSONAL OR EMOTIO ATTACHMENTS COULD THE STRONGEST SLAY TO EVER SERVE.
ONE THAT WILL ACTUALLY **HEED ORDERS** AND NOT CAUSE CATASTROPHIC SETBACKS, AT ANY RATE.
AND THE SERUM?

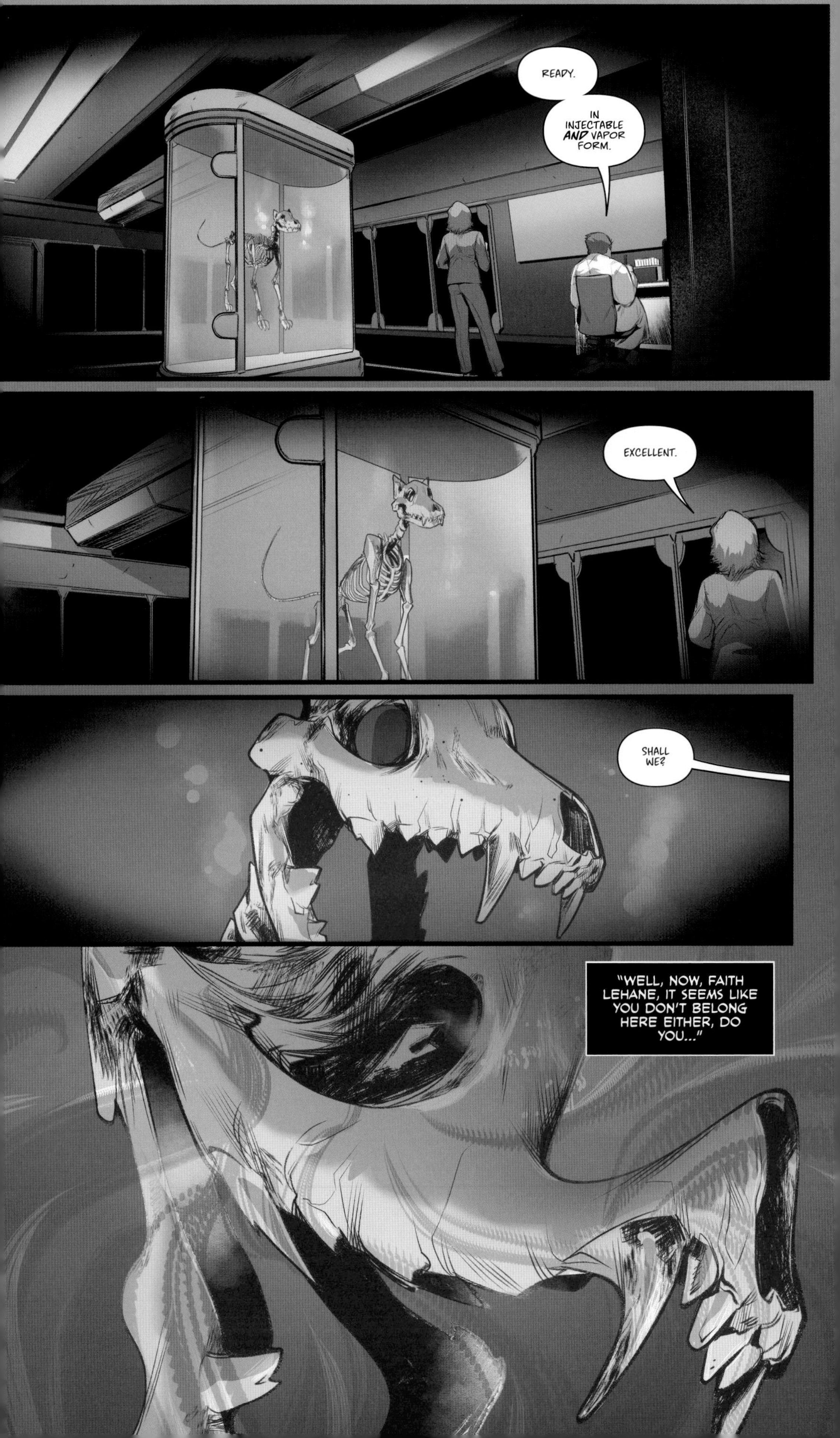
READY.
IN INJECTABLE AND VAPOR FORM.
EXCELLENT.
SHALL WE?
"WELL, NOW, FAITH LEHANE, IT SEEMS LIKE YOU DON'T BELONG HERE EITHER, DO YOU..."

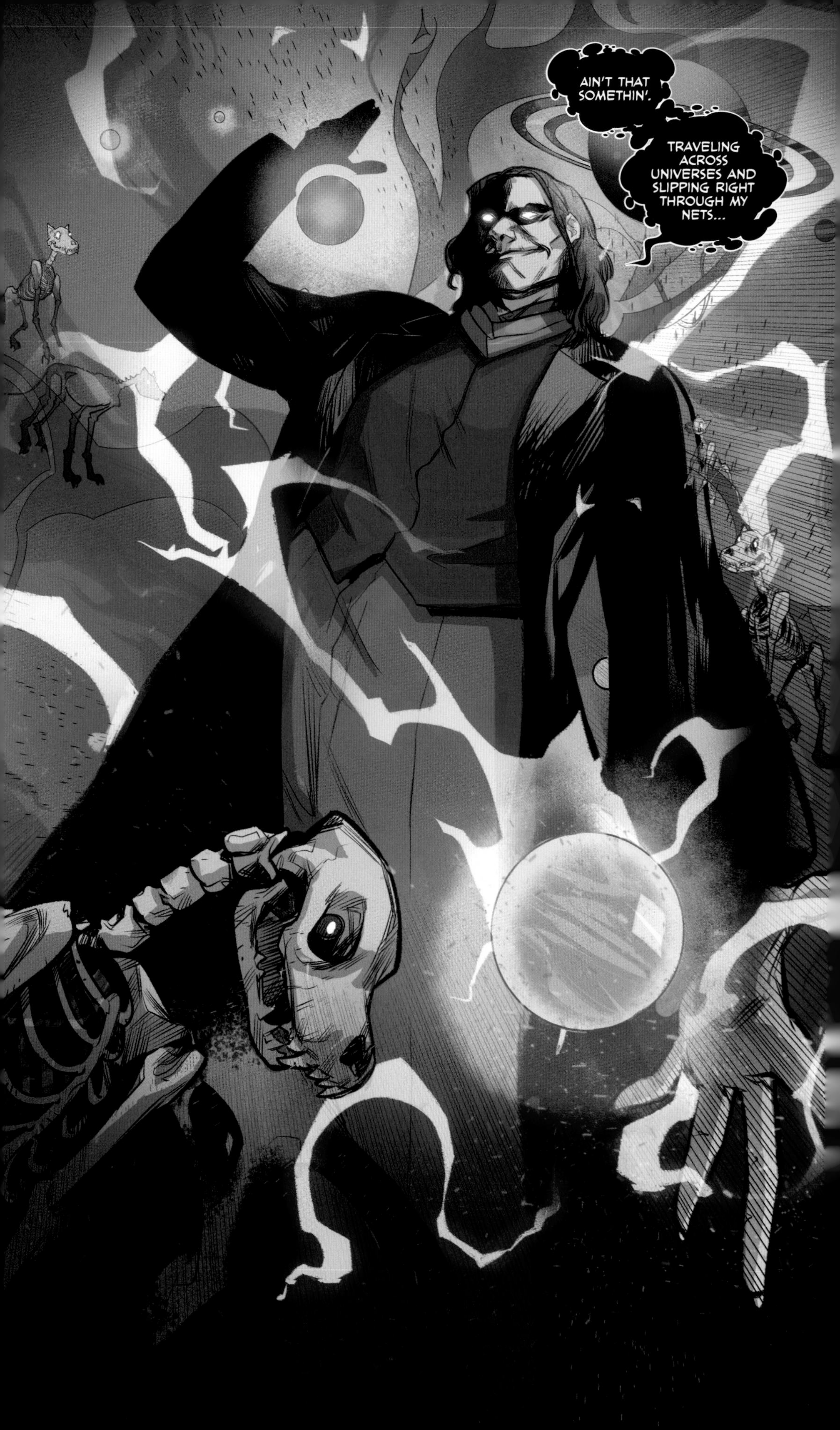
AIN'T THAT SOMETHIN'.
TRAVELING ACROSS UNIVERSES AND SLIPPING RIGHT THROUGH MY NETS...

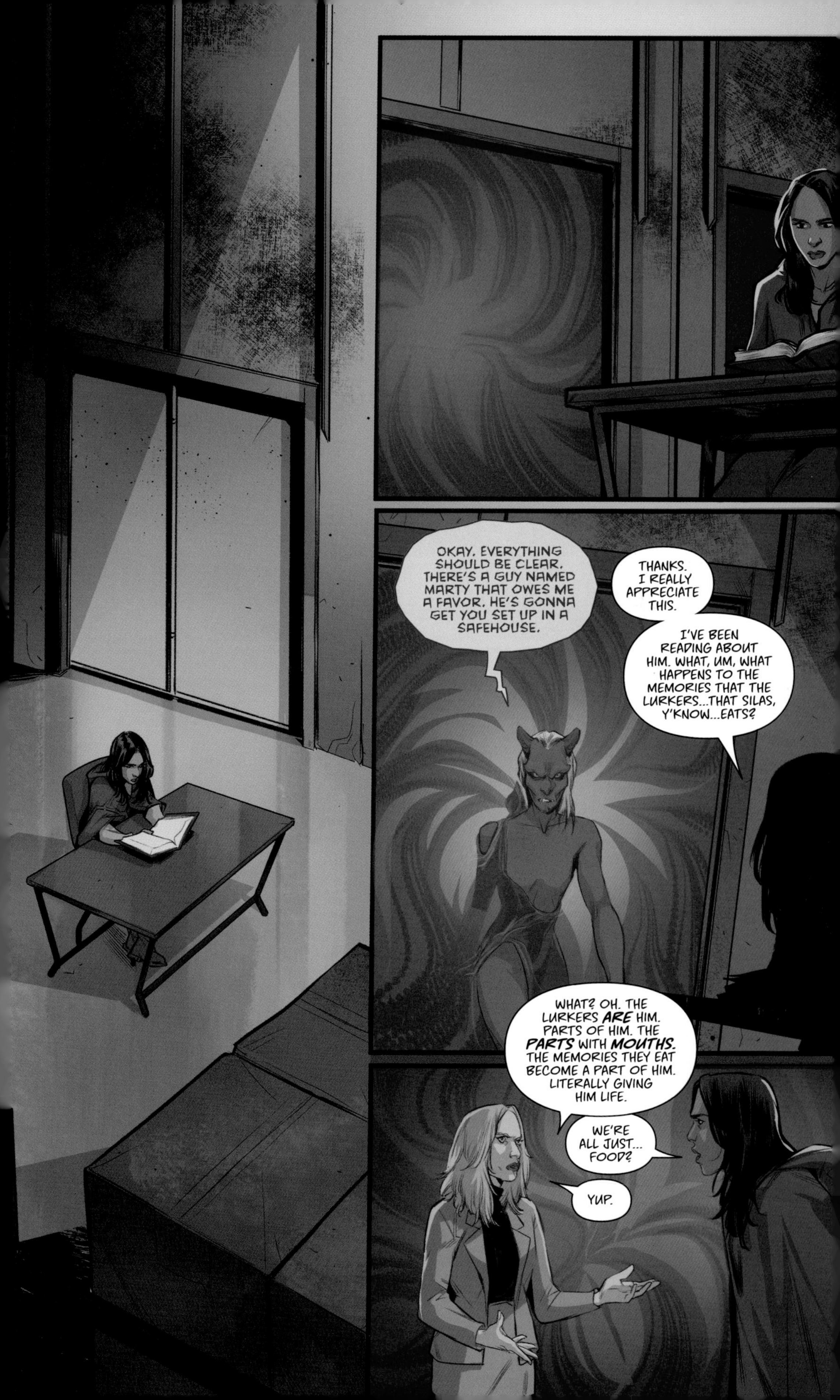
OKAY. EVERYTHING SHOULD BE CLEAR. THERE'S A GUY NAMED MARTY THAT OWES ME A FAVOR. HE'S GONNA GET YOU SET UP IN A SAFEHOUSE.
THANKS. I REALLY APPRECIATE THIS.
I'VE BEEN READING ABOUT HIM. WHAT, UM, WHAT HAPPENS TO THE MEMORIES THAT THE LURKERS...THAT SILAS, Y'KNOW...EATS?
WHAT? OH. THE LURKERS ARE HIM. PARTS OF HIM. THE PARTS WITH MOUTHS. THE MEMORIES THEY EAT BECOME A PART OF HIM. LITERALLY GIVING HIM LIFE.
WE'RE ALL JUST... FOOD?
YUP.

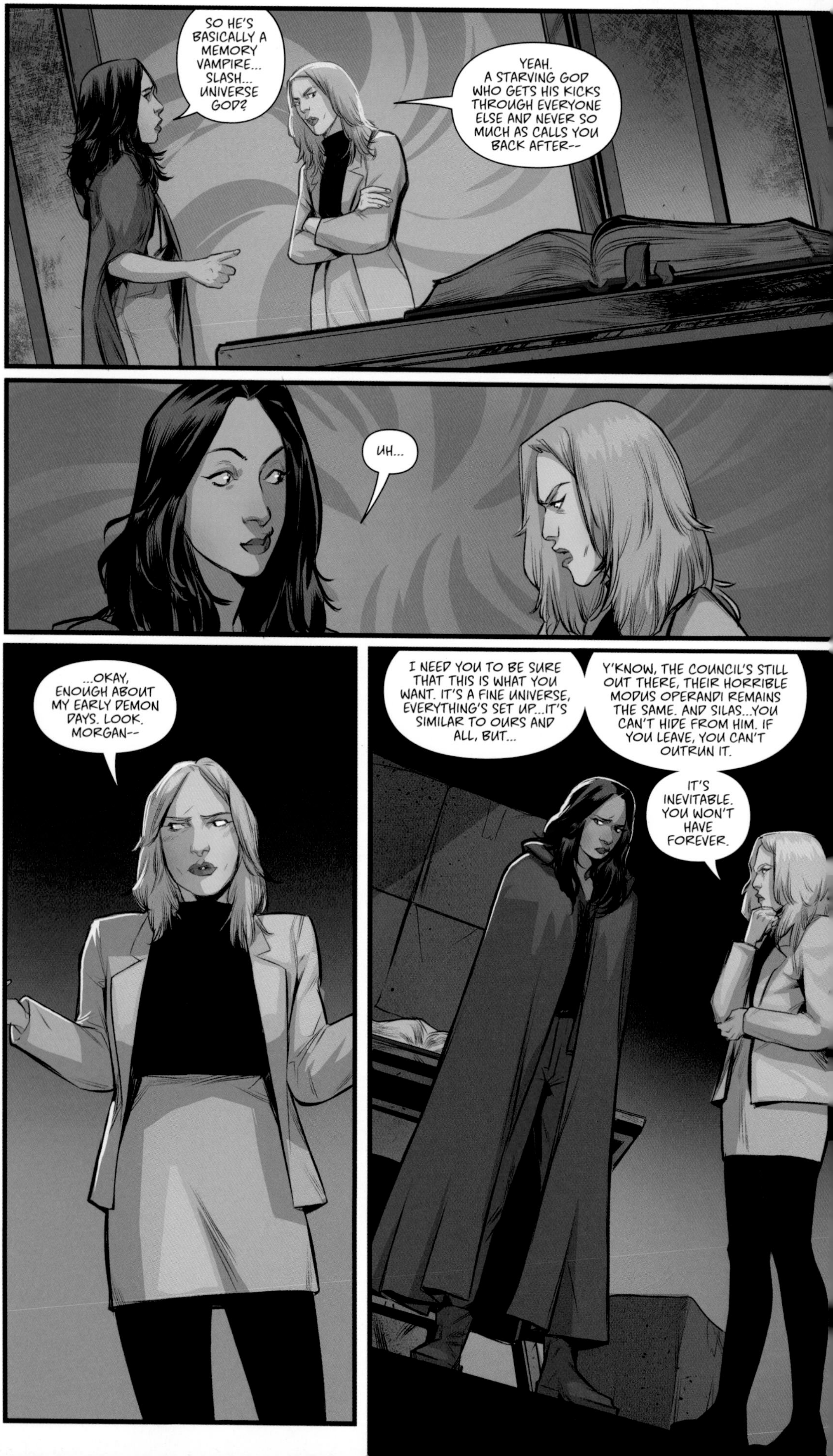
SO HE'S BASICALLY A MEMORY VAMPIRE... SLASH... UNIVERSE GOD?
YEAH. A STARVING GOD WHO GETS HIS KICKS THROUGH EVERYONE ELSE AND NEVER SO MUCH AS CALLS YOU BACK AFTER--
UH...
...OKAY, ENOUGH ABOUT MY EARLY DEMON DAYS. LOOK. MORGAN--
I NEED YOU TO BE SURE THAT THIS IS WHAT YOU WANT. IT'S A FINE UNIVERSE, EVERYTHING'S SET UP...IT'S SIMILAR TO OURS AND ALL, BUT...
Y'KNOW, THE COUNCIL'S STILL OUT THERE, THEIR HORRIBLE MODUS OPERANDI REMAINS THE SAME. AND SILAS...YOU CAN'T HIDE FROM HIM. IF YOU LEAVE, YOU CAN'T OUTRUN IT.
IT'S INEVITABLE. YOU WON'T HAVE FOREVER.

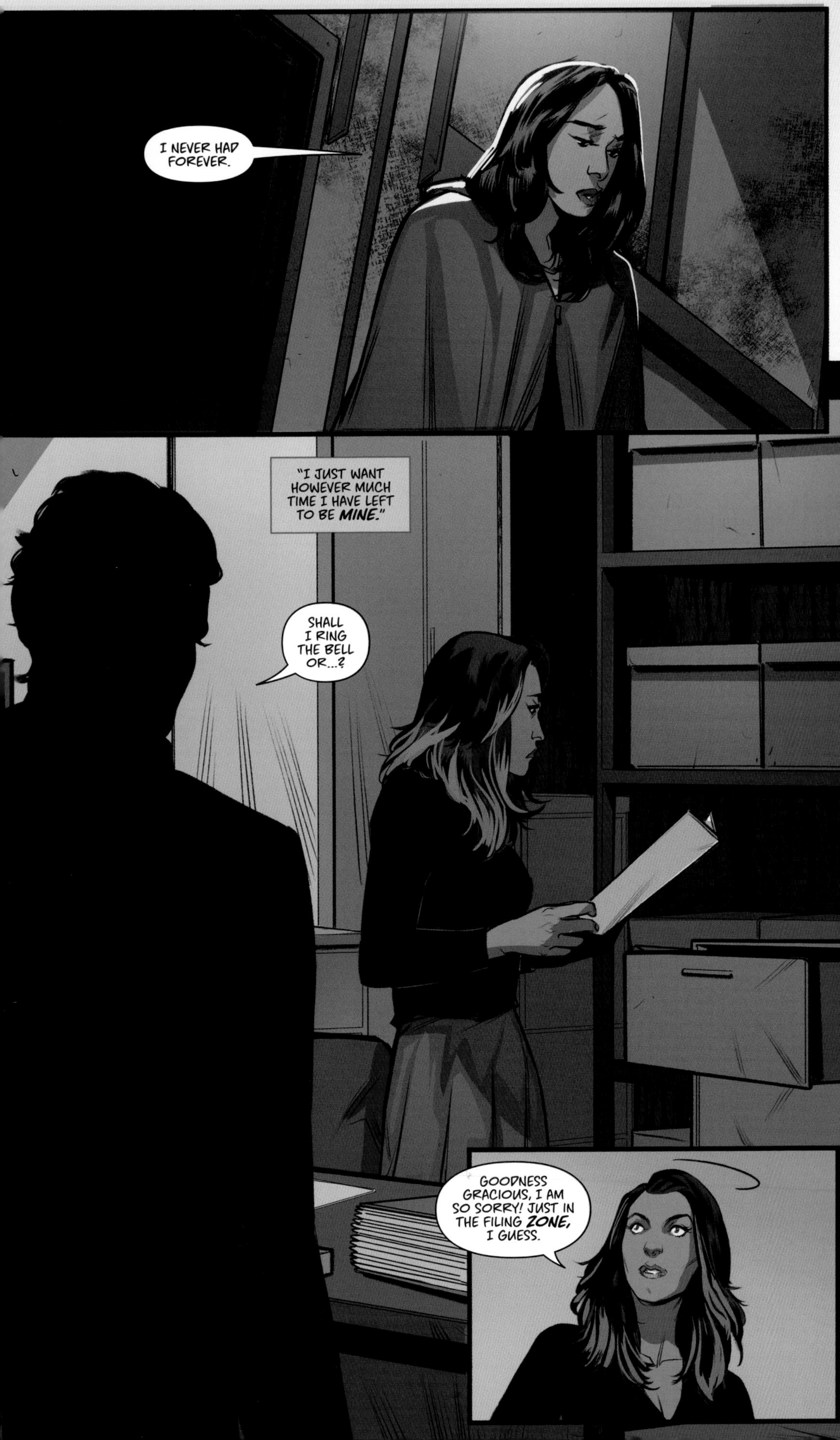
I NEVER HAD FOREVER.
"I JUST WANT HOWEVER MUCH TIME I HAVE LEFT TO BE ***MINE.***"
SHALL I RING THE BELL OR...?
GOODNESS GRACIOUS, I AM SO SORRY! JUST IN THE FILING ***ZONE,*** I GUESS.

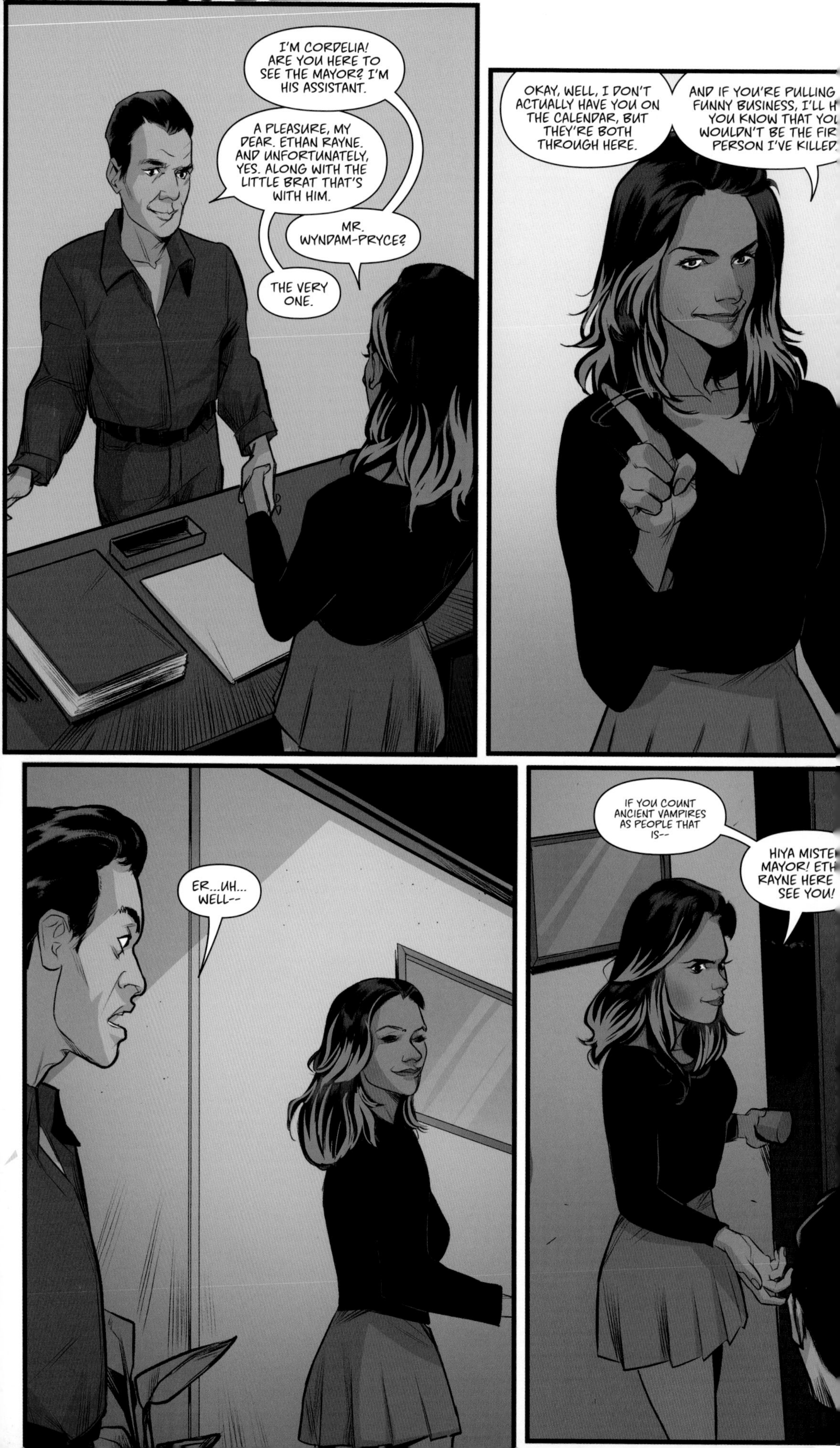
I'M CORDELIA! ARE YOU HERE TO SEE THE MAYOR? I'M HIS ASSISTANT.
A PLEASURE, MY DEAR. ETHAN RAYNE. AND UNFORTUNATELY, YES. ALONG WITH THE LITTLE BRAT THAT'S WITH HIM.
MR. WYNDAM-PRYCE?
THE VERY ONE.
OKAY, WELL, I DON'T ACTUALLY HAVE YOU ON THE CALENDAR, BUT THEY'RE BOTH THROUGH HERE.
AND IF YOU'RE PULLING FUNNY BUSINESS, I'LL H YOU KNOW THAT YOU WOULDN'T BE THE FIR PERSON I'VE KILLED.
ER...UH... WELL--
IF YOU COUNT ANCIENT VAMPIRES AS PEOPLE THAT IS--
HIYA MISTE MAYOR! ETH RAYNE HERE SEE YOU!

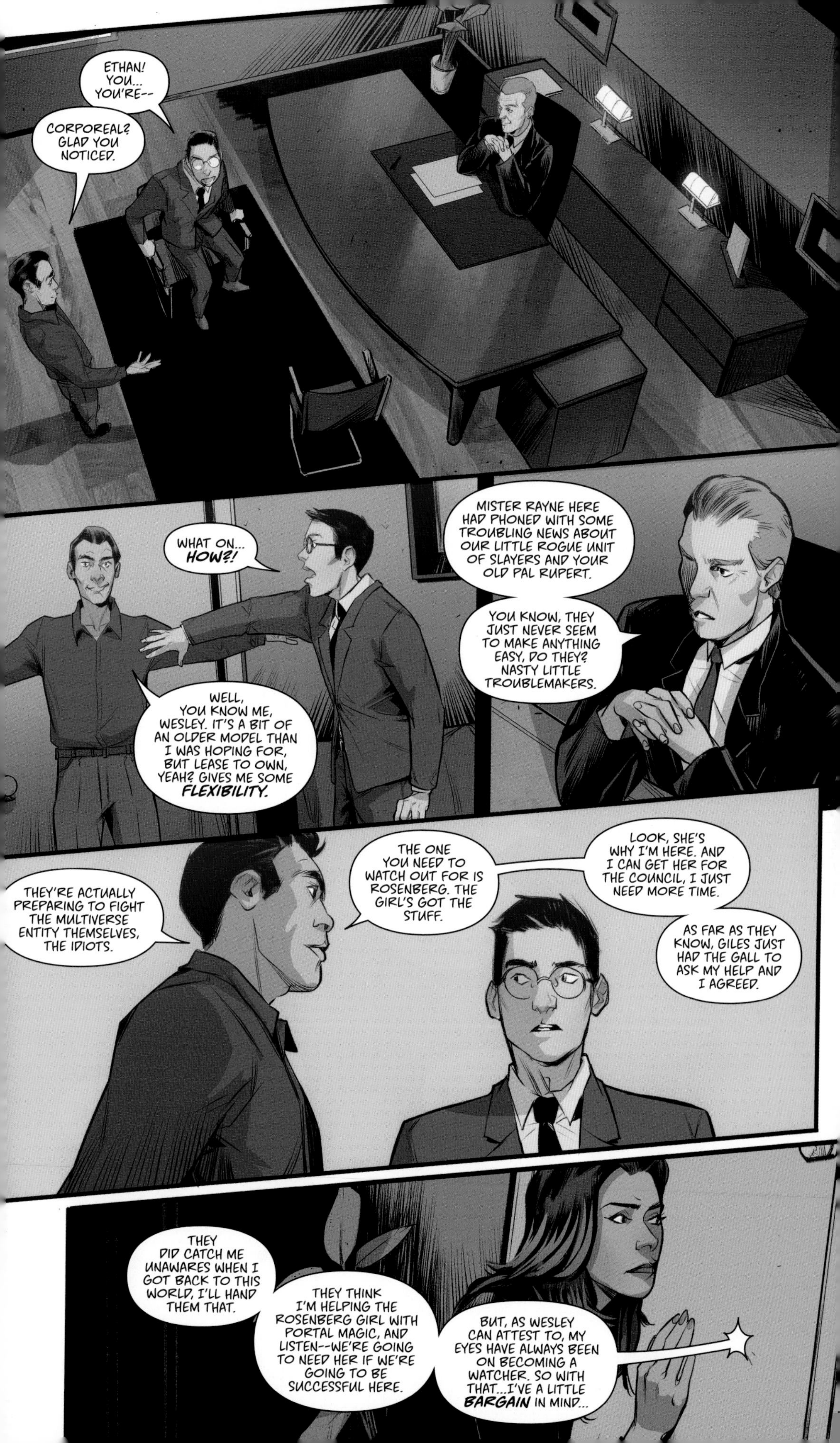
ETHAN! YOU... YOU'RE--
CORPOREAL? GLAD YOU NOTICED.
WHAT ON... HOW?!
WELL, YOU KNOW ME, WESLEY. IT'S A BIT OF AN OLDER MODEL THAN I WAS HOPING FOR, BUT LEASE TO OWN, YEAH? GIVES ME SOME FLEXIBILITY.
MISTER RAYNE HERE HAD PHONED WITH SOME TROUBLING NEWS ABOUT OUR LITTLE ROGUE UNIT OF SLAYERS AND YOUR OLD PAL RUPERT.
YOU KNOW, THEY JUST NEVER SEEM TO MAKE ANYTHING EASY, DO THEY? NASTY LITTLE TROUBLEMAKERS.
THEY'RE ACTUALLY PREPARING TO FIGHT THE MULTIVERSE ENTITY THEMSELVES, THE IDIOTS.
THE ONE YOU NEED TO WATCH OUT FOR IS ROSENBERG. THE GIRL'S GOT THE STUFF.
LOOK, SHE'S WHY I'M HERE. AND I CAN GET HER FOR THE COUNCIL, I JUST NEED MORE TIME.
AS FAR AS THEY KNOW, GILES JUST HAD THE GALL TO ASK MY HELP AND I AGREED.
THEY DID CATCH ME UNAWARES WHEN I GOT BACK TO THIS WORLD, I'LL HAND THEM THAT.
THEY THINK I'M HELPING THE ROSENBERG GIRL WITH PORTAL MAGIC, AND LISTEN--WE'RE GOING TO NEED HER IF WE'RE GOING TO BE SUCCESSFUL HERE.
BUT, AS WESLEY CAN ATTEST TO, MY EYES HAVE ALWAYS BEEN ON BECOMING A WATCHER. SO WITH THAT...I'VE A LITTLE BARGAIN IN MIND...

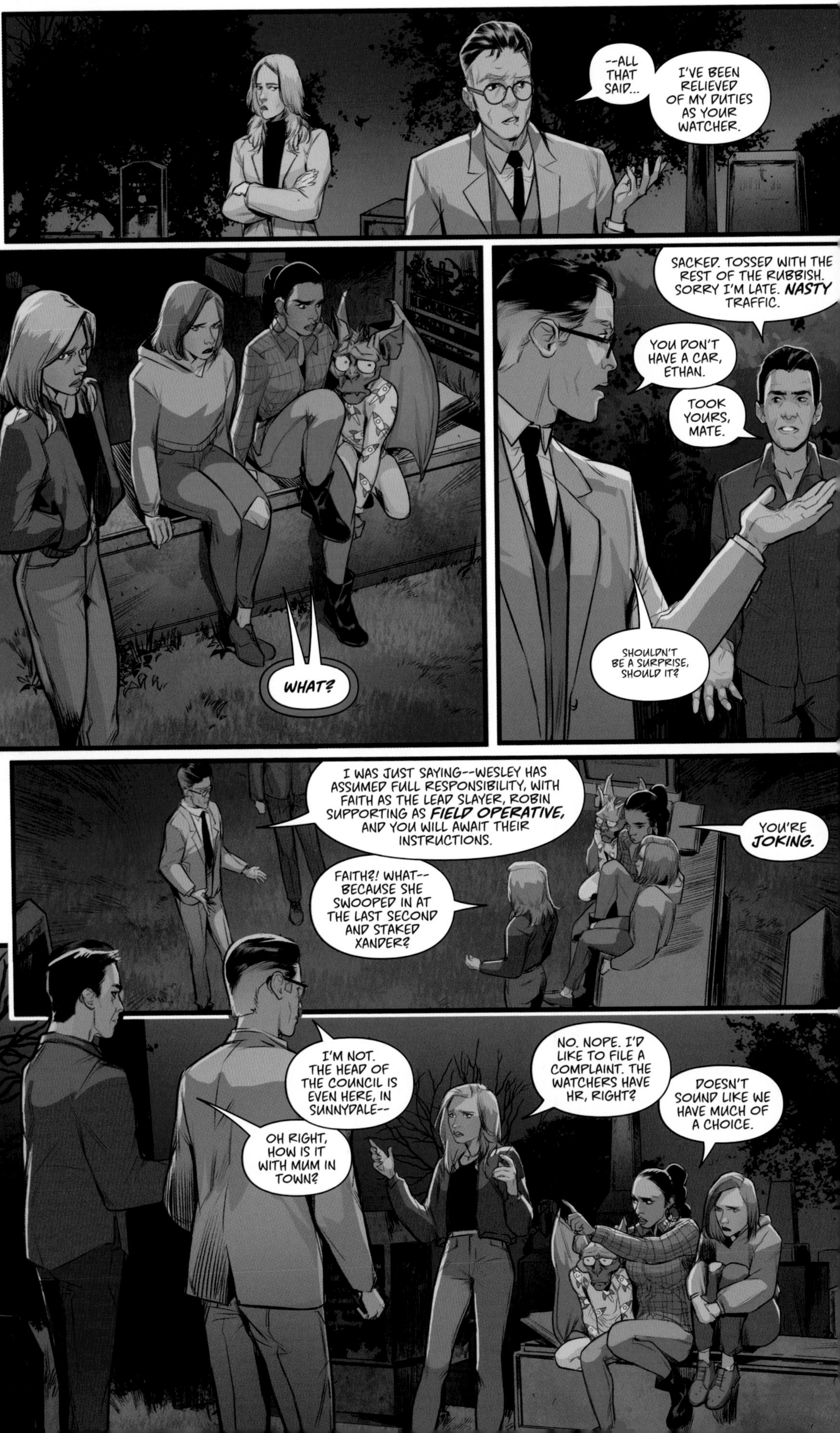
--ALL THAT SAID...
I'VE BEEN RELIEVED OF MY DUTIES AS YOUR WATCHER.
WHAT?
SACKED. TOSSED WITH THE REST OF THE RUBBISH. SORRY I'M LATE. ***NASTY*** TRAFFIC.
YOU DON'T HAVE A CAR, ETHAN.
TOOK YOURS, MATE.
SHOULDN'T BE A SURPRISE, SHOULD IT?
I WAS JUST SAYING--WESLEY HAS ASSUMED FULL RESPONSIBILITY, WITH FAITH AS THE LEAD SLAYER, ROBIN SUPPORTING AS ***FIELD OPERATIVE,*** AND YOU WILL AWAIT THEIR INSTRUCTIONS.
FAITH?! WHAT--BECAUSE SHE SWOOPED IN AT THE LAST SECOND AND STAKED XANDER?
YOU'RE ***JOKING.***
I'M NOT. THE HEAD OF THE COUNCIL IS EVEN HERE, IN SUNNYDALE--
OH RIGHT, HOW IS IT WITH MUM IN TOWN?
NO. NOPE. I'D LIKE TO FILE A COMPLAINT. THE WATCHERS HAVE HR, RIGHT?
DOESN'T SOUND LIKE WE HAVE MUCH OF A CHOICE.

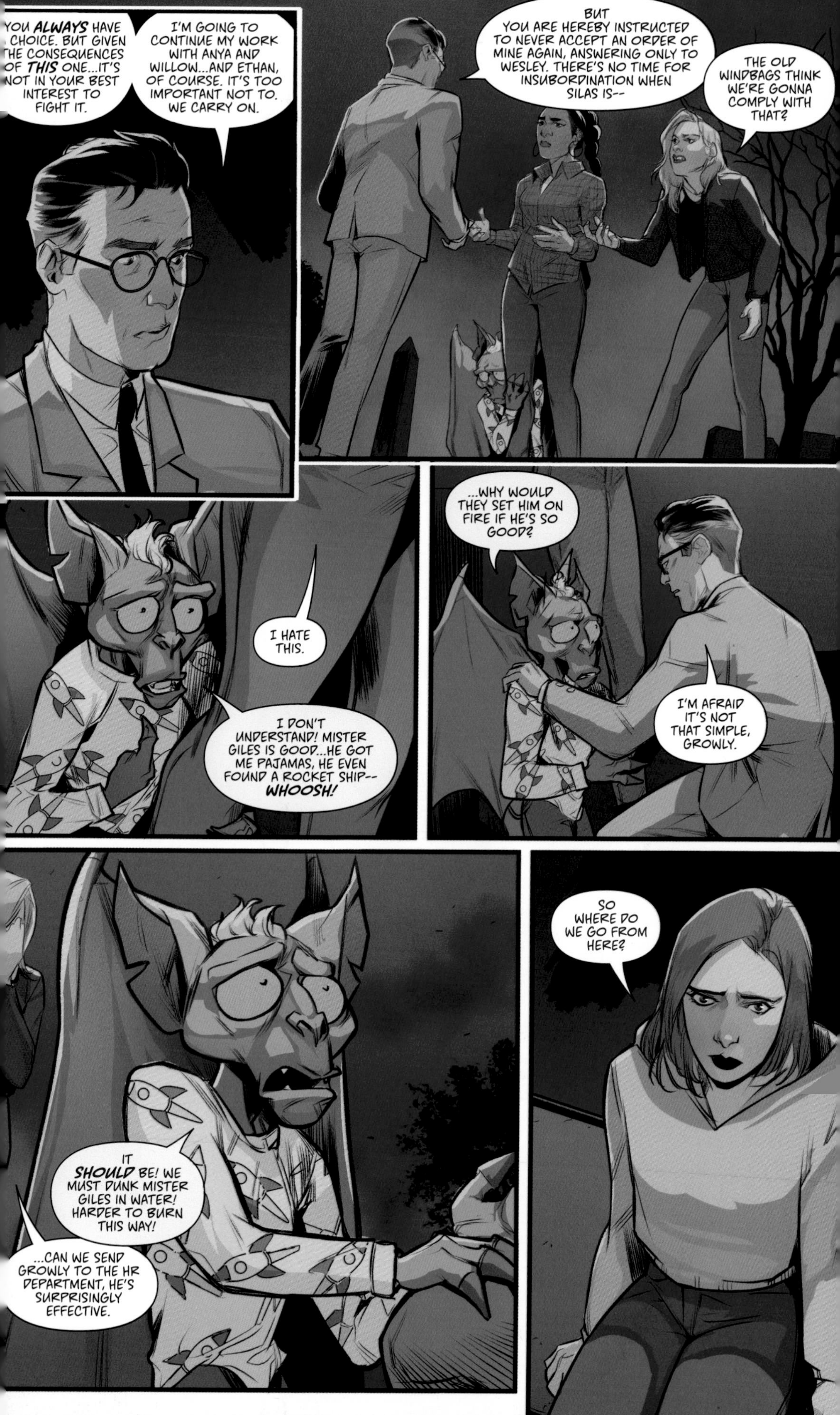
YOU ALWAYS HAVE A CHOICE. BUT GIVEN THE CONSEQUENCES OF THIS ONE...IT'S NOT IN YOUR BEST INTEREST TO FIGHT IT.
I'M GOING TO CONTINUE MY WORK WITH ANYA AND WILLOW...AND ETHAN, OF COURSE. IT'S TOO IMPORTANT NOT TO. WE CARRY ON.
BUT YOU ARE HEREBY INSTRUCTED TO NEVER ACCEPT AN ORDER OF MINE AGAIN, ANSWERING ONLY TO WESLEY. THERE'S NO TIME FOR INSUBORDINATION WHEN SILAS IS--
THE OLD WINDBAGS THINK WE'RE GONNA COMPLY WITH THAT?
I HATE THIS.
I DON'T UNDERSTAND! MISTER GILES IS GOOD...HE GOT ME PAJAMAS, HE EVEN FOUND A ROCKET SHIP-- WHOOSH!
...WHY WOULD THEY SET HIM ON FIRE IF HE'S SO GOOD?
I'M AFRAID IT'S NOT THAT SIMPLE, GROWLY.
IT SHOULD BE! WE MUST DUNK MISTER GILES IN WATER! HARDER TO BURN THIS WAY!
...CAN WE SEND GROWLY TO THE HR DEPARTMENT, HE'S SURPRISINGLY EFFECTIVE.
SO WHERE DO WE GO FROM HERE?

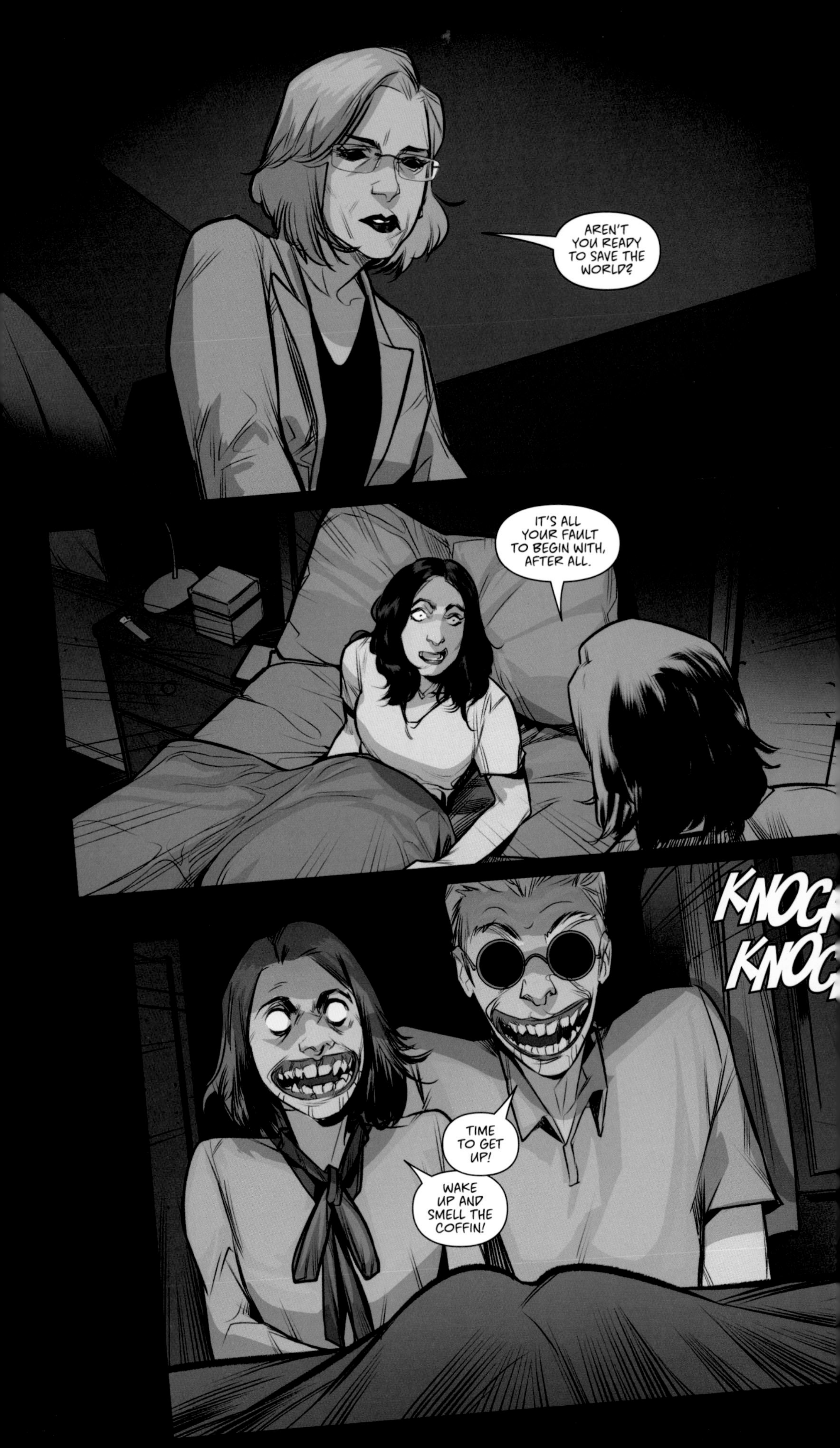
AREN'T YOU READY TO SAVE THE WORLD?
IT'S ALL YOUR FAULT TO BEGIN WITH, AFTER ALL.
KNOC KNOC
TIME TO GET UP!
WAKE UP AND SMELL THE COFFIN!

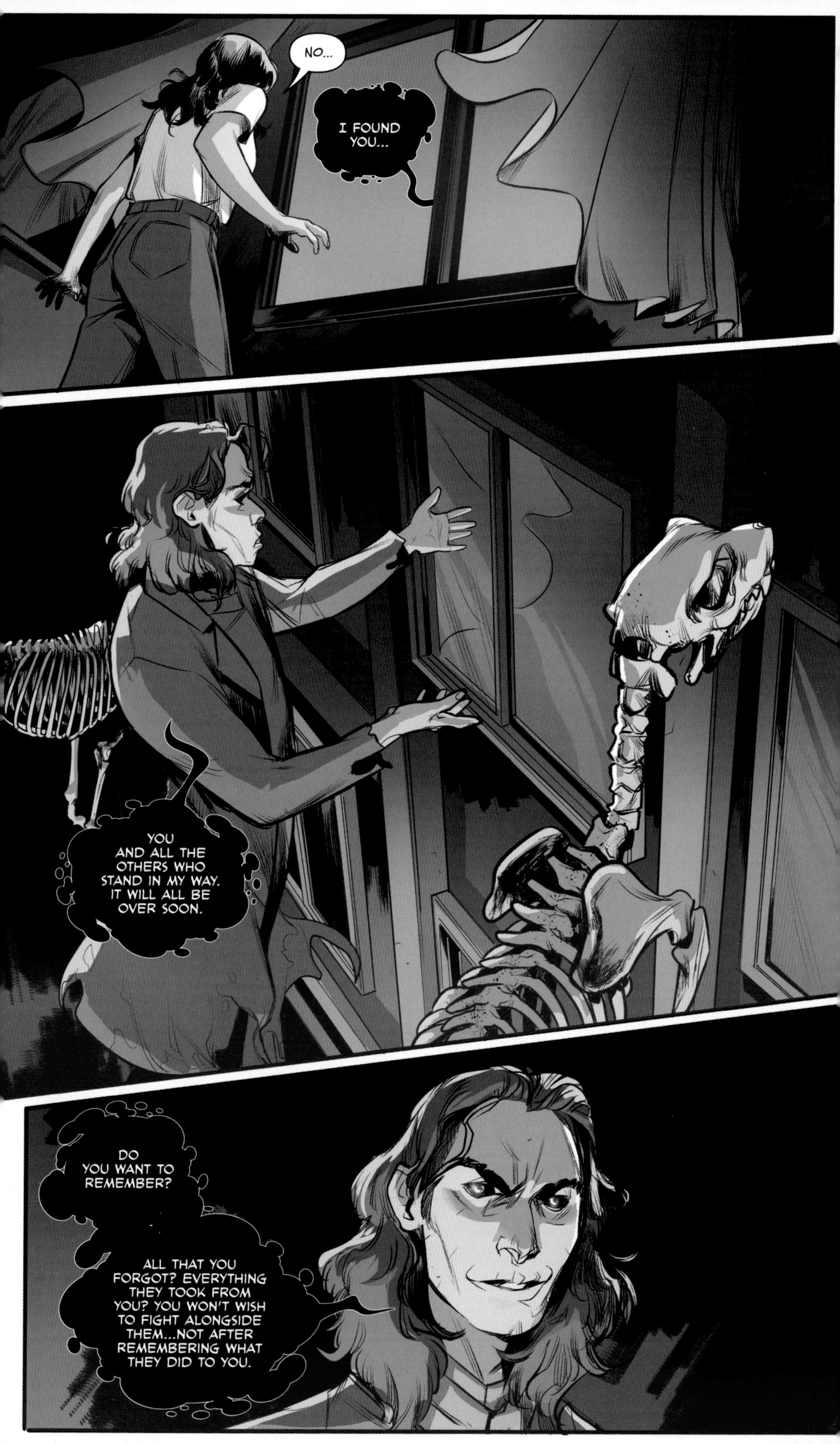
NO...
I FOUND YOU...
YOU AND ALL THE OTHERS WHO STAND IN MY WAY. IT WILL ALL BE OVER SOON.
DO YOU WANT TO REMEMBER?
ALL THAT YOU FORGOT? EVERYTHING THEY TOOK FROM YOU? YOU WON'T WISH TO FIGHT ALONGSIDE THEM...NOT AFTER REMEMBERING WHAT THEY DID TO YOU.

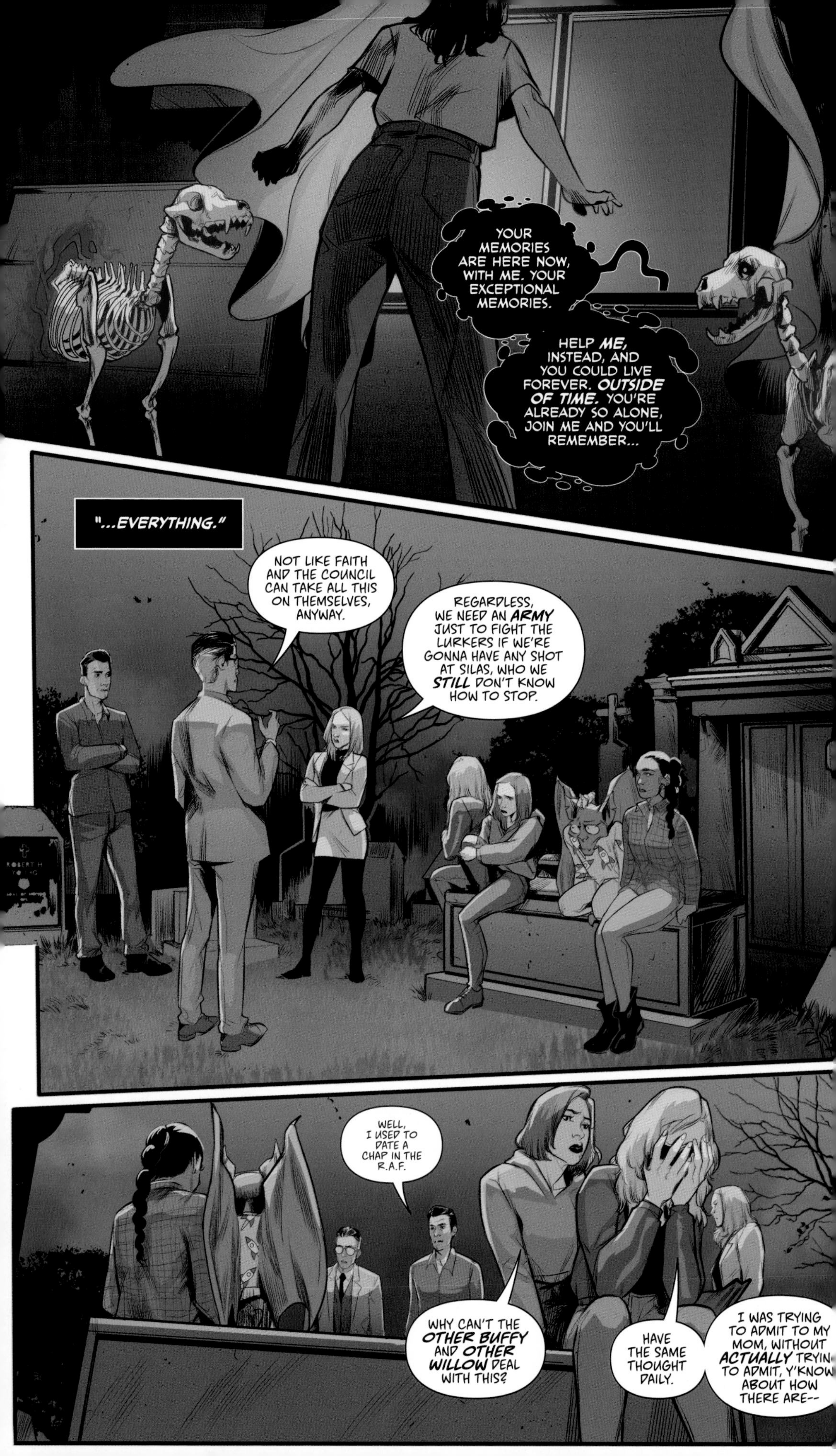
YOUR MEMORIES ARE HERE NOW, WITH ME. YOUR EXCEPTIONAL MEMORIES.
HELP ME, INSTEAD, AND YOU COULD LIVE FOREVER. OUTSIDE OF TIME. YOU'RE ALREADY SO ALONE, JOIN ME AND YOU'LL REMEMBER...
"...EVERYTHING."
NOT LIKE FAITH AND THE COUNCIL CAN TAKE ALL THIS ON THEMSELVES, ANYWAY.
REGARDLESS, WE NEED AN ARMY JUST TO FIGHT THE LURKERS IF WE'RE GONNA HAVE ANY SHOT AT SILAS, WHO WE STILL DON'T KNOW HOW TO STOP.
WELL, I USED TO DATE A CHAP IN THE R.A.F.
WHY CAN'T THE OTHER BUFFY AND OTHER WILLOW DEAL WITH THIS?
HAVE THE SAME THOUGHT DAILY.
I WAS TRYING TO ADMIT TO MY MOM, WITHOUT ACTUALLY TRYIN TO ADMIT, Y'KNOW ABOUT HOW THERE ARE--

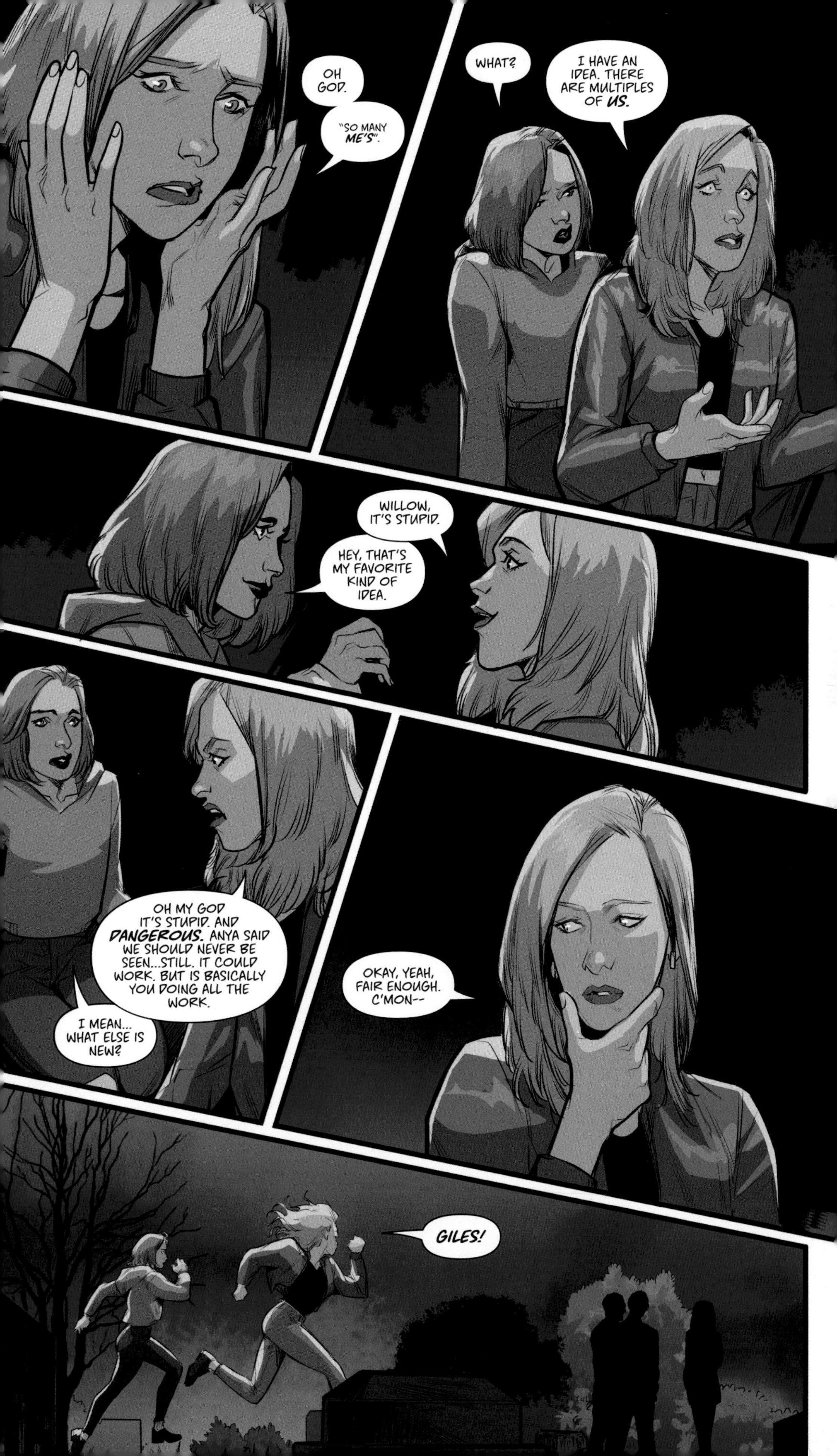

OH GOD.
"SO MANY ME'S".
WHAT?
I HAVE AN IDEA. THERE ARE MULTIPLES OF US.
WILLOW, IT'S STUPID.
HEY, THAT'S MY FAVORITE KIND OF IDEA.
OH MY GOD IT'S STUPID. AND DANGEROUS. ANYA SAID WE SHOULD NEVER BE SEEN...STILL. IT COULD WORK. BUT IS BASICALLY YOU DOING ALL THE WORK.
I MEAN... WHAT ELSE IS NEW?
OKAY, YEAH, FAIR ENOUGH. C'MON--
GILES!

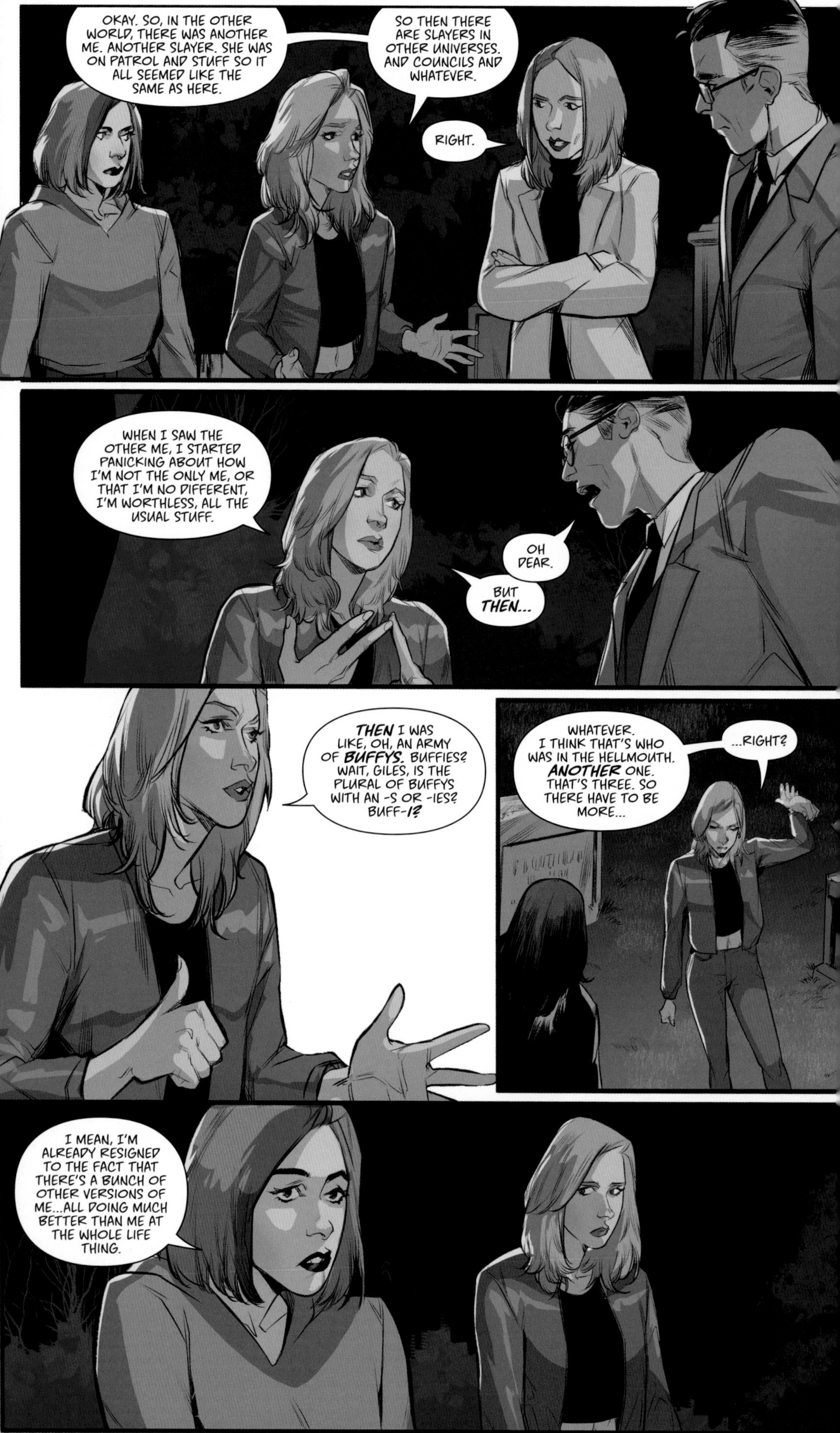
OKAY. SO, IN THE OTHER WORLD, THERE WAS ANOTHER ME. ANOTHER SLAYER. SHE WAS ON PATROL AND STUFF SO IT ALL SEEMED LIKE THE SAME AS HERE.
SO THEN THERE ARE SLAYERS IN OTHER UNIVERSES. AND COUNCILS AND WHATEVER.
RIGHT.
WHEN I SAW THE OTHER ME, I STARTED PANICKING ABOUT HOW I'M NOT THE ONLY ME, OR THAT I'M NO DIFFERENT, I'M WORTHLESS, ALL THE USUAL STUFF.
OH DEAR.
BUT **THEN...**
THEN I WAS LIKE, OH, AN ARMY OF **BUFFYS.** BUFFIES? WAIT, GILES, IS THE PLURAL OF BUFFYS WITH AN -S OR -IES? BUFF-**I?**
WHATEVER. I THINK THAT'S WHO WAS IN THE HELLMOUTH. **ANOTHER** ONE. THAT'S THREE. SO THERE HAVE TO BE MORE...
...RIGHT?
I MEAN, I'M ALREADY RESIGNED TO THE FACT THAT THERE'S A BUNCH OF OTHER VERSIONS OF ME...ALL DOING MUCH BETTER THAN ME AT THE WHOLE LIFE THING.

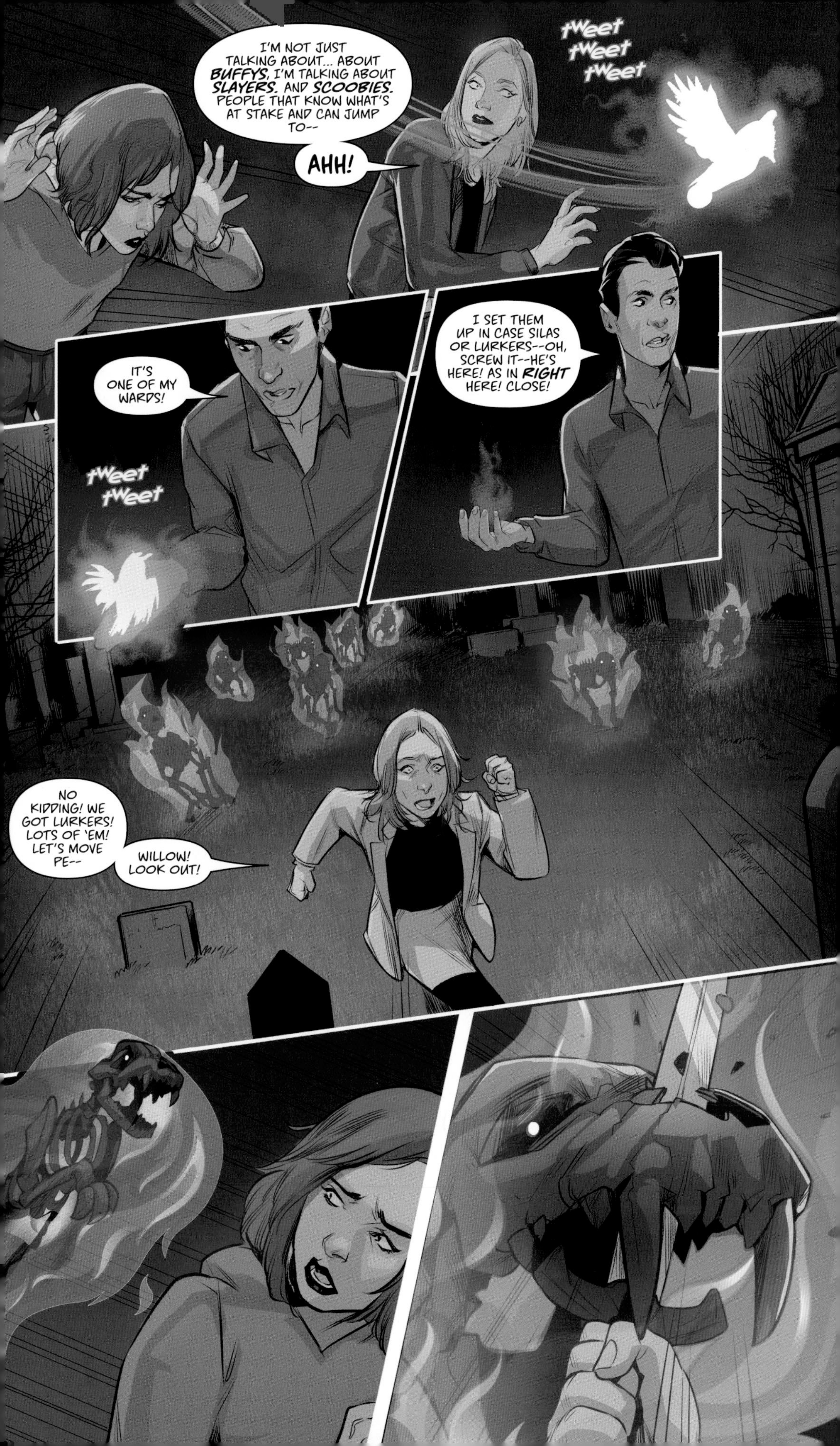

I'M NOT JUST TALKING ABOUT... ABOUT **BUFFYS**, I'M TALKING ABOUT **SLAYERS.** AND **SCOOBIES.** PEOPLE THAT KNOW WHAT'S AT STAKE AND CAN JUMP TO--
AHH!
tweet tweet tweet
IT'S ONE OF MY WARDS!
tweet tweet
I SET THEM UP IN CASE SILAS OR LURKERS--OH, SCREW IT--HE'S HERE! AS IN **RIGHT** HERE! CLOSE!
NO KIDDING! WE GOT LURKERS! LOTS OF 'EM! LET'S MOVE PE--
WILLOW! LOOK OUT!

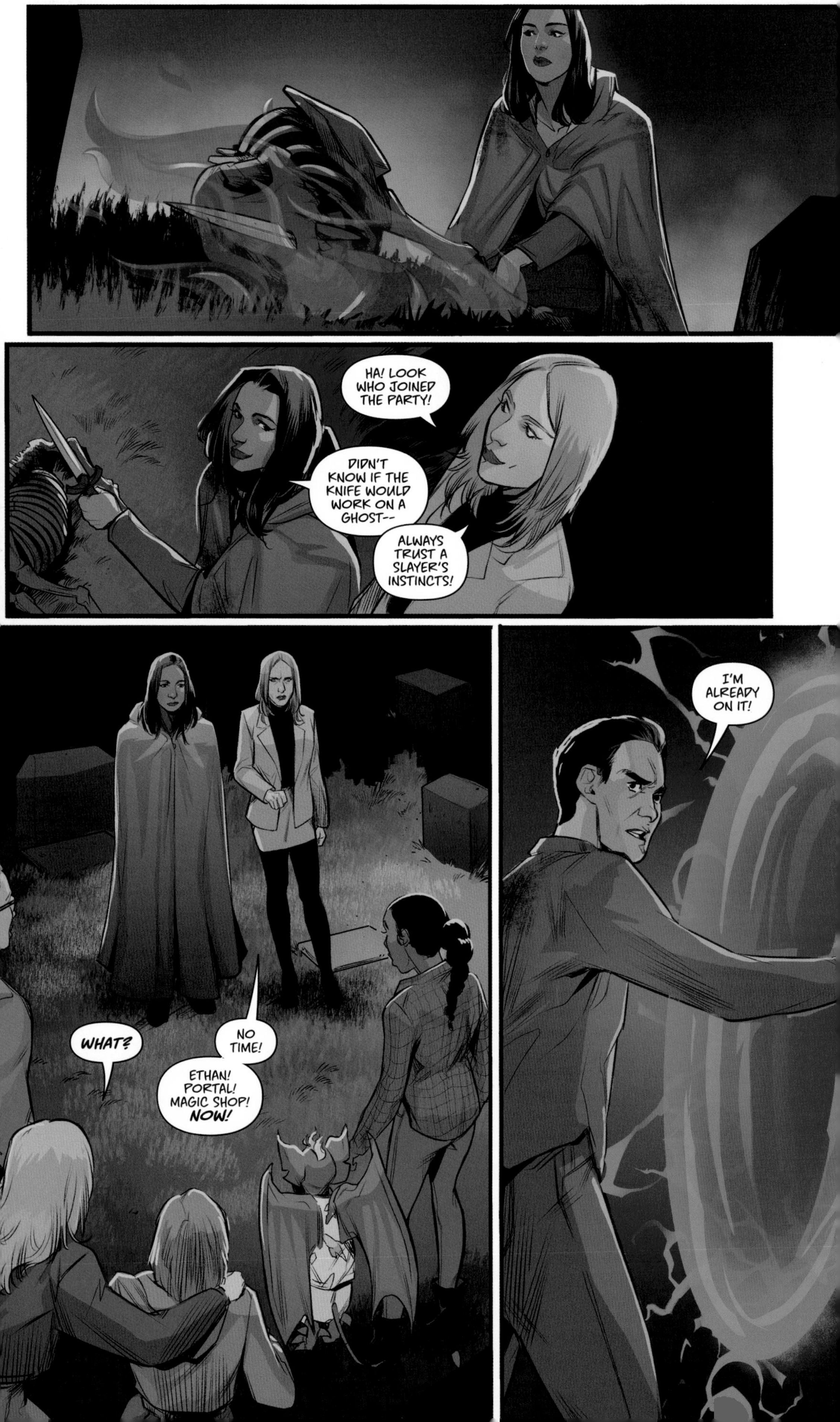
HA! LOOK WHO JOINED THE PARTY!
DIDN'T KNOW IF THE KNIFE WOULD WORK ON A GHOST--
ALWAYS TRUST A SLAYER'S INSTINCTS!
WHAT?
NO TIME!
ETHAN! PORTAL! MAGIC SHOP! **NOW!**
I'M ALREADY ON IT!

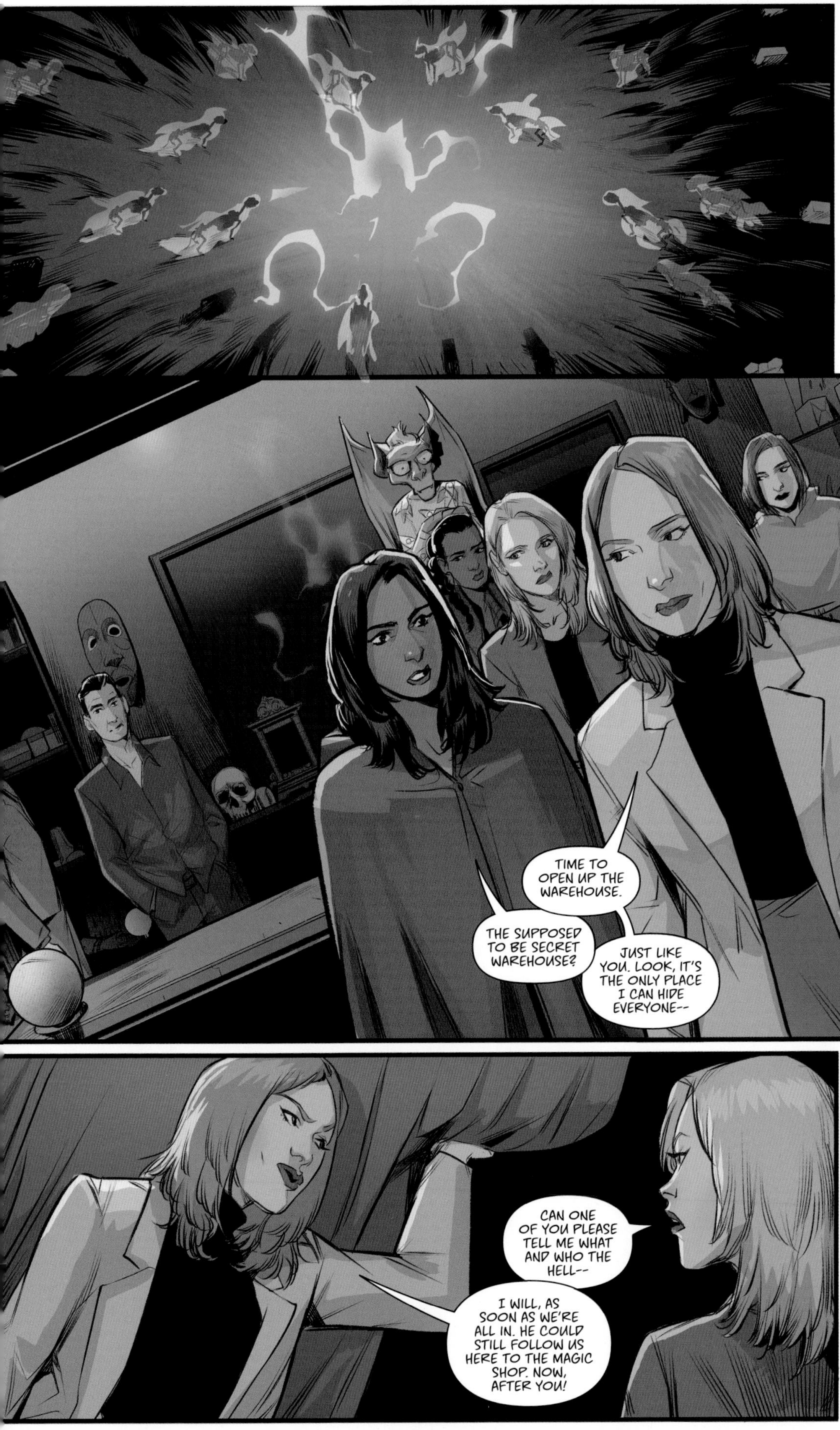
TIME TO OPEN UP THE WAREHOUSE.
THE SUPPOSED TO BE SECRET WAREHOUSE?
JUST LIKE YOU. LOOK, IT'S THE ONLY PLACE I CAN HIDE EVERYONE--
CAN ONE OF YOU PLEASE TELL ME WHAT AND WHO THE HELL--
I WILL, AS SOON AS WE'RE ALL IN. HE COULD STILL FOLLOW US HERE TO THE MAGIC SHOP. NOW, AFTER YOU!

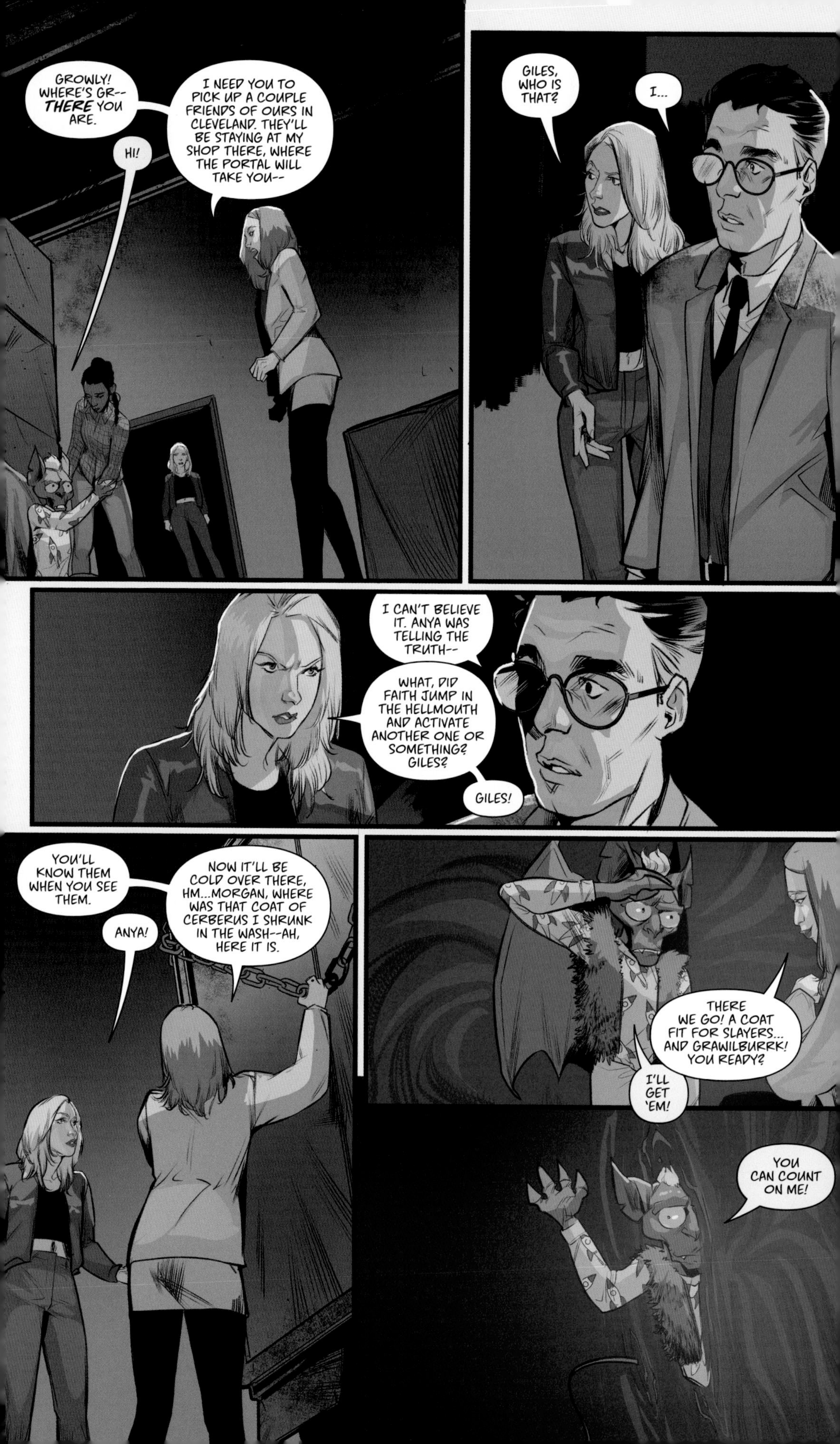
GROWLY! WHERE'S GR-- **THERE** YOU ARE.
I NEED YOU TO PICK UP A COUPLE FRIENDS OF OURS IN CLEVELAND. THEY'LL BE STAYING AT MY SHOP THERE, WHERE THE PORTAL WILL TAKE YOU--
HI!
GILES, WHO IS THAT?
I...
I CAN'T BELIEVE IT. ANYA WAS TELLING THE TRUTH--
WHAT, DID FAITH JUMP IN THE HELLMOUTH AND ACTIVATE ANOTHER ONE OR SOMETHING? GILES?
GILES!
YOU'LL KNOW THEM WHEN YOU SEE THEM.
NOW IT'LL BE COLD OVER THERE, HM...MORGAN, WHERE WAS THAT COAT OF CERBERUS I SHRUNK IN THE WASH--AH, HERE IT IS.
ANYA!
THERE WE GO! A COAT FIT FOR SLAYERS... AND GRAWILBURRK! YOU READY?
I'LL GET 'EM!
YOU CAN COUNT ON ME!

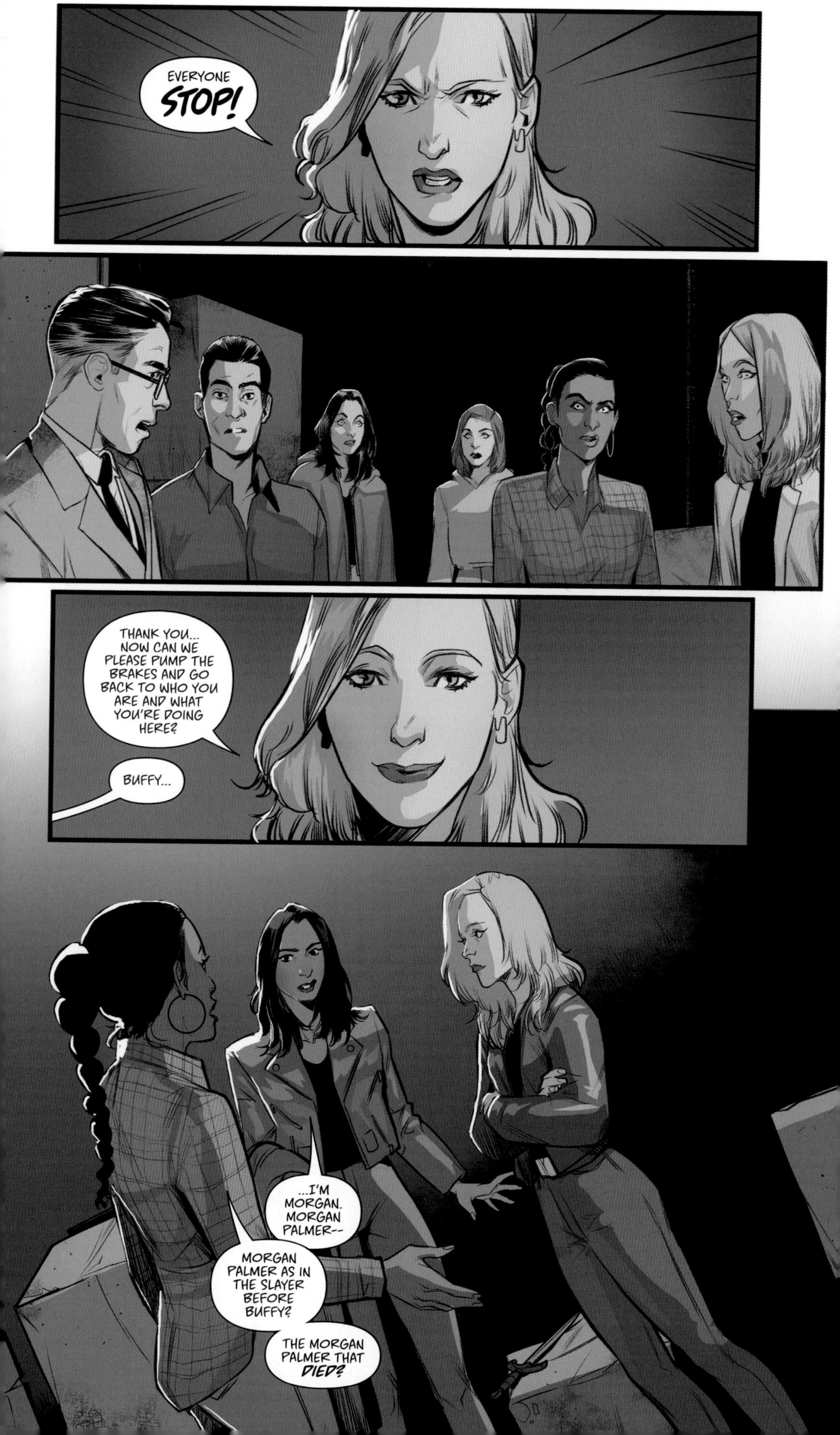
EVERYONE STOP!
THANK YOU... NOW CAN WE PLEASE PUMP THE BRAKES AND GO BACK TO WHO YOU ARE AND WHAT YOU'RE DOING HERE?
BUFFY...
...I'M MORGAN. MORGAN PALMER--
MORGAN PALMER AS IN THE SLAYER BEFORE BUFFY?
THE MORGAN PALMER THAT DIED?

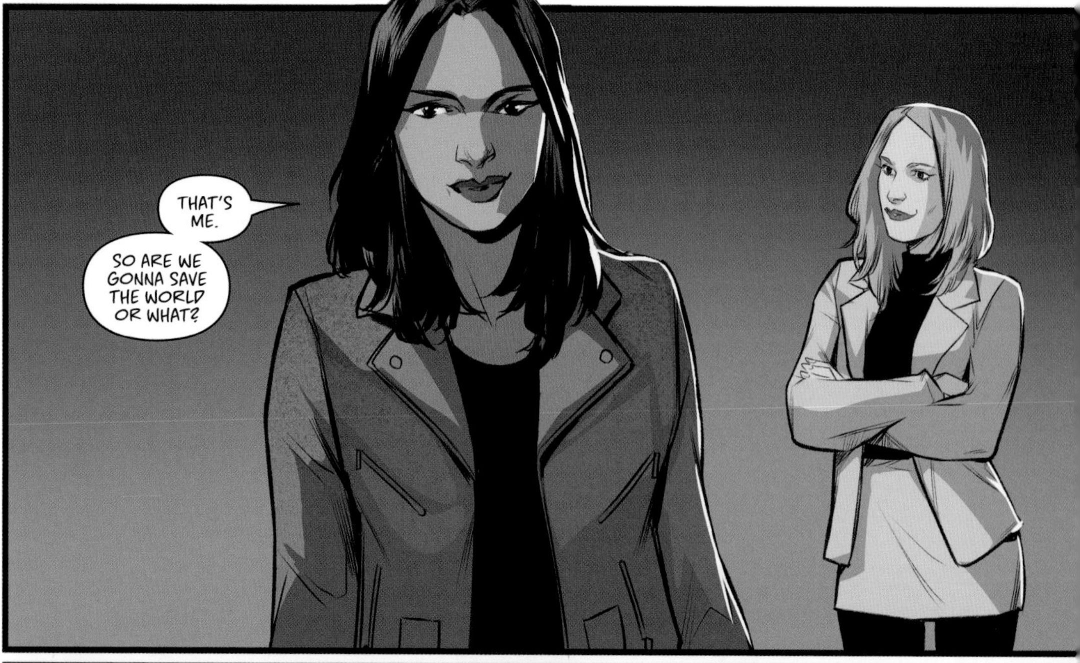
THAT'S ME.
SO ARE WE GONNA SAVE THE WORLD OR WHAT?

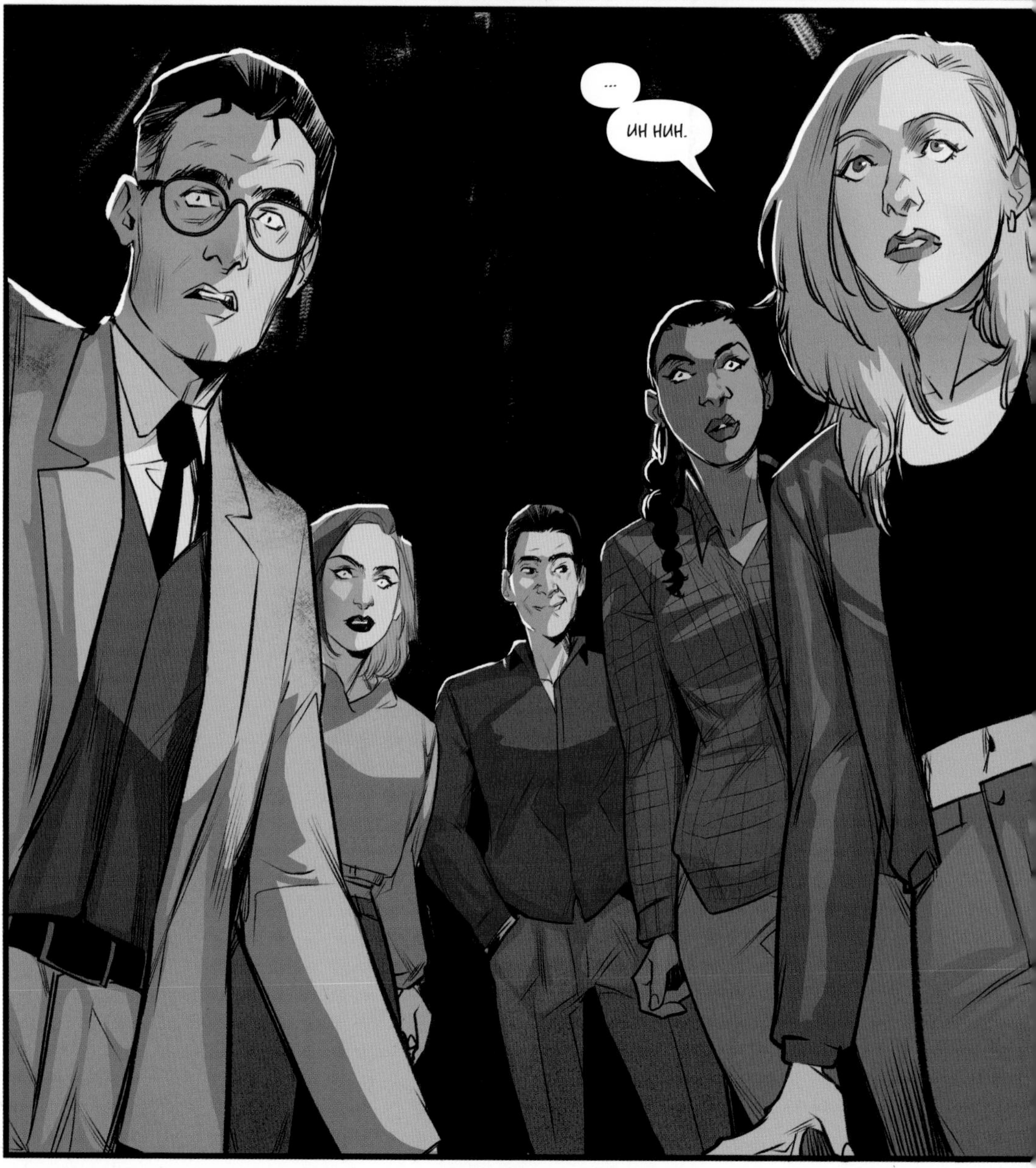
...
UH HUH.

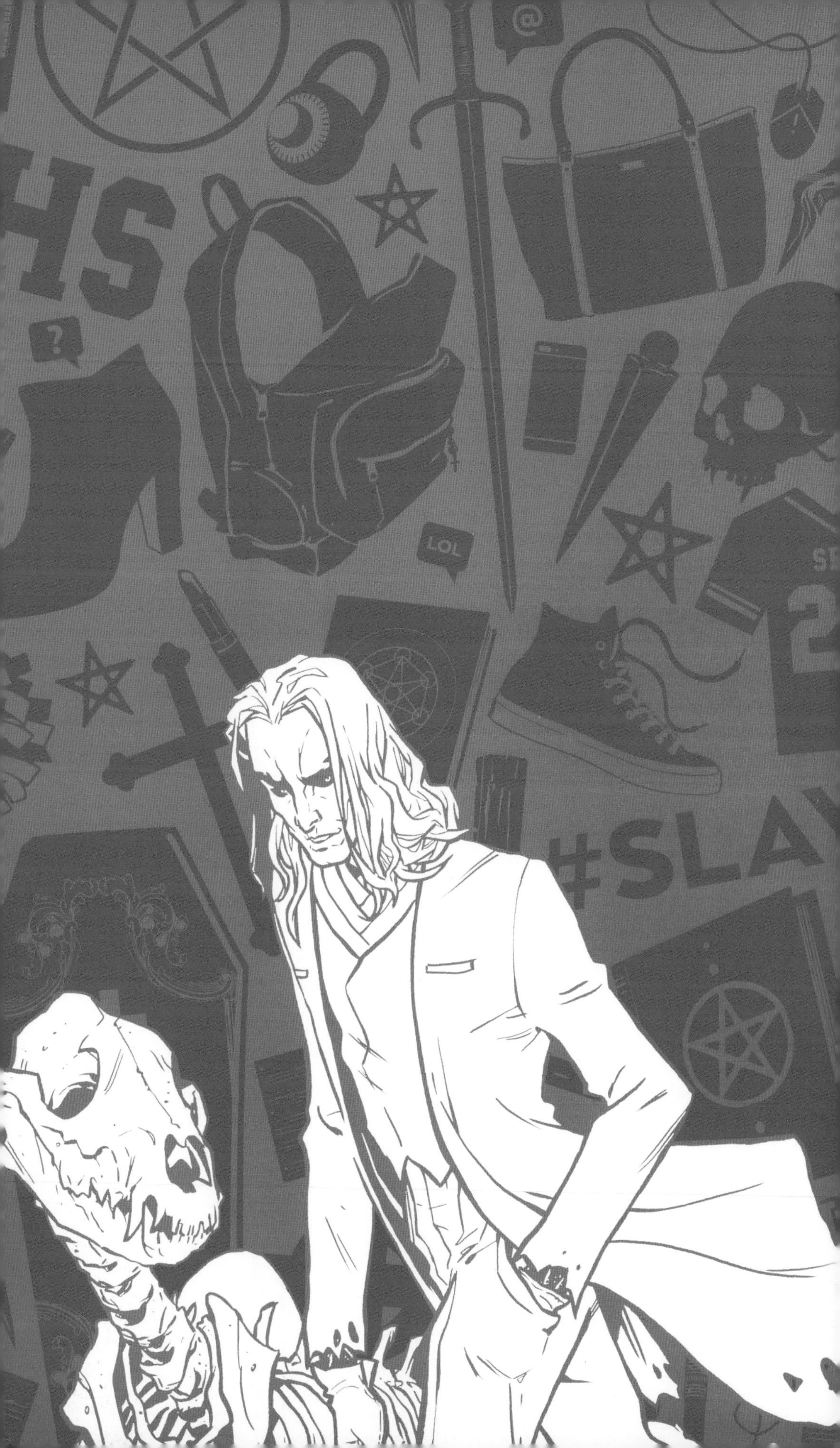
LOL

MULTIVERSAL INTERLUDE:

TEA TIME

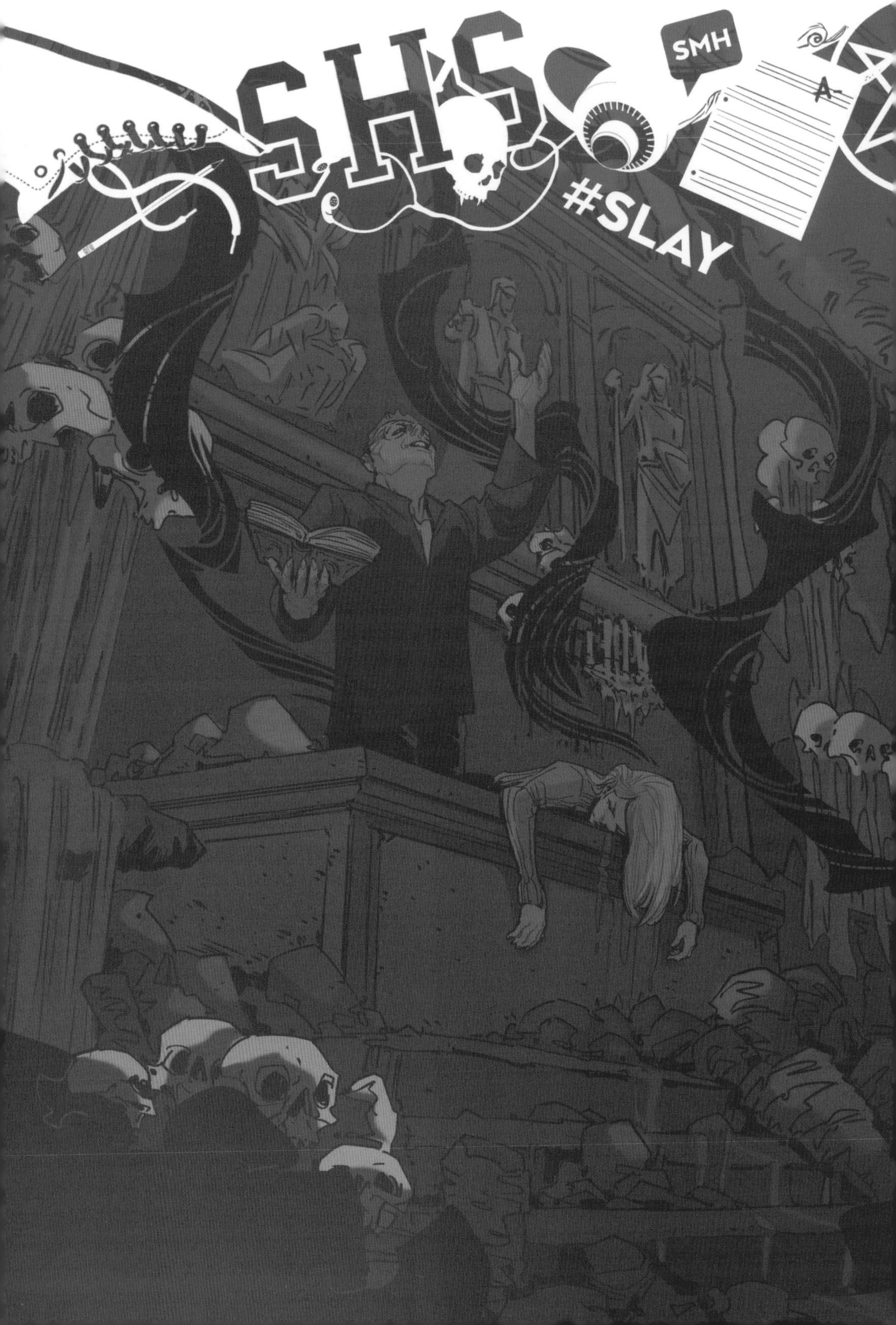
S.H.S.
SMH
#SLAY

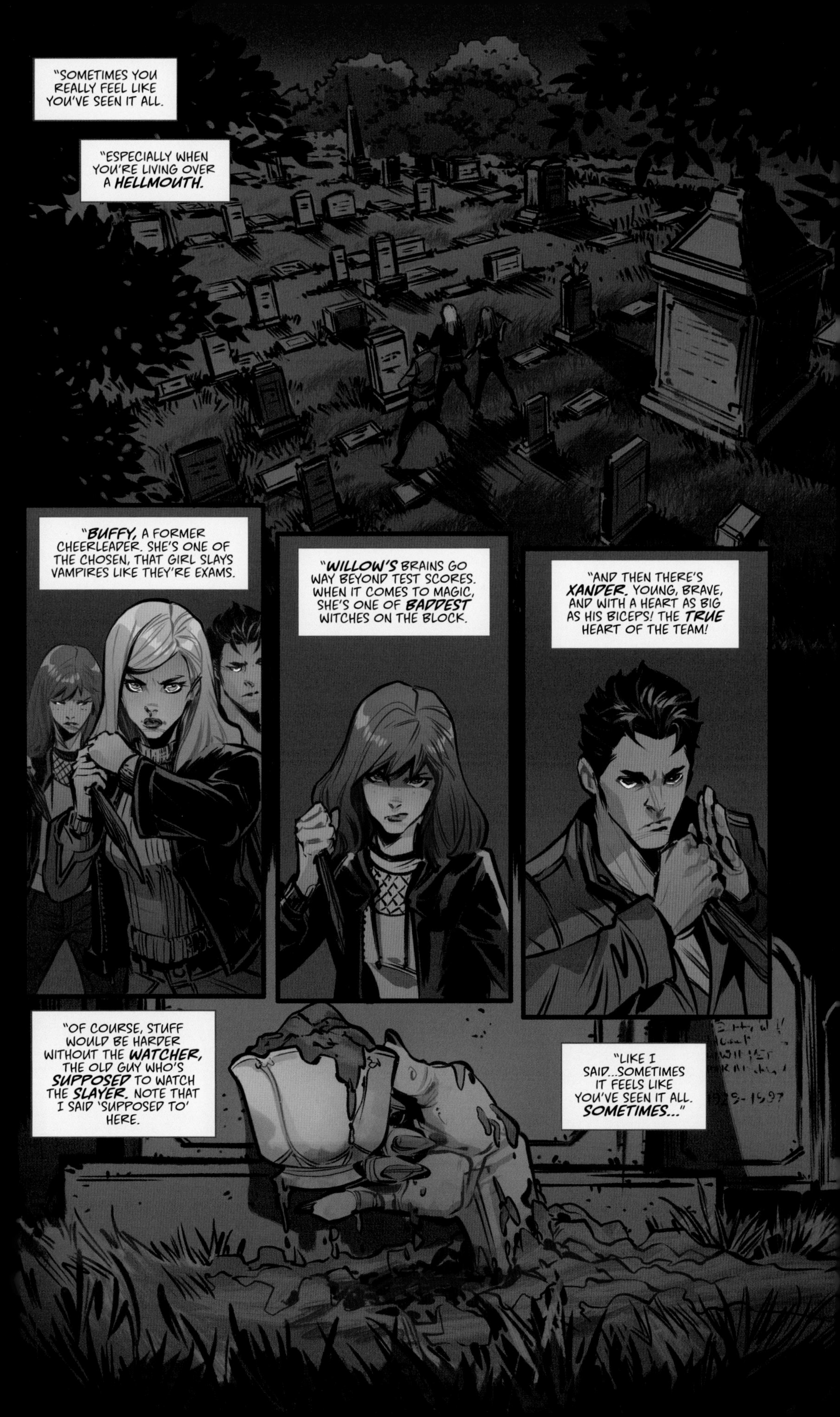
"SOMETIMES YOU REALLY FEEL LIKE YOU'VE SEEN IT ALL.
"ESPECIALLY WHEN YOU'RE LIVING OVER A HELLMOUTH.
"BUFFY, A FORMER CHEERLEADER. SHE'S ONE OF THE CHOSEN, THAT GIRL SLAYS VAMPIRES LIKE THEY'RE EXAMS.
"WILLOW'S BRAINS GO WAY BEYOND TEST SCORES. WHEN IT COMES TO MAGIC, SHE'S ONE OF BADDEST WITCHES ON THE BLOCK.
"AND THEN THERE'S XANDER. YOUNG, BRAVE, AND WITH A HEART AS BIG AS HIS BICEPS! THE TRUE HEART OF THE TEAM!
"OF COURSE, STUFF WOULD BE HARDER WITHOUT THE WATCHER, THE OLD GUY WHO'S SUPPOSED TO WATCH THE SLAYER. NOTE THAT I SAID 'SUPPOSED TO' HERE.
"LIKE I SAID...SOMETIMES IT FEELS LIKE YOU'VE SEEN IT ALL. SOMETIMES..."

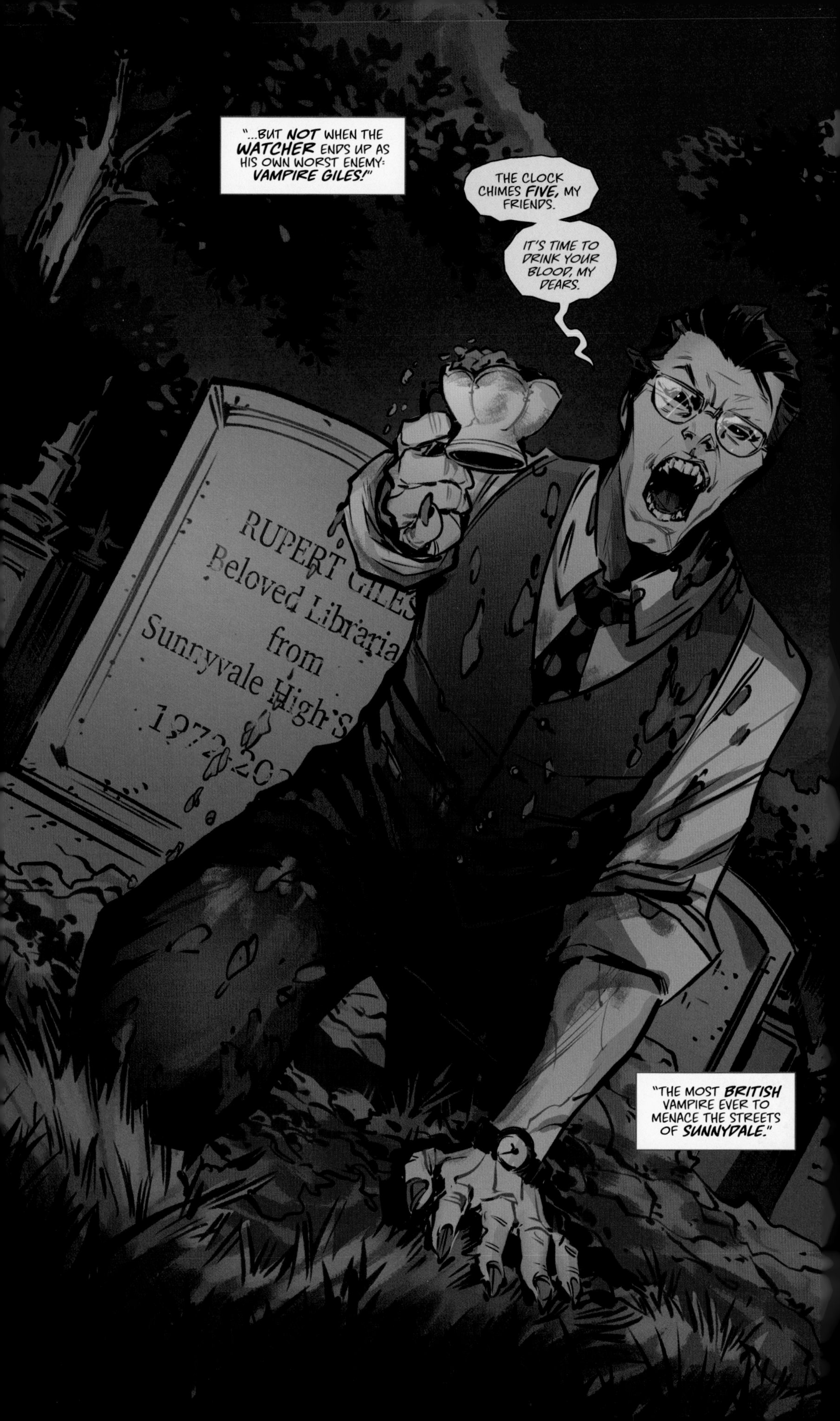
"...BUT NOT WHEN THE WATCHER ENDS UP AS HIS OWN WORST ENEMY: VAMPIRE GILES!"
THE CLOCK CHIMES FIVE, MY FRIENDS.
IT'S TIME TO DRINK YOUR BLOOD, MY DEARS.
RUPERT GILES
Beloved Libraria
from
Sunnyvale High S
"THE MOST BRITISH VAMPIRE EVER TO MENACE THE STREETS OF SUNNYDALE."

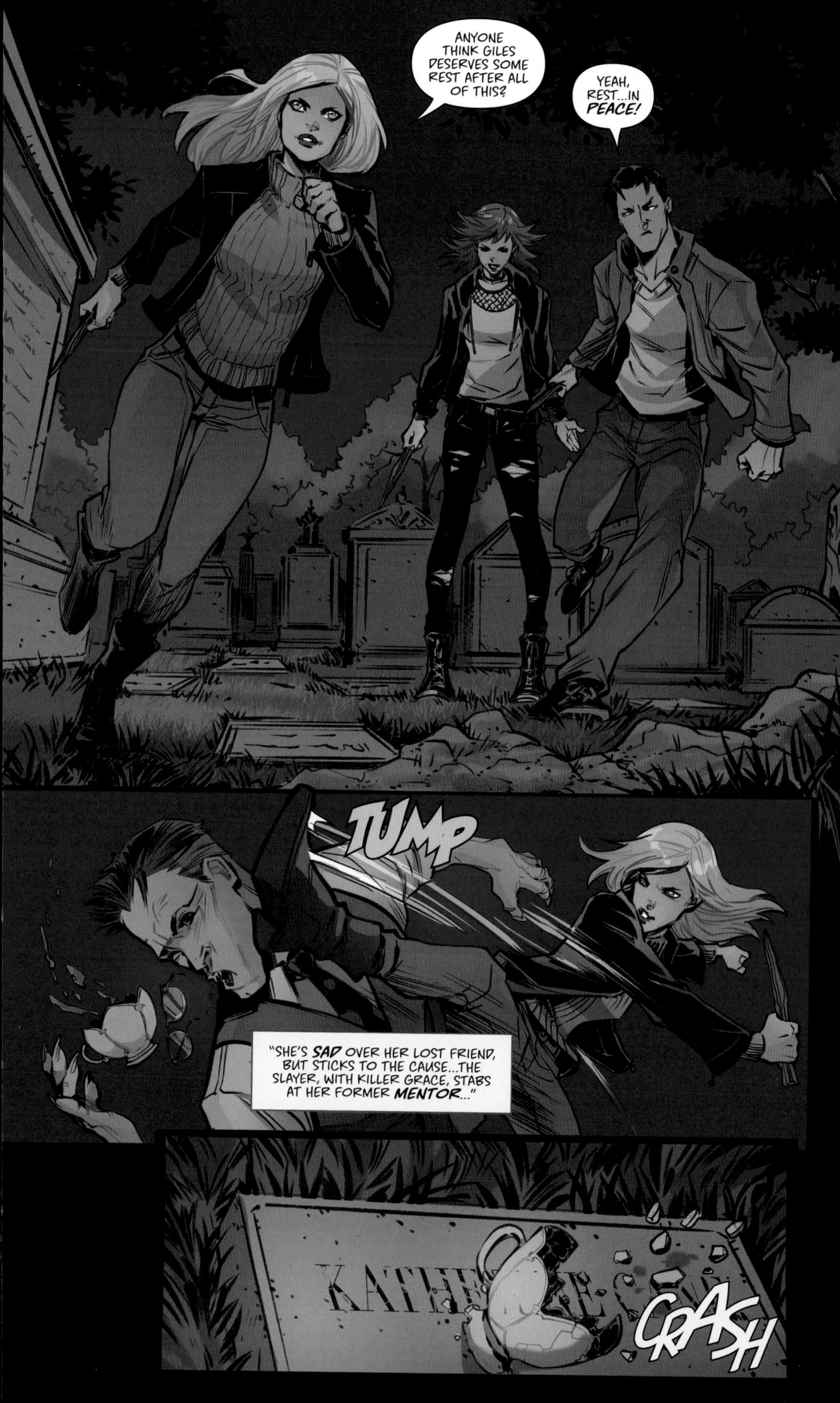

ANYONE THINK GILES DESERVES SOME REST AFTER ALL OF THIS?
YEAH, REST...IN PEACE!
TUMP
"SHE'S SAD OVER HER LOST FRIEND, BUT STICKS TO THE CAUSE...THE SLAYER, WITH KILLER GRACE, STABS AT HER FORMER MENTOR..."
CRASH

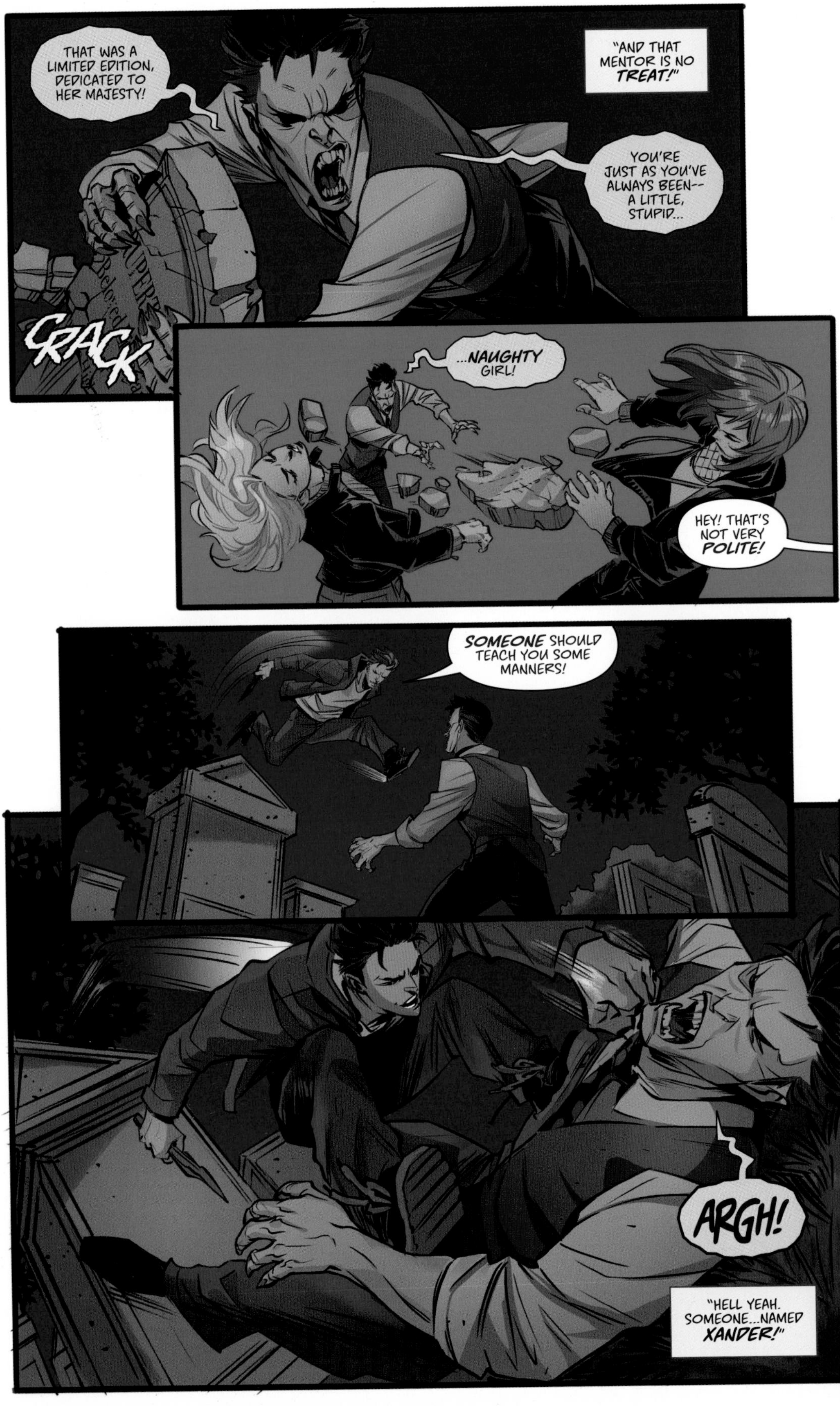
THAT WAS A LIMITED EDITION, DEDICATED TO HER MAJESTY!
"AND THAT MENTOR IS NO TREAT!"
YOU'RE JUST AS YOU'VE ALWAYS BEEN-- A LITTLE, STUPID...
CRACK
...NAUGHTY GIRL!
HEY! THAT'S NOT VERY POLITE!
SOMEONE SHOULD TEACH YOU SOME MANNERS!
ARGH!
"HELL YEAH. SOMEONE...NAMED XANDER!"

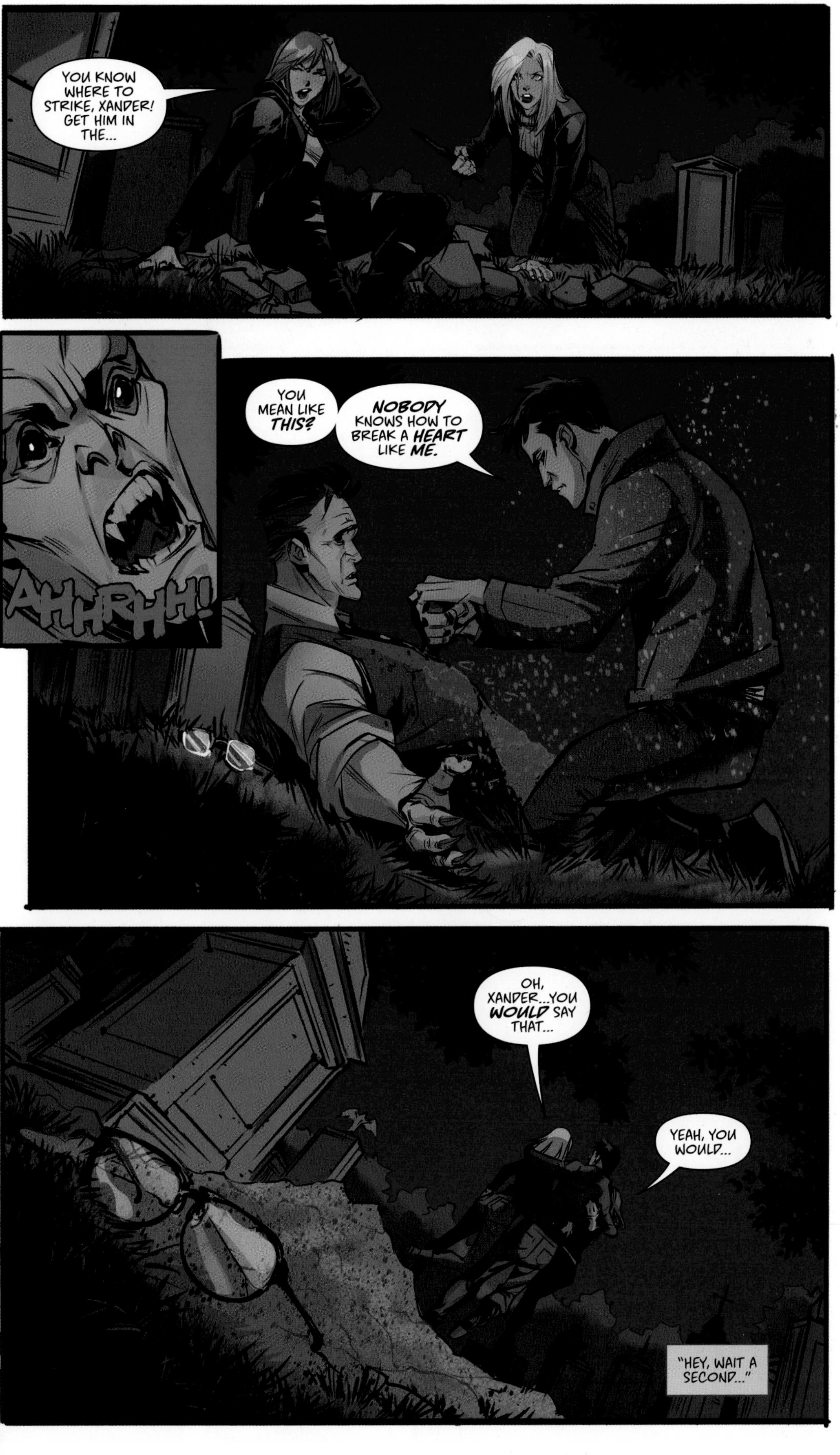
YOU KNOW WHERE TO STRIKE, XANDER! GET HIM IN THE...
AHHRHH!
YOU MEAN LIKE THIS?
NOBODY KNOWS HOW TO BREAK A HEART LIKE ME.
OH, XANDER...YOU WOULD SAY THAT...
YEAH, YOU WOULD...
"HEY, WAIT A SECOND..."

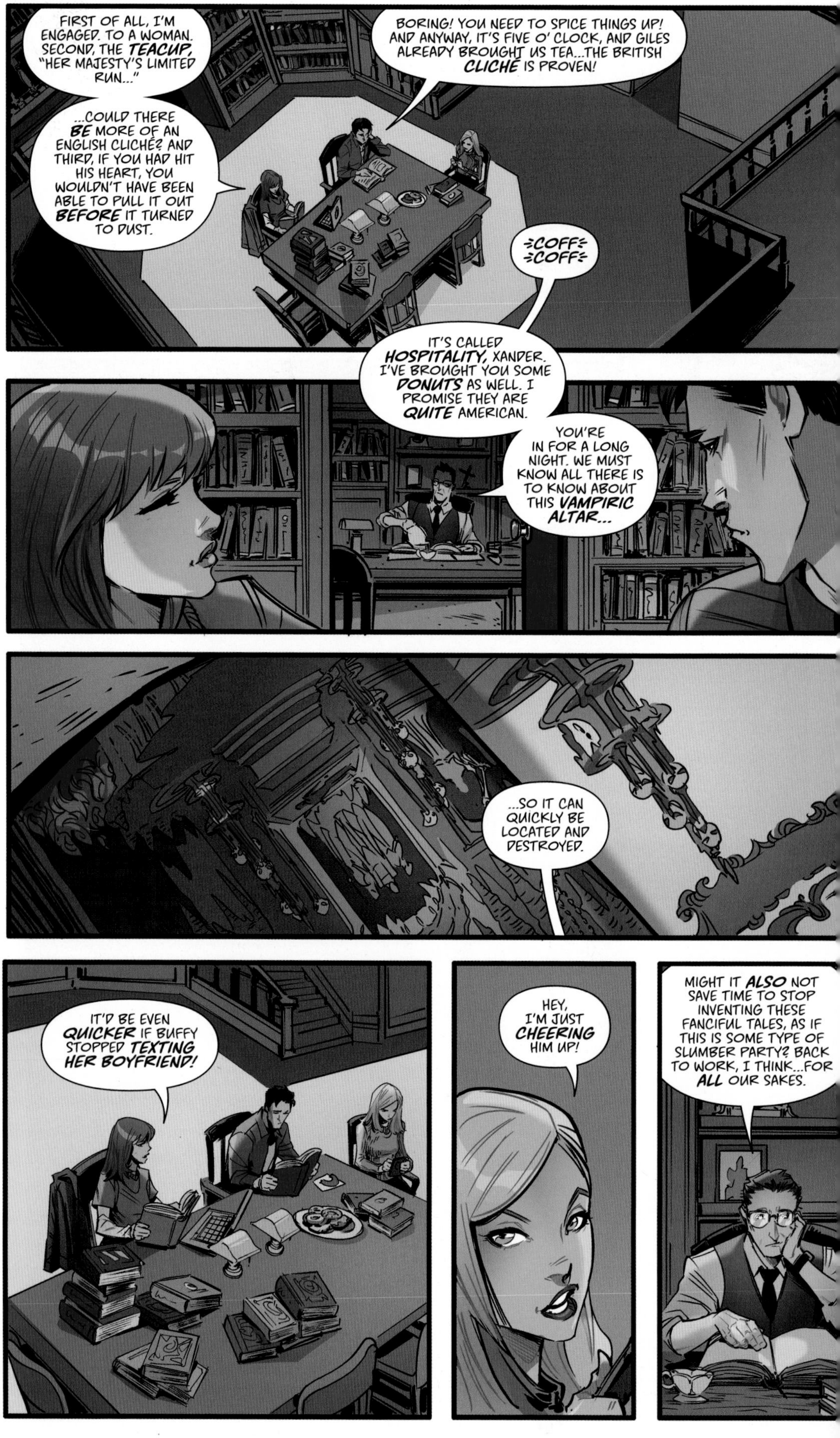
FIRST OF ALL, I'M ENGAGED. TO A WOMAN. SECOND, THE TEACUP, "HER MAJESTY'S LIMITED RUN..."
...COULD THERE BE MORE OF AN ENGLISH CLICHÉ? AND THIRD, IF YOU HAD HIT HIS HEART, YOU WOULDN'T HAVE BEEN ABLE TO PULL IT OUT BEFORE IT TURNED TO DUST.
BORING! YOU NEED TO SPICE THINGS UP! AND ANYWAY, IT'S FIVE O' CLOCK, AND GILES ALREADY BROUGHT US TEA...THE BRITISH CLICHÉ IS PROVEN!
COFF COFF
IT'S CALLED HOSPITALITY, XANDER. I'VE BROUGHT YOU SOME DONUTS AS WELL. I PROMISE THEY ARE QUITE AMERICAN.
YOU'RE IN FOR A LONG NIGHT. WE MUST KNOW ALL THERE IS TO KNOW ABOUT THIS VAMPIRIC ALTAR...
...SO IT CAN QUICKLY BE LOCATED AND DESTROYED.
IT'D BE EVEN QUICKER IF BUFFY STOPPED TEXTING HER BOYFRIEND!
HEY, I'M JUST CHEERING HIM UP!
MIGHT IT ALSO NOT SAVE TIME TO STOP INVENTING THESE FANCIFUL TALES, AS IF THIS IS SOME TYPE OF SLUMBER PARTY? BACK TO WORK, I THINK...FOR ALL OUR SAKES.

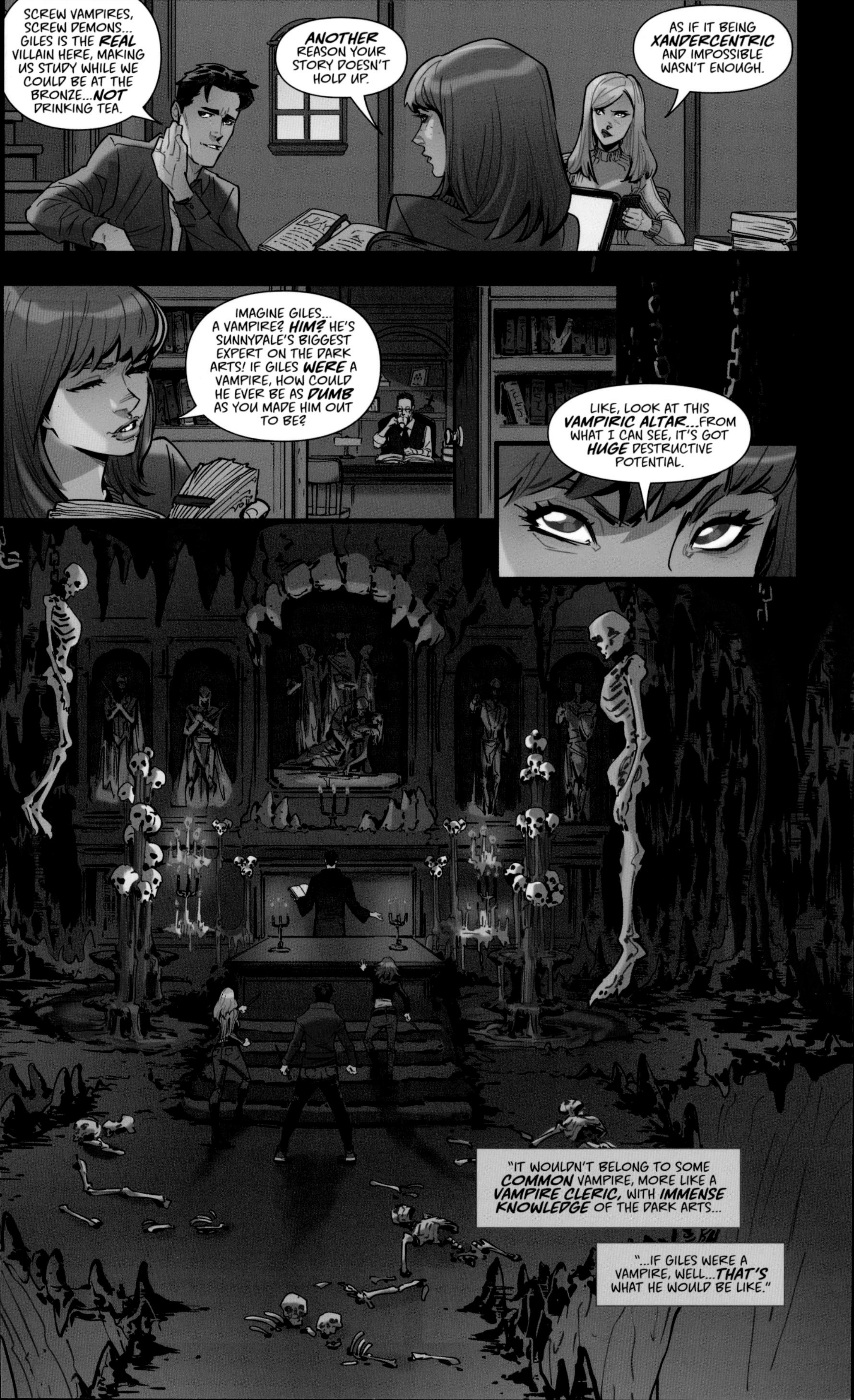
SCREW VAMPIRES, SCREW DEMONS... GILES IS THE REAL VILLAIN HERE, MAKING US STUDY WHILE WE COULD BE AT THE BRONZE...NOT DRINKING TEA.
ANOTHER REASON YOUR STORY DOESN'T HOLD UP.
AS IF IT BEING XANDERCENTRIC AND IMPOSSIBLE WASN'T ENOUGH.
IMAGINE GILES... A VAMPIRE? HIM? HE'S SUNNYDALE'S BIGGEST EXPERT ON THE DARK ARTS! IF GILES WERE A VAMPIRE, HOW COULD HE EVER BE AS DUMB AS YOU MADE HIM OUT TO BE?
LIKE, LOOK AT THIS VAMPIRIC ALTAR...FROM WHAT I CAN SEE, IT'S GOT HUGE DESTRUCTIVE POTENTIAL.
"IT WOULDN'T BELONG TO SOME COMMON VAMPIRE, MORE LIKE A VAMPIRE CLERIC, WITH IMMENSE KNOWLEDGE OF THE DARK ARTS...
"...IF GILES WERE A VAMPIRE, WELL...THAT'S WHAT HE WOULD BE LIKE."

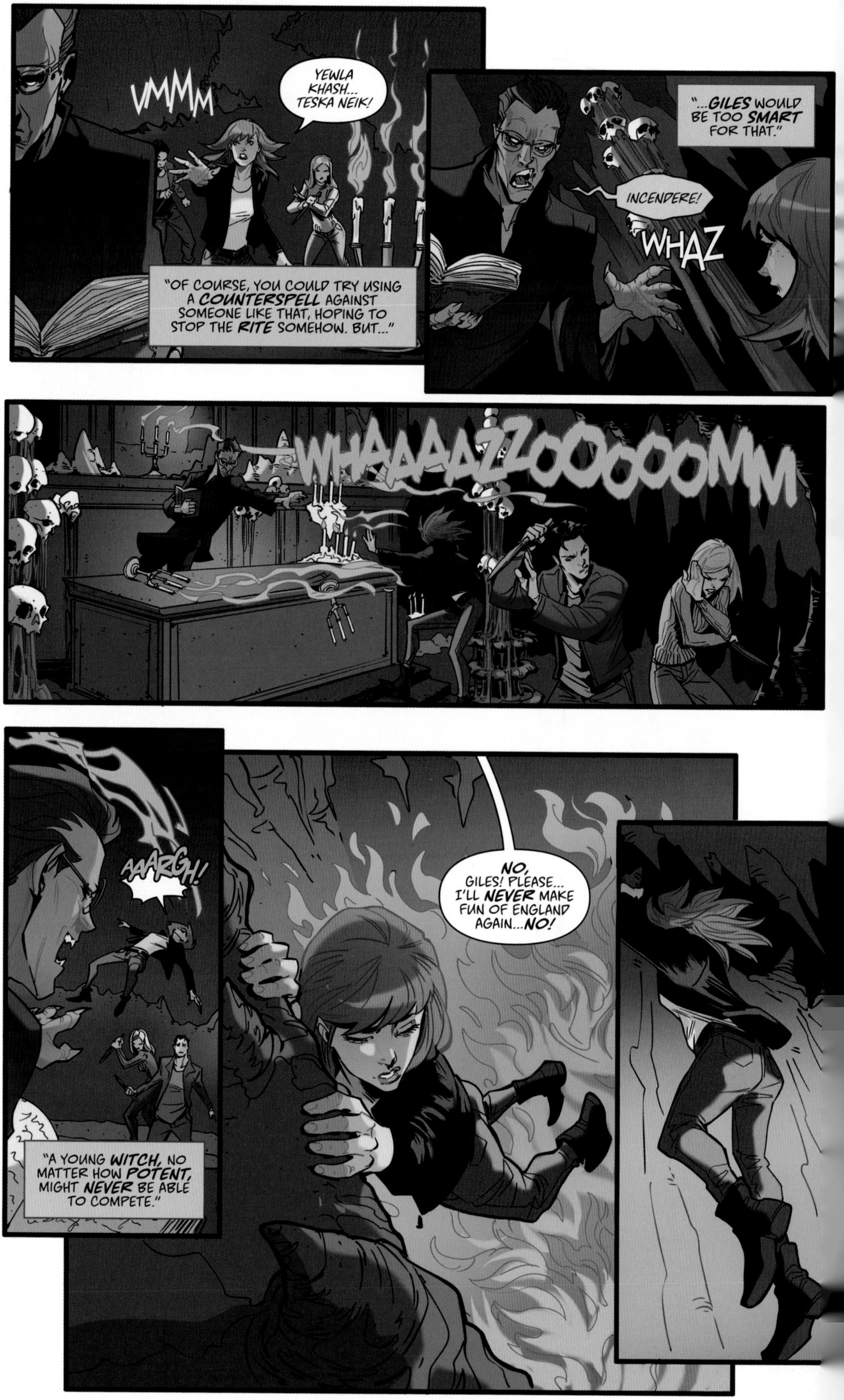
VMMM
YEWLA KHASH... TESKA NEIK!
"OF COURSE, YOU COULD TRY USING A COUNTERSPELL AGAINST SOMEONE LIKE THAT, HOPING TO STOP THE RITE SOMEHOW. BUT..."
"...GILES WOULD BE TOO SMART FOR THAT."
INCENDERE!
WHAZ
WHAAAAZZOOOOOOMM
AAARGH!
"A YOUNG WITCH, NO MATTER HOW POTENT, MIGHT NEVER BE ABLE TO COMPETE."
NO, GILES! PLEASE... I'LL NEVER MAKE FUN OF ENGLAND AGAIN...NO!

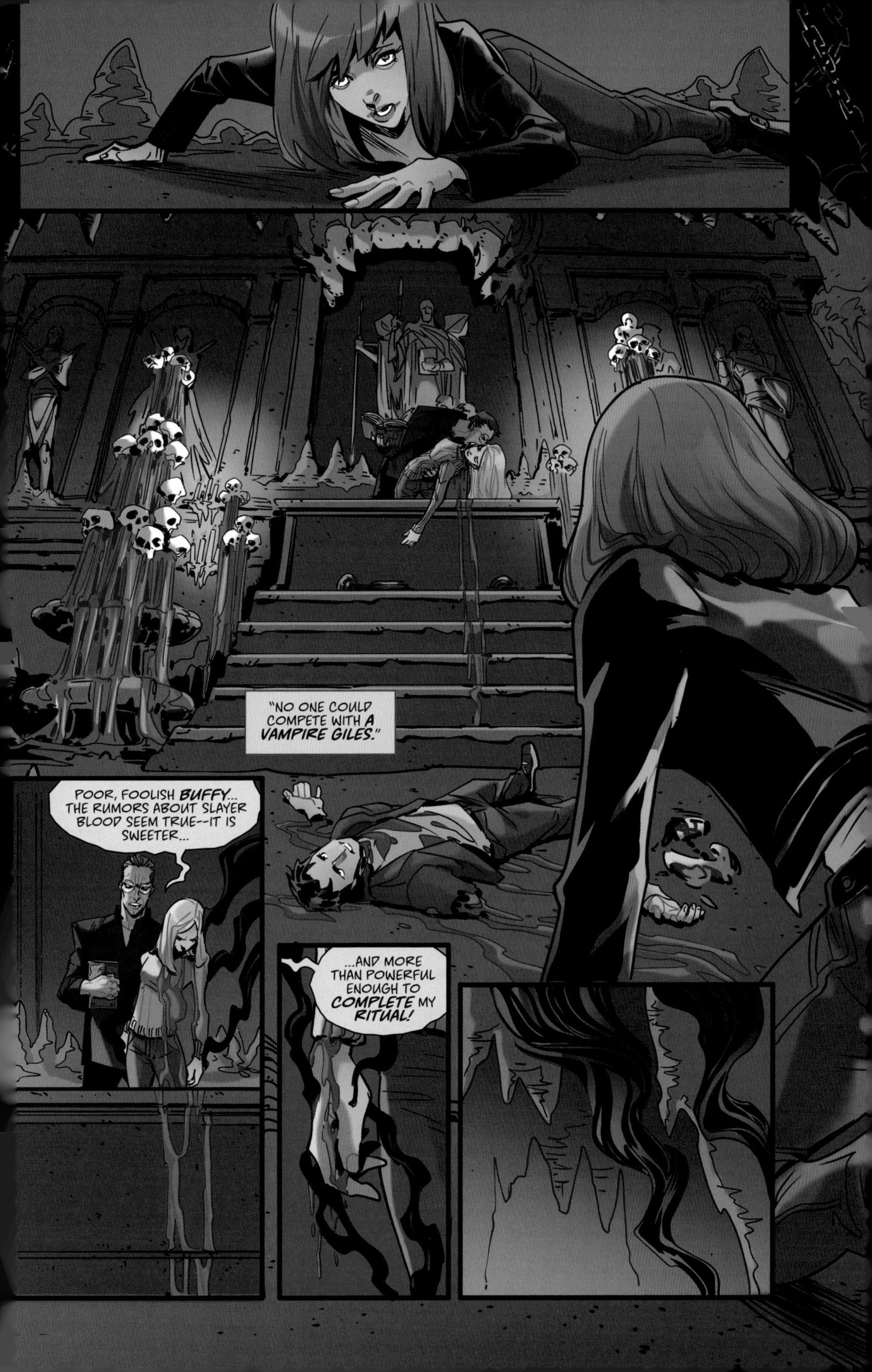
"NO ONE COULD COMPETE WITH A VAMPIRE GILES."
POOR, FOOLISH BUFFY... THE RUMORS ABOUT SLAYER BLOOD SEEM TRUE--IT IS SWEETER...
...AND MORE THAN POWERFUL ENOUGH TO COMPLETE MY RITUAL!

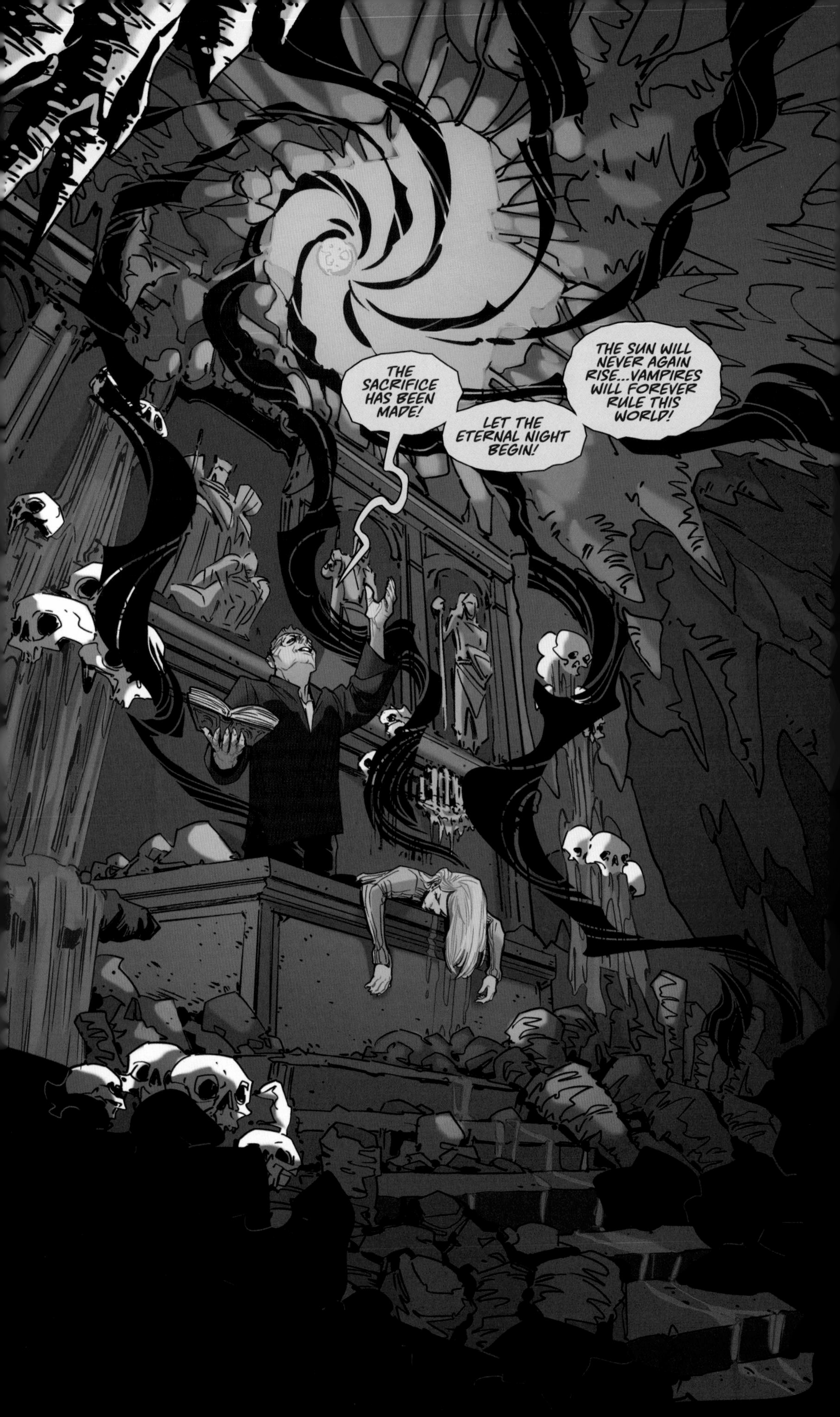
THE SACRIFICE HAS BEEN MADE!
LET THE ETERNAL NIGHT BEGIN!
THE SUN WILL NEVER AGAIN RISE...VAMPIRES WILL FOREVER RULE THIS WORLD!

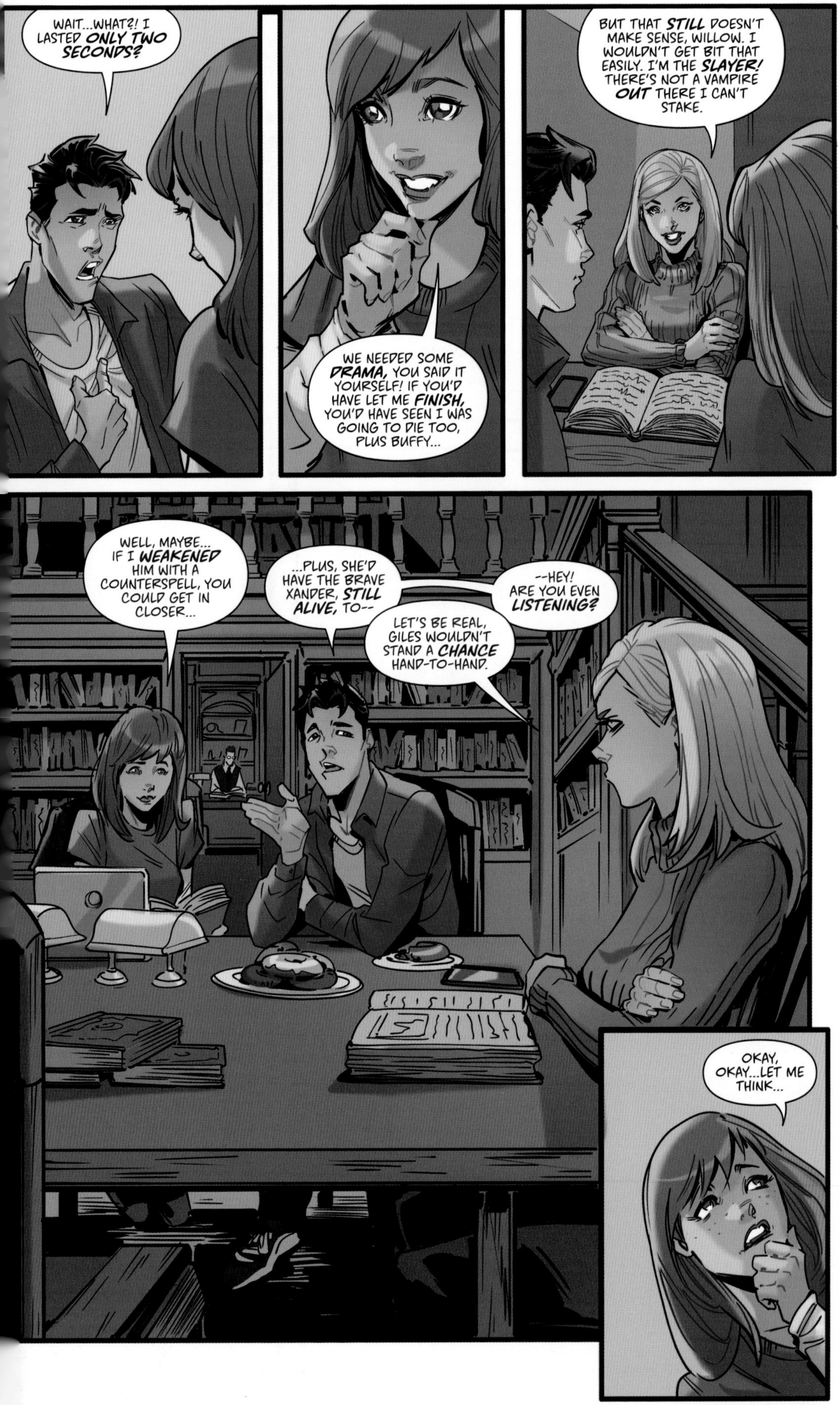

WAIT...WHAT?! I LASTED ONLY TWO SECONDS?
WE NEEDED SOME DRAMA, YOU SAID IT YOURSELF! IF YOU'D HAVE LET ME FINISH, YOU'D HAVE SEEN I WAS GOING TO DIE TOO, PLUS BUFFY...
BUT THAT STILL DOESN'T MAKE SENSE, WILLOW. I WOULDN'T GET BIT THAT EASILY. I'M THE SLAYER! THERE'S NOT A VAMPIRE OUT THERE I CAN'T STAKE.
WELL, MAYBE... IF I WEAKENED HIM WITH A COUNTERSPELL, YOU COULD GET IN CLOSER...
...PLUS, SHE'D HAVE THE BRAVE XANDER, STILL ALIVE, TO--
--HEY! ARE YOU EVEN LISTENING?
LET'S BE REAL, GILES WOULDN'T STAND A CHANCE HAND-TO-HAND.
OKAY, OKAY...LET ME THINK...

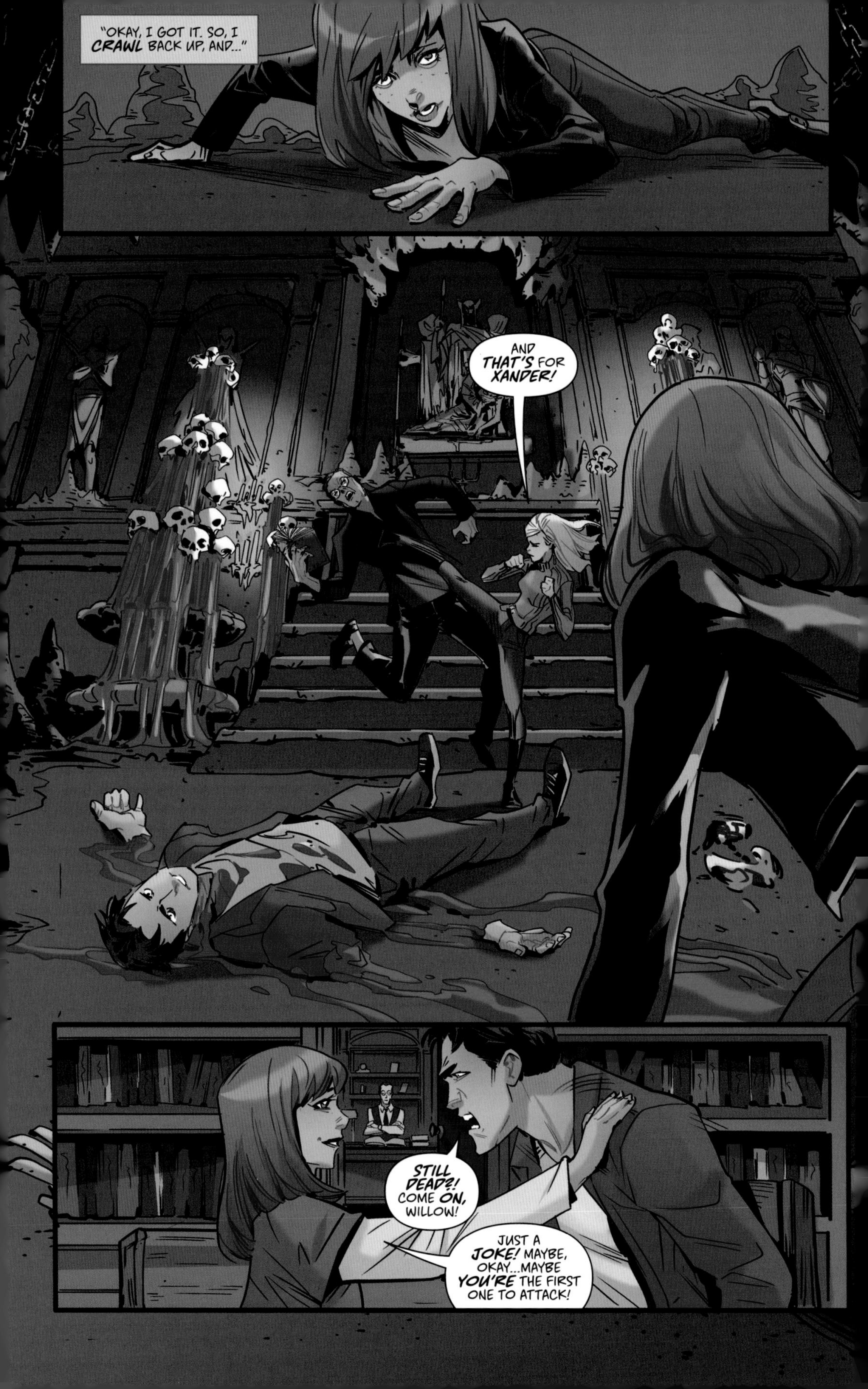
"OKAY, I GOT IT. SO, I CRAWL BACK UP, AND..."
AND THAT'S FOR XANDER!
STILL DEAD?! COME ON, WILLOW!
JUST A JOKE! MAYBE, OKAY...MAYBE YOU'RE THE FIRST ONE TO ATTACK!

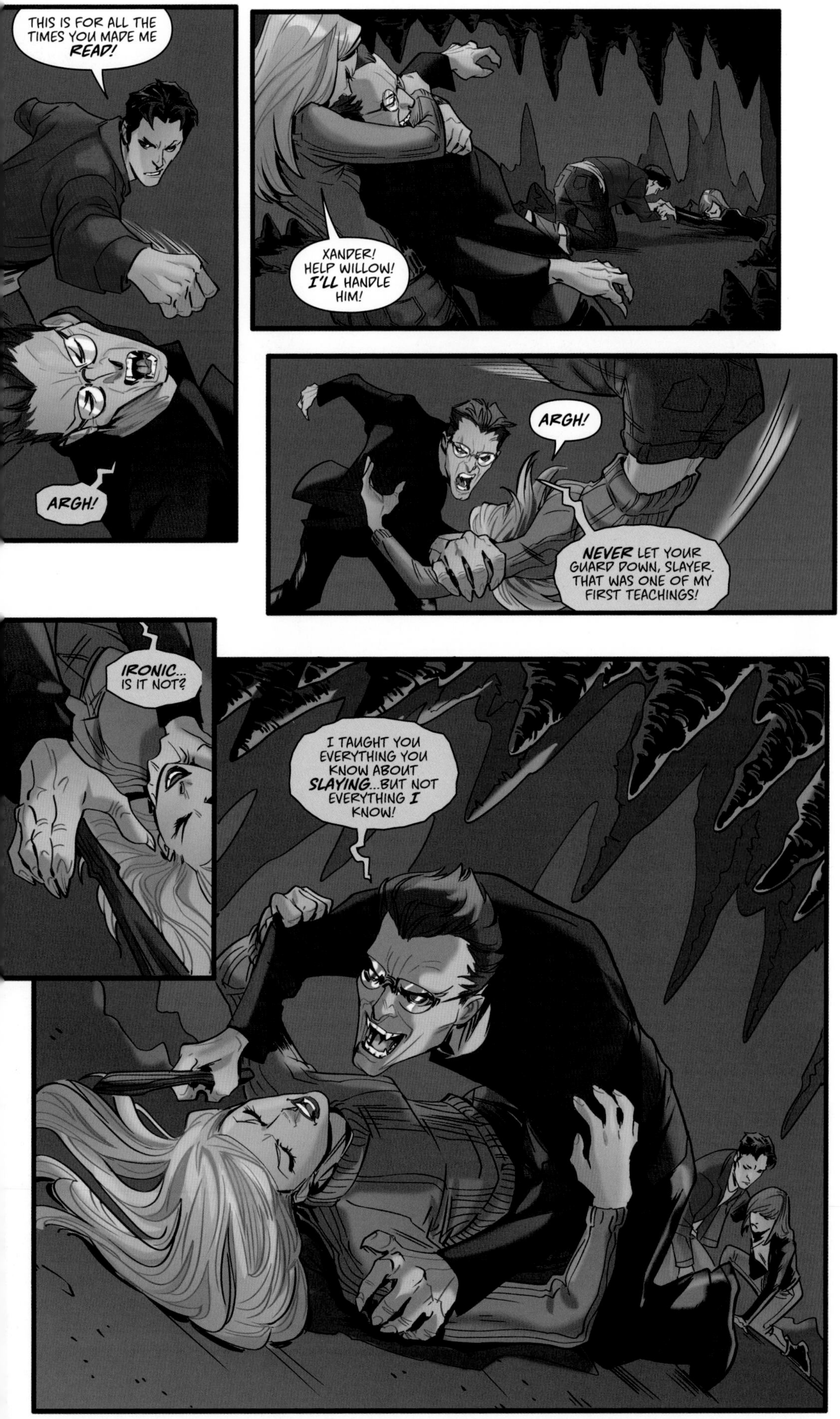
THIS IS FOR ALL THE TIMES YOU MADE ME **READ!**
ARGH!
XANDER! HELP WILLOW! ***I'LL*** HANDLE HIM!
ARGH!
NEVER LET YOUR GUARD DOWN, SLAYER. THAT WAS ONE OF MY FIRST TEACHINGS!
IRONIC... IS IT NOT?
I TAUGHT YOU EVERYTHING YOU KNOW ABOUT **SLAYING**...BUT NOT EVERYTHING ***I*** KNOW!

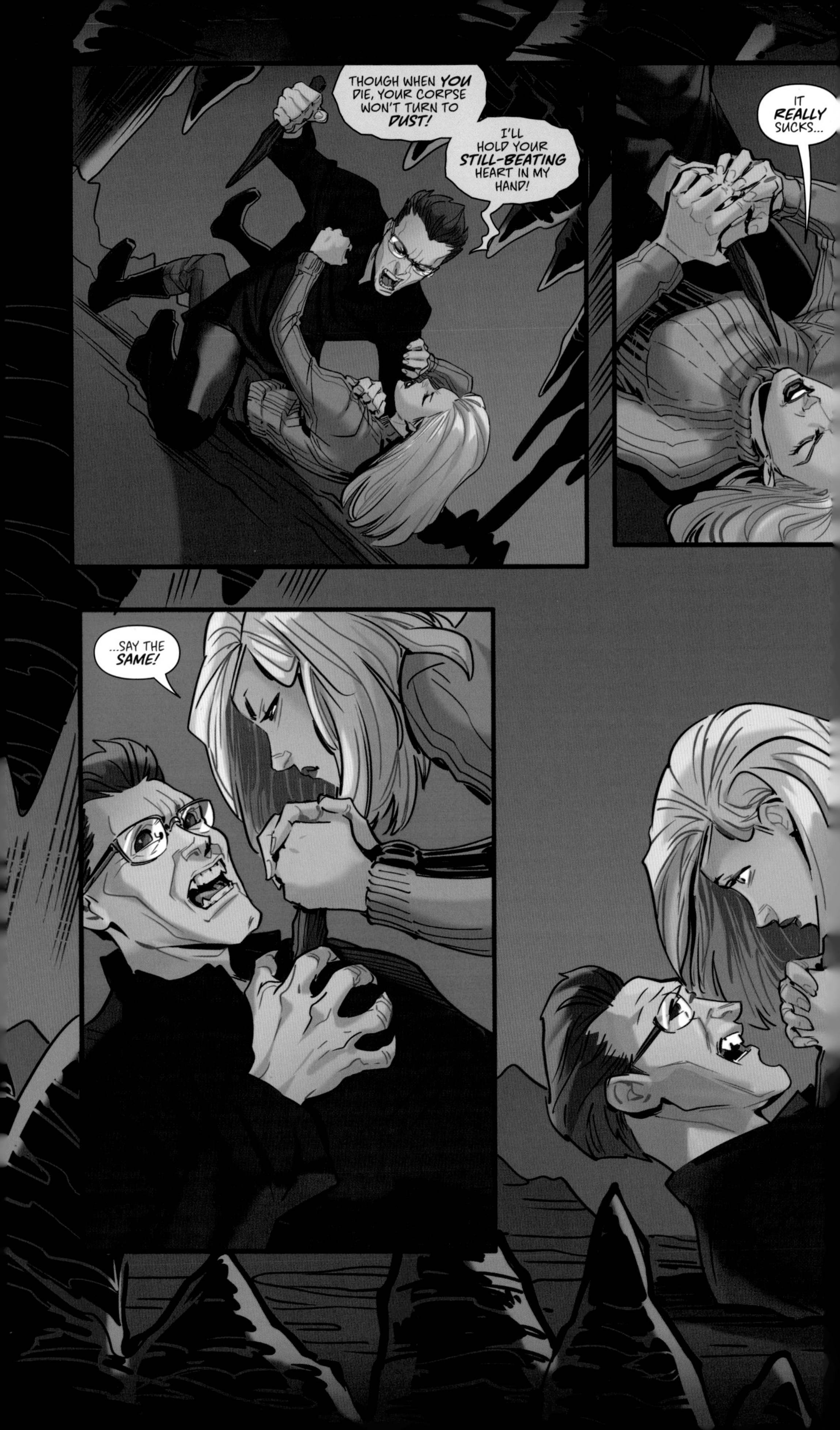
THOUGH WHEN YOU DIE, YOUR CORPSE WON'T TURN TO DUST!
I'LL HOLD YOUR STILL-BEATING HEART IN MY HAND!
IT REALLY SUCKS...
...SAY THE SAME!

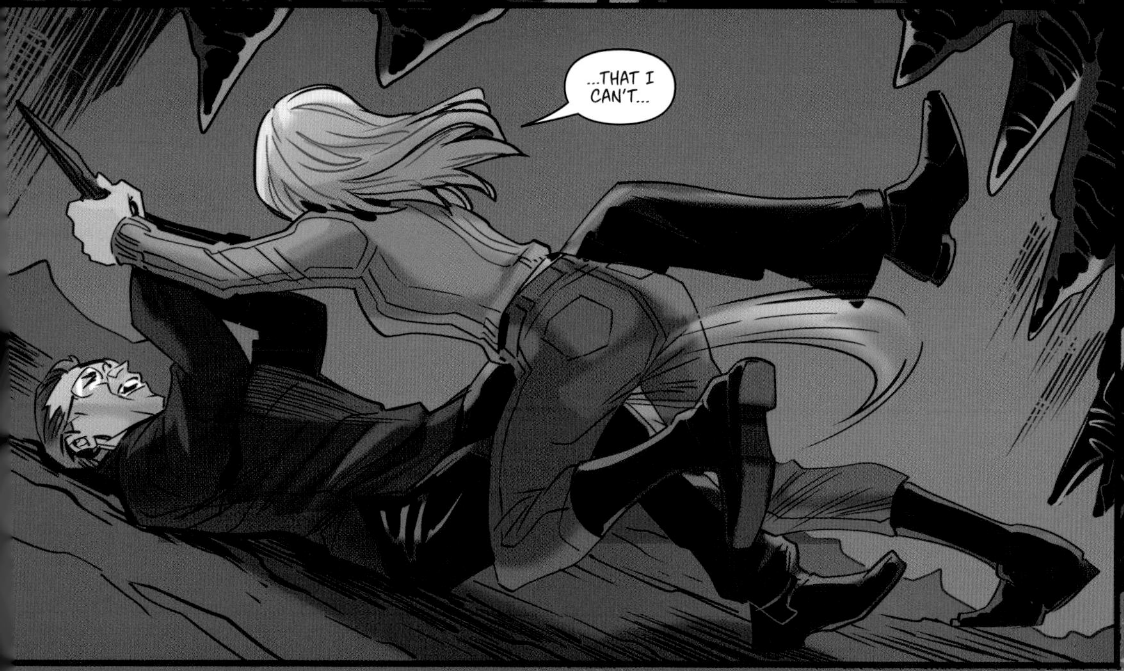
...THAT I CAN'T...

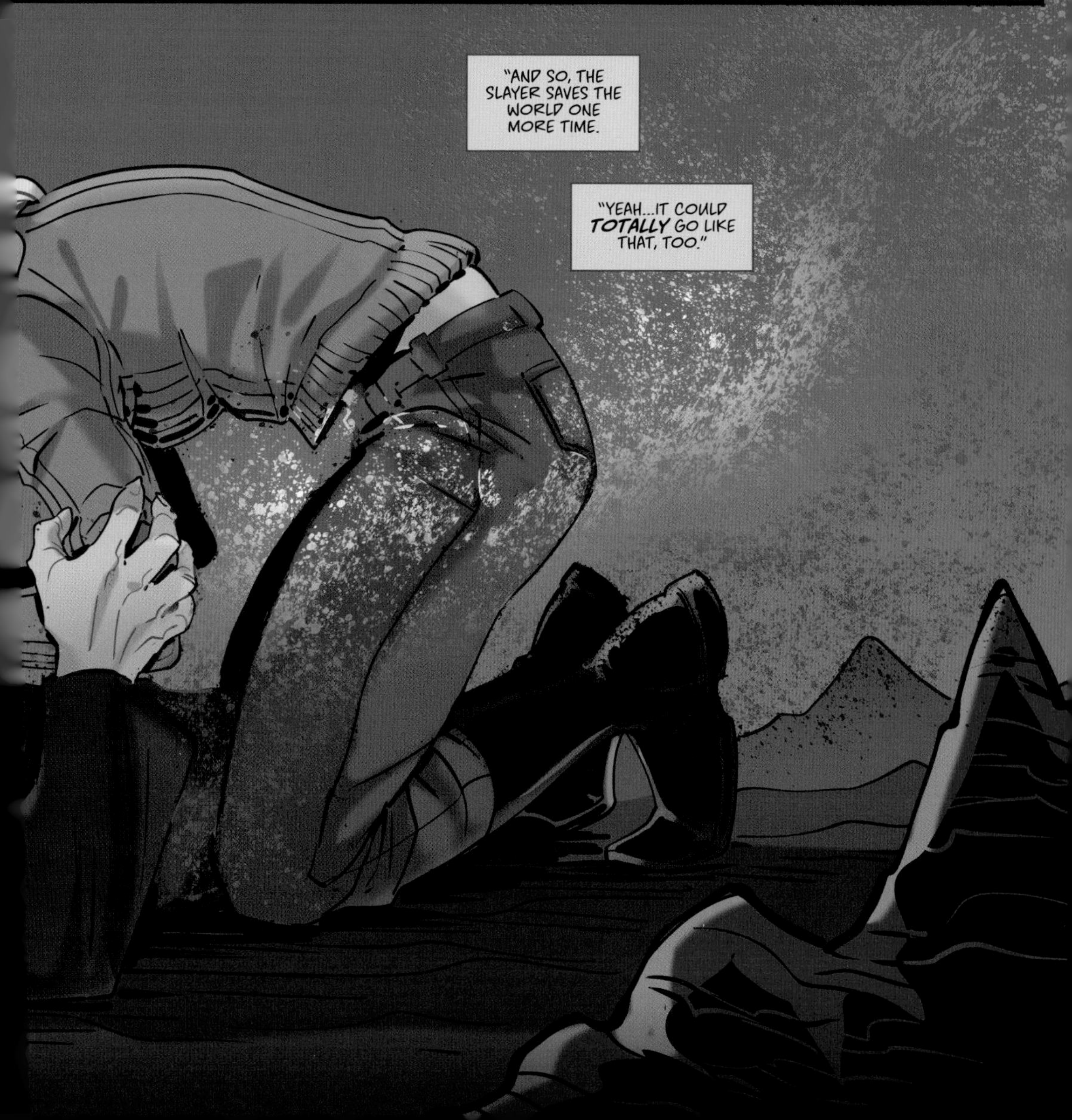
"AND SO, THE SLAYER SAVES THE WORLD ONE MORE TIME.
"YEAH...IT COULD **TOTALLY** GO LIKE THAT, TOO."

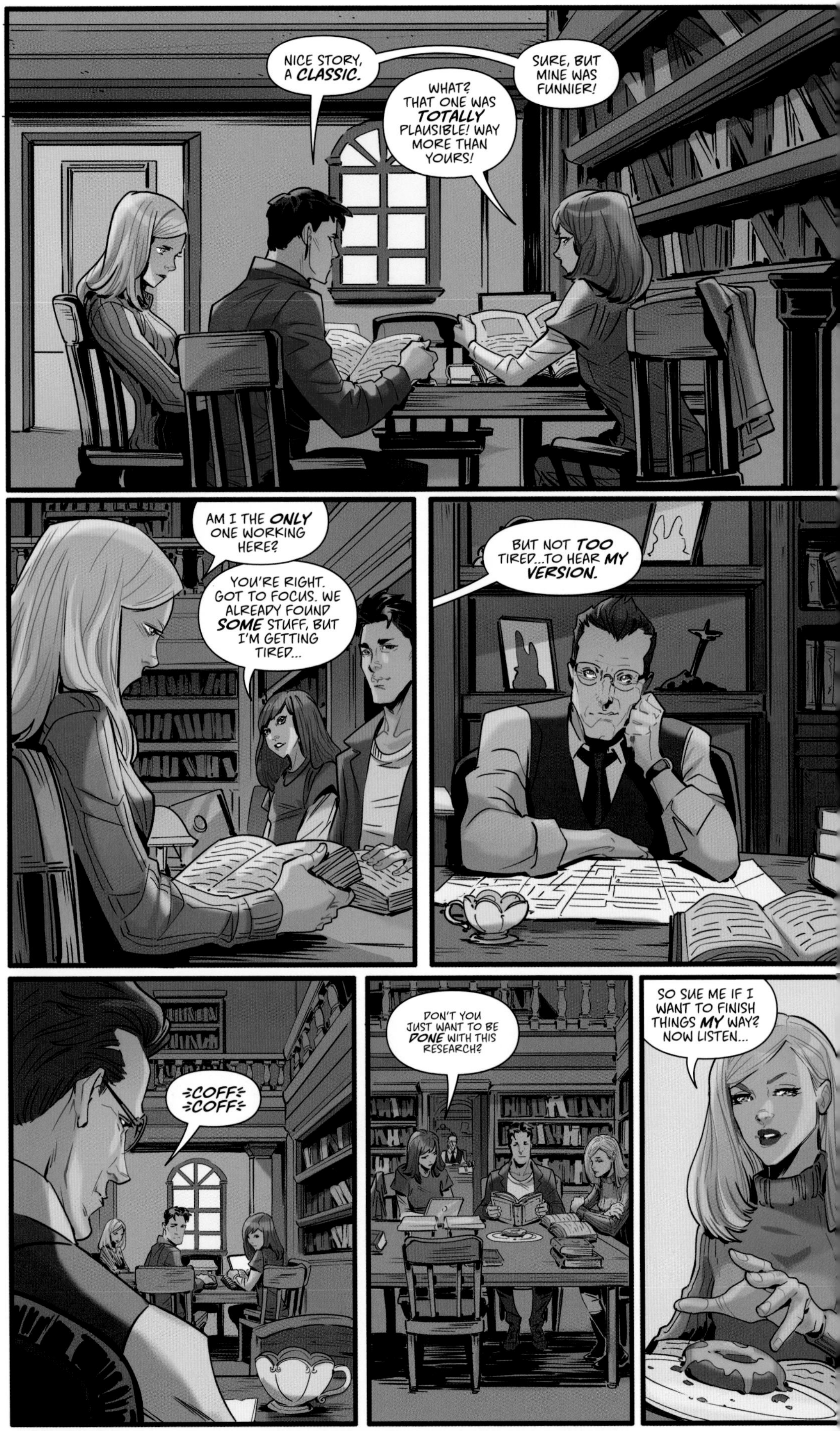
NICE STORY, A CLASSIC.
SURE, BUT MINE WAS FUNNIER!
WHAT? THAT ONE WAS TOTALLY PLAUSIBLE! WAY MORE THAN YOURS!
AM I THE ONLY ONE WORKING HERE?
YOU'RE RIGHT. GOT TO FOCUS. WE ALREADY FOUND SOME STUFF, BUT I'M GETTING TIRED...
BUT NOT TOO TIRED...TO HEAR MY VERSION.
COFF COFF
DON'T YOU JUST WANT TO BE DONE WITH THIS RESEARCH?
SO SUE ME IF I WANT TO FINISH THINGS MY WAY? NOW LISTEN...

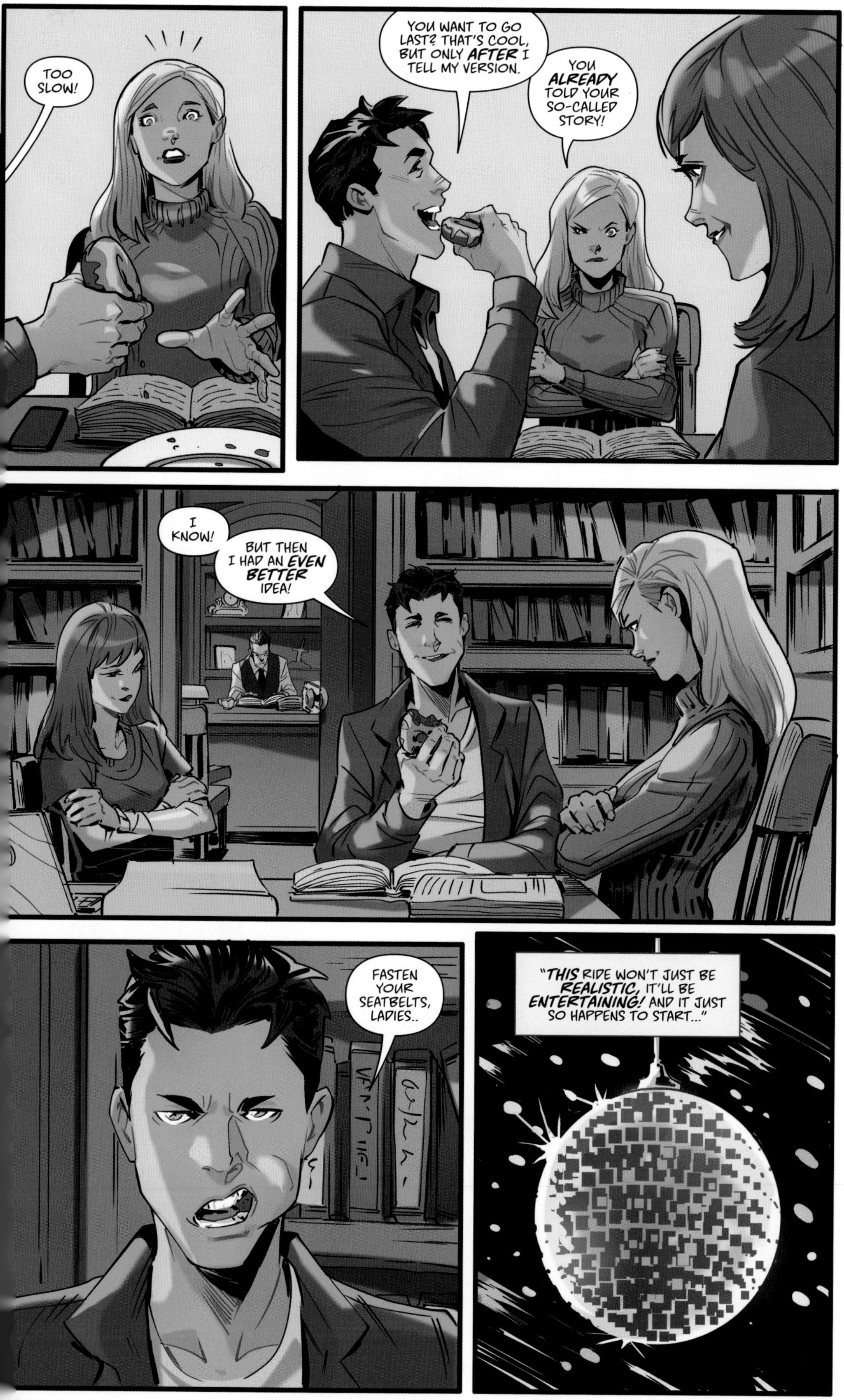
TOO SLOW!
YOU WANT TO GO LAST? THAT'S COOL, BUT ONLY **AFTER** I TELL MY VERSION.
YOU **ALREADY** TOLD YOUR SO-CALLED STORY!
I KNOW!
BUT THEN I HAD AN **EVEN BETTER** IDEA!
FASTEN YOUR SEATBELTS, LADIES..
"**THIS** RIDE WON'T JUST BE **REALISTIC**, IT'LL BE **ENTERTAINING!** AND IT JUST SO HAPPENS TO START..."

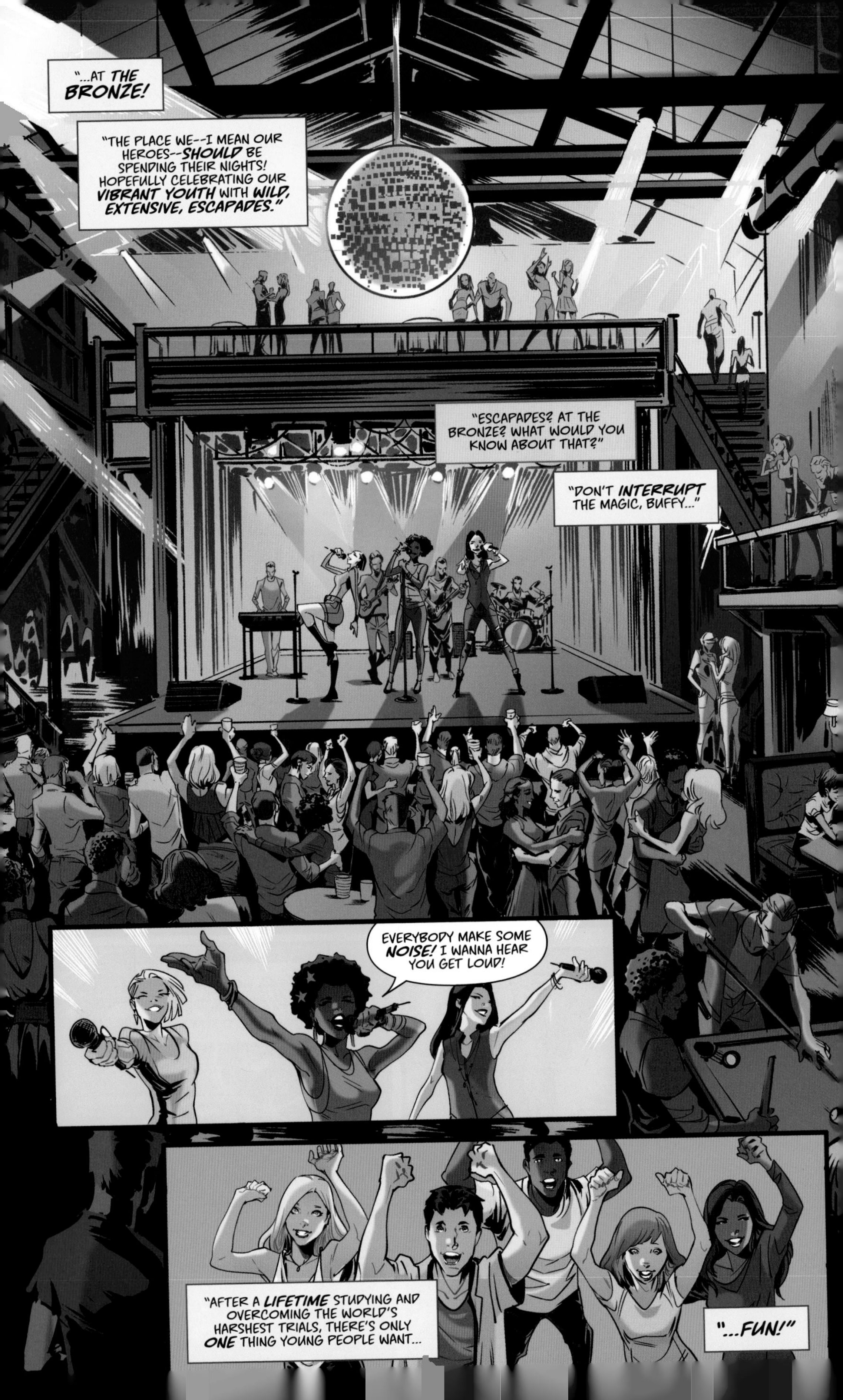
"...AT THE BRONZE!
"THE PLACE WE--I MEAN OUR HEROES--SHOULD BE SPENDING THEIR NIGHTS! HOPEFULLY CELEBRATING OUR VIBRANT YOUTH WITH WILD, EXTENSIVE, ESCAPADES."
"ESCAPADES? AT THE BRONZE? WHAT WOULD YOU KNOW ABOUT THAT?"
"DON'T INTERRUPT THE MAGIC, BUFFY..."
EVERYBODY MAKE SOME NOISE! I WANNA HEAR YOU GET LOUD!
"AFTER A LIFETIME STUDYING AND OVERCOMING THE WORLD'S HARSHEST TRIALS, THERE'S ONLY ONE THING YOUNG PEOPLE WANT...
"...FUN!"

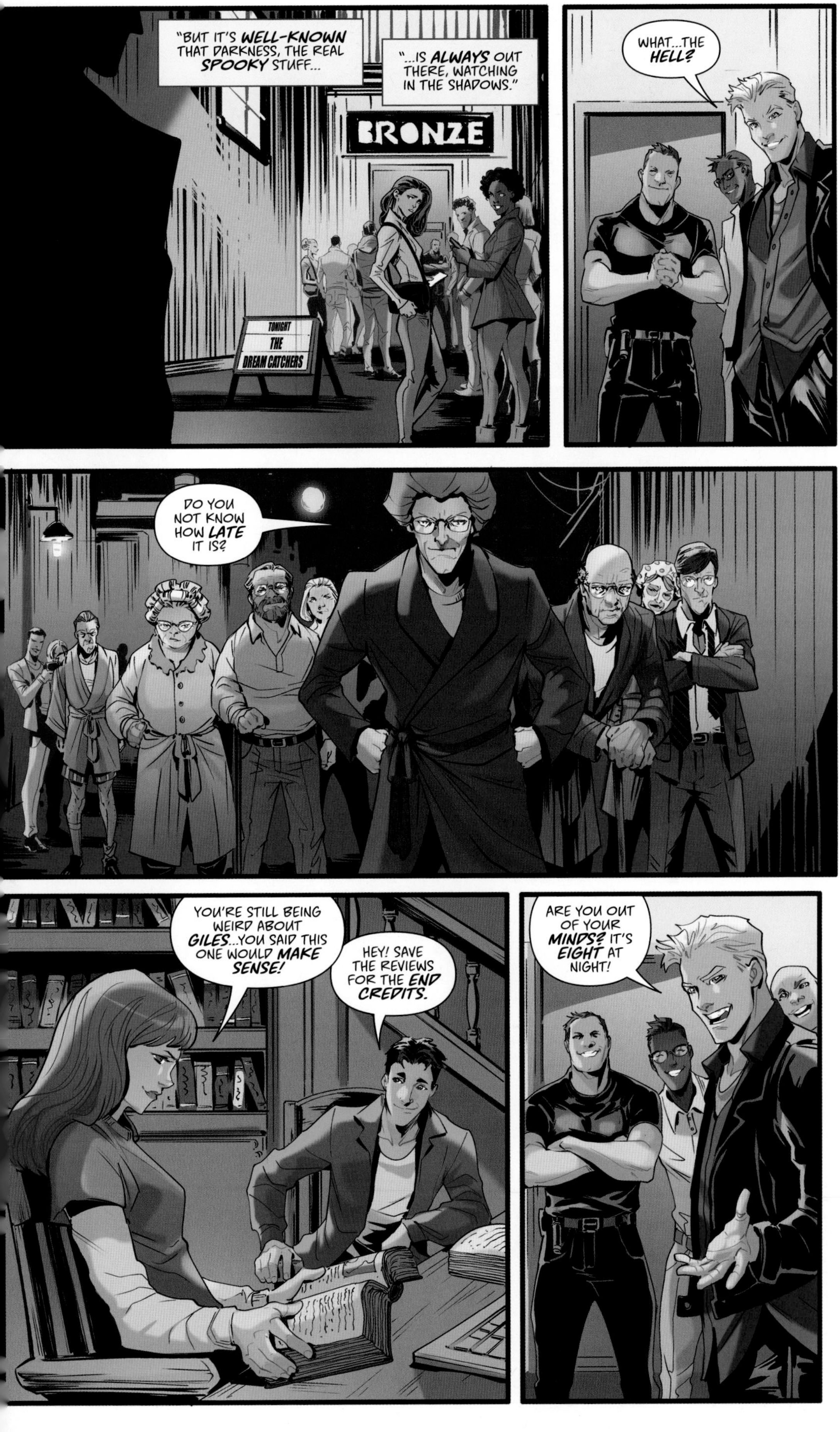
"BUT IT'S WELL-KNOWN THAT DARKNESS, THE REAL SPOOKY STUFF...
"...IS ALWAYS OUT THERE, WATCHING IN THE SHADOWS."
BRONZE
TONIGHT THE DREAM CATCHERS
WHAT...THE HELL?
DO YOU NOT KNOW HOW LATE IT IS?
YOU'RE STILL BEING WEIRD ABOUT GILES...YOU SAID THIS ONE WOULD MAKE SENSE!
HEY! SAVE THE REVIEWS FOR THE END CREDITS.
ARE YOU OUT OF YOUR MINDS? IT'S EIGHT AT NIGHT!

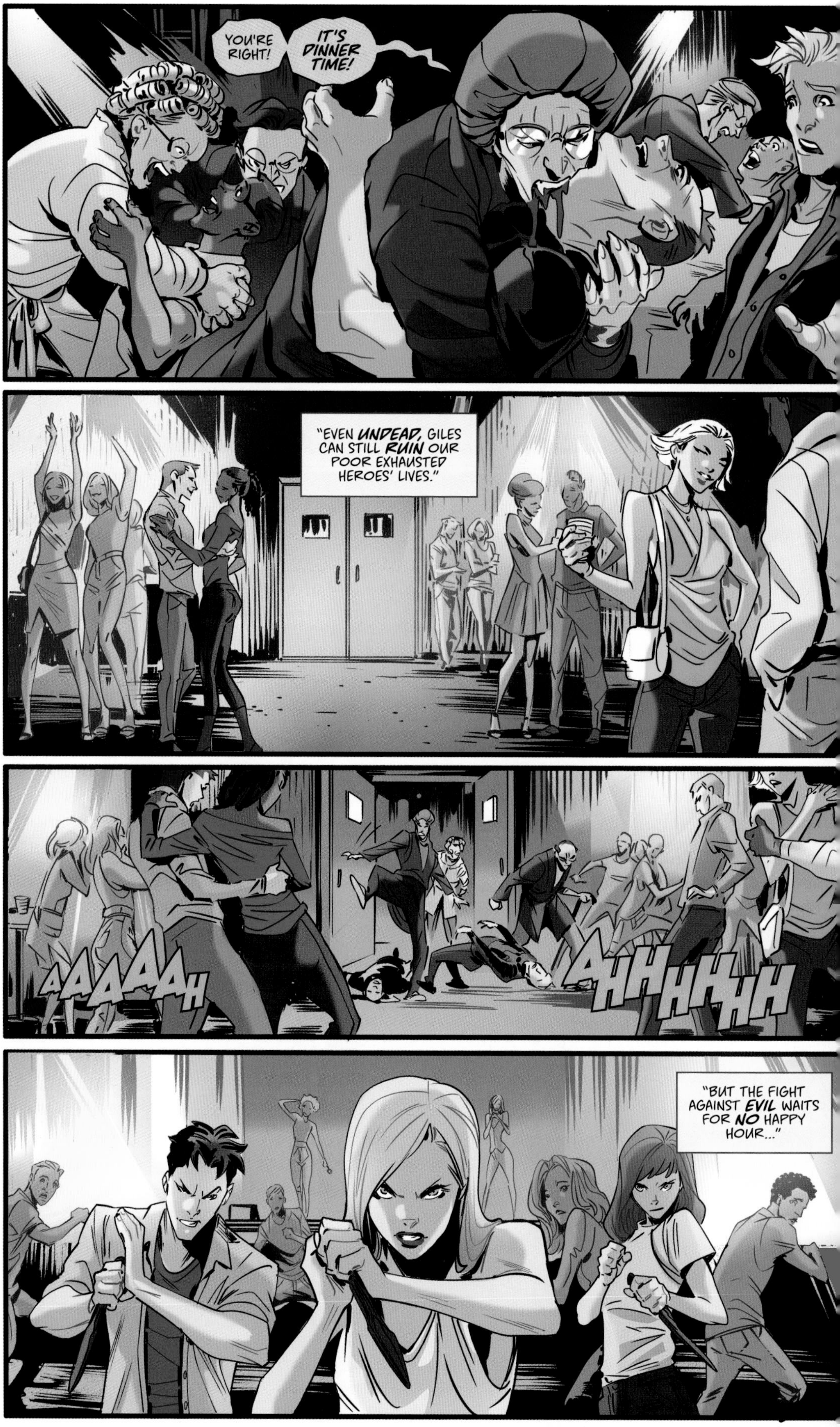
YOU'RE RIGHT!
IT'S DINNER TIME!
"EVEN UNDEAD, GILES CAN STILL RUIN OUR POOR EXHAUSTED HEROES' LIVES."
AAAAAH
AHHHHHHH
"BUT THE FIGHT AGAINST EVIL WAITS FOR NO HAPPY HOUR..."

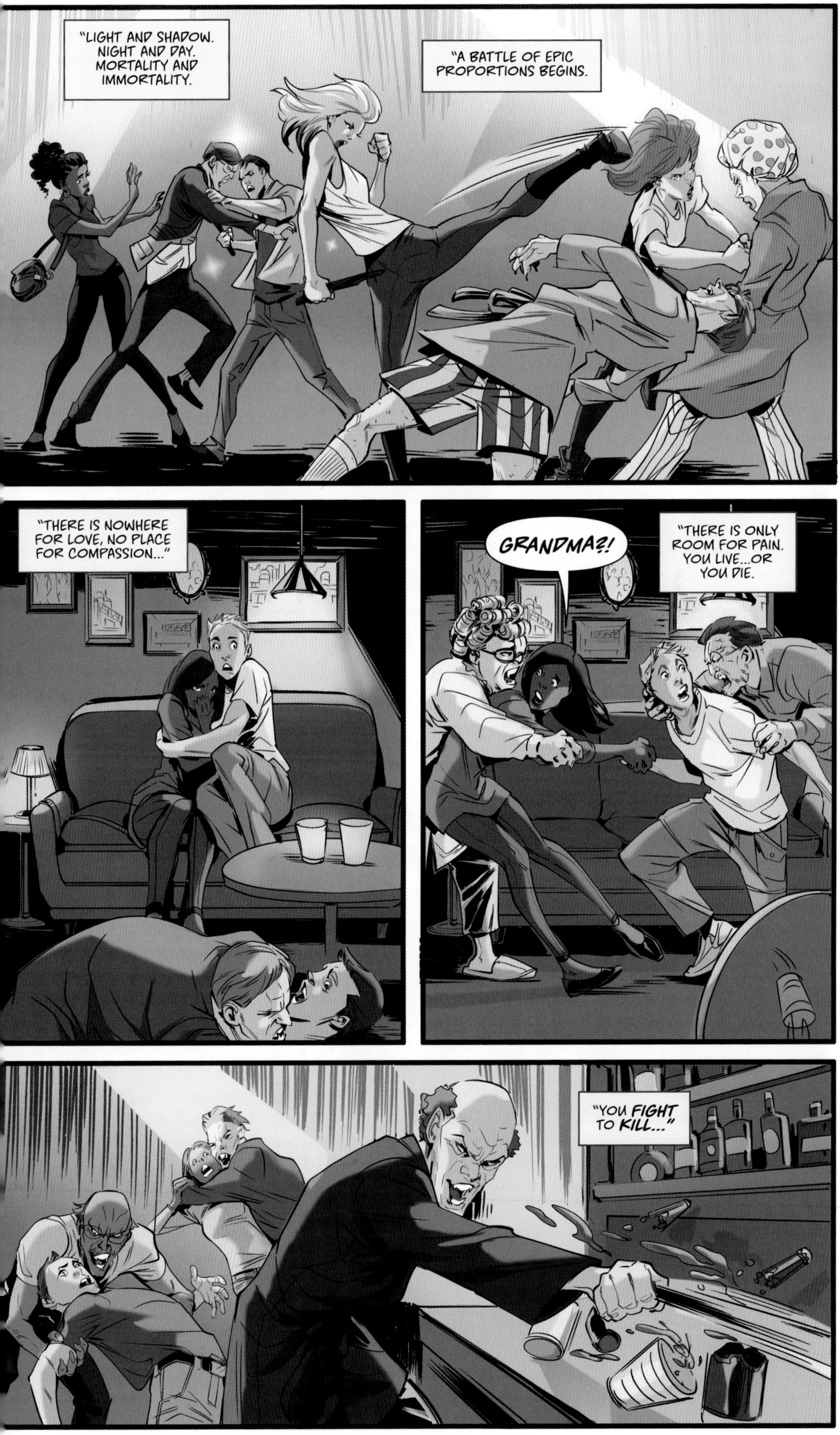
"LIGHT AND SHADOW. NIGHT AND DAY. MORTALITY AND IMMORTALITY.
"A BATTLE OF EPIC PROPORTIONS BEGINS.
"THERE IS NOWHERE FOR LOVE, NO PLACE FOR COMPASSION..."
GRANDMA?!
"THERE IS ONLY ROOM FOR PAIN. YOU LIVE...OR YOU DIE.
"YOU FIGHT TO KILL..."

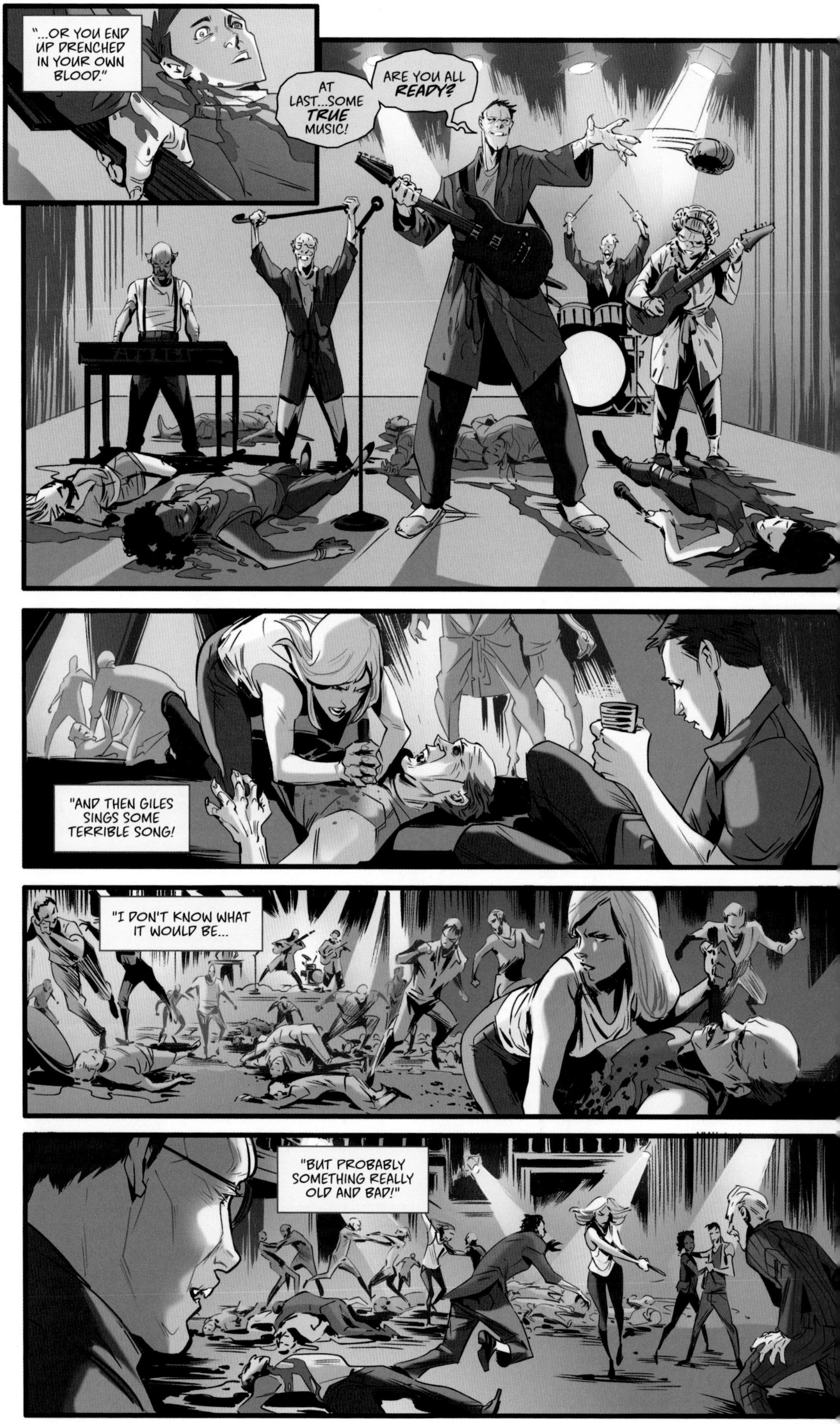
"...OR YOU END UP DRENCHED IN YOUR OWN BLOOD."
AT LAST...SOME TRUE MUSIC!
ARE YOU ALL READY?
"AND THEN GILES SINGS SOME TERRIBLE SONG!
"I DON'T KNOW WHAT IT WOULD BE...
"BUT PROBABLY SOMETHING REALLY OLD AND BAD!"

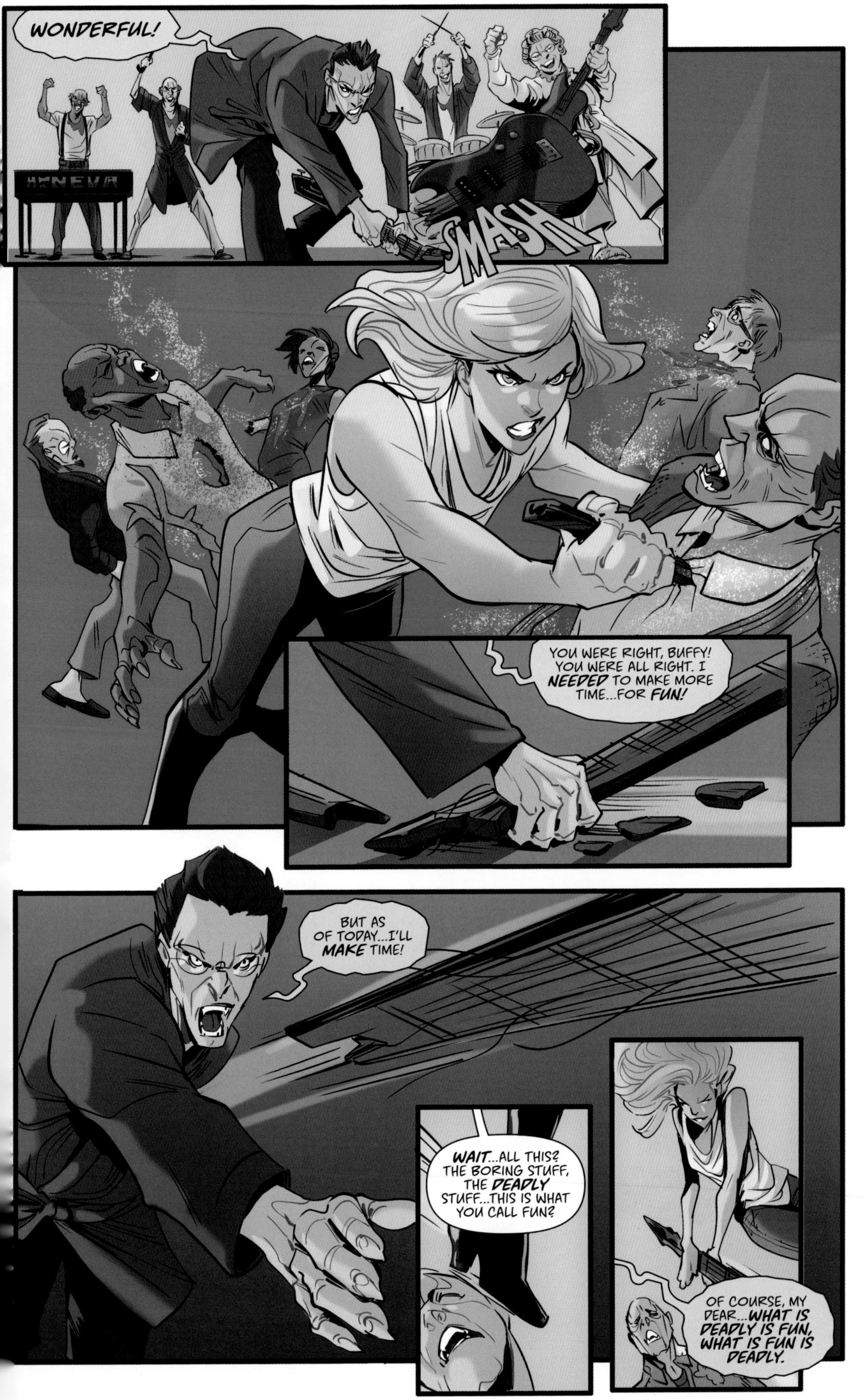

WONDERFUL!
HENEVA
SMASH
YOU WERE RIGHT, BUFFY! YOU WERE ALL RIGHT. I **NEEDED** TO MAKE MORE TIME...FOR **FUN!**
BUT AS OF TODAY...I'LL **MAKE** TIME!
WAIT...ALL THIS? THE BORING STUFF, THE **DEADLY** STUFF...THIS IS WHAT YOU CALL FUN?
OF COURSE, MY DEAR...**WHAT IS DEADLY IS FUN, WHAT IS FUN IS DEADLY.**

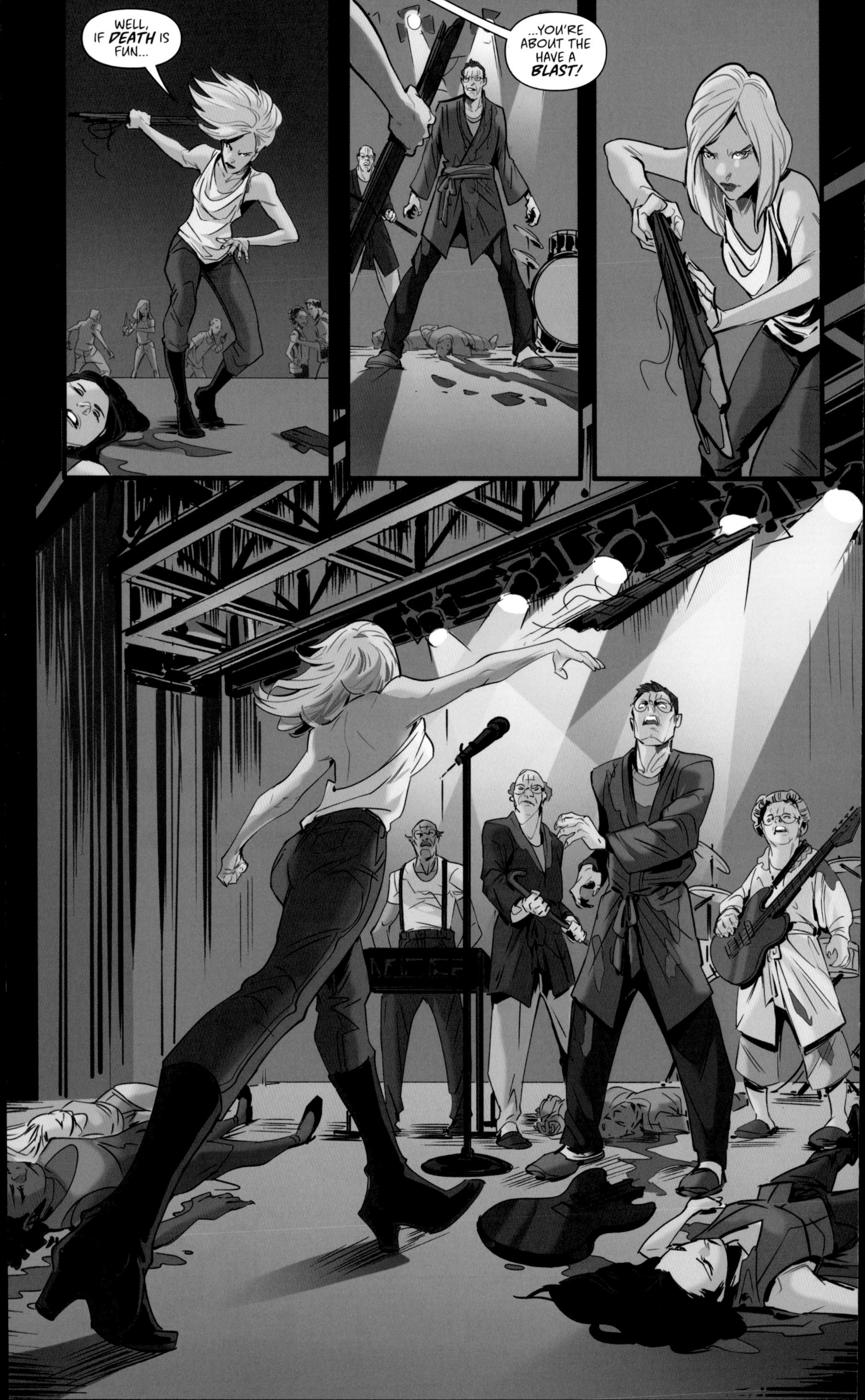
WELL, IF DEATH IS FUN...
...YOU'RE ABOUT THE HAVE A BLAST!

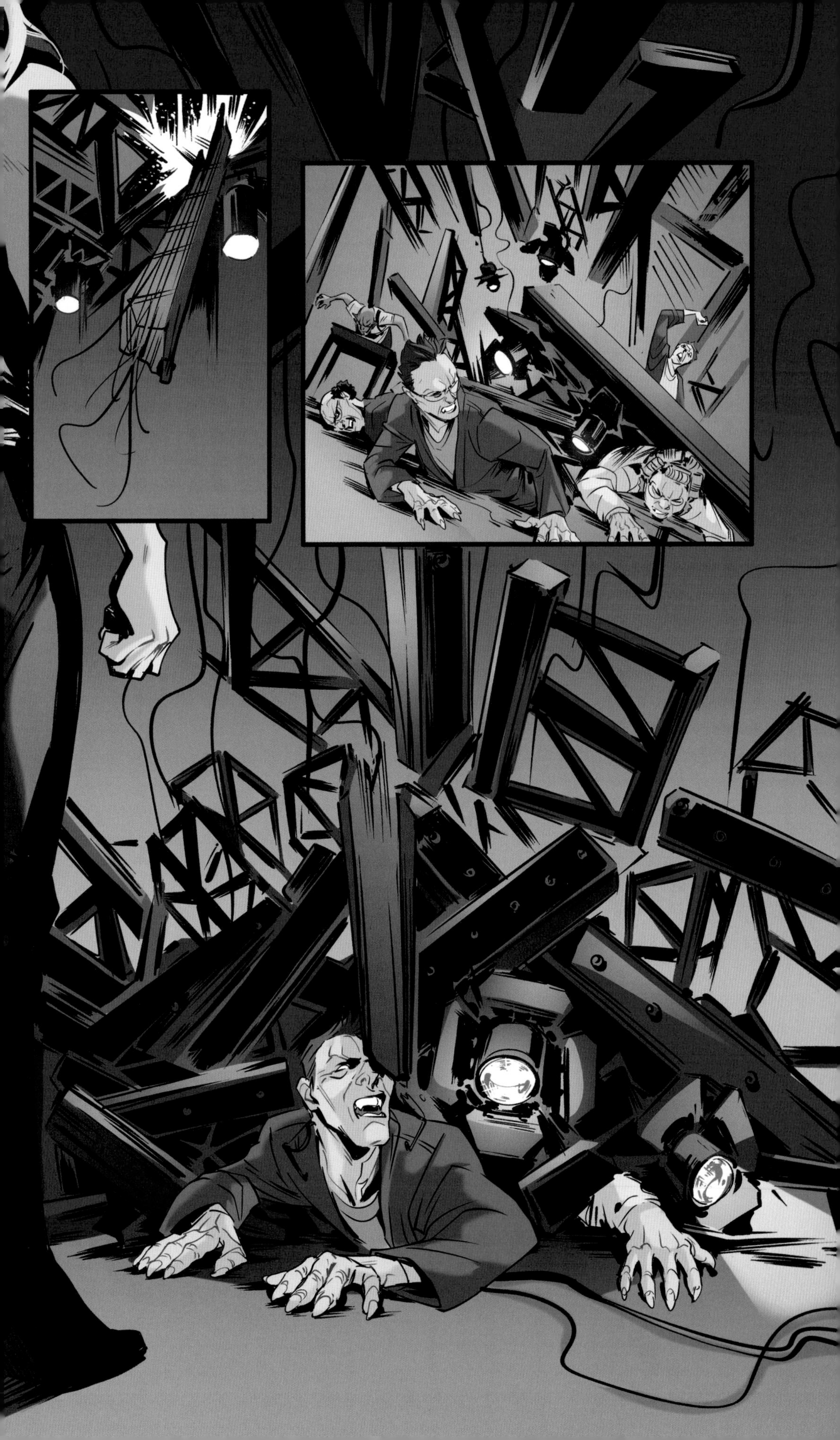

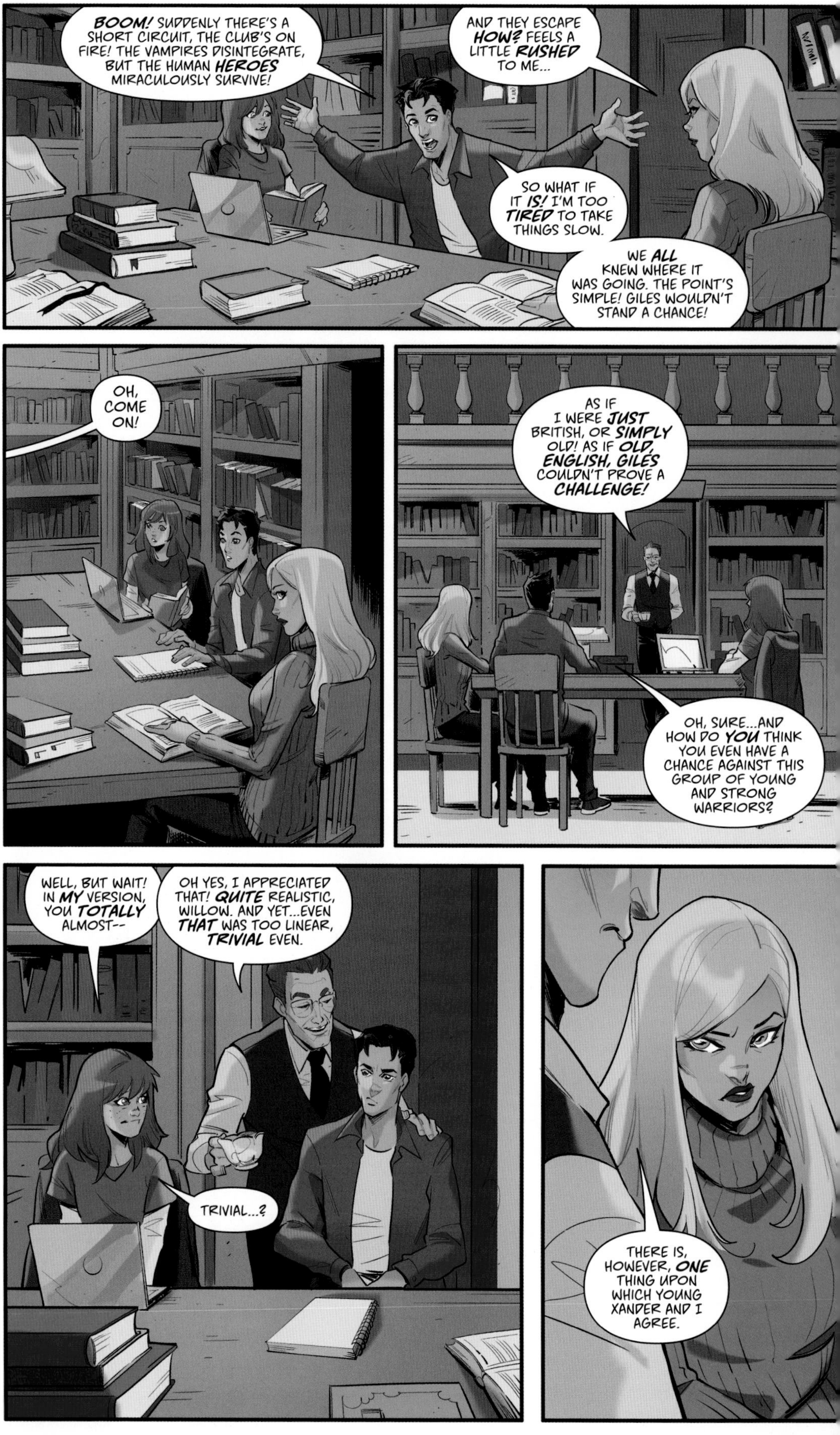
BOOM! SUDDENLY THERE'S A SHORT CIRCUIT, THE CLUB'S ON FIRE! THE VAMPIRES DISINTEGRATE, BUT THE HUMAN HEROES MIRACULOUSLY SURVIVE!
AND THEY ESCAPE HOW? FEELS A LITTLE RUSHED TO ME...
SO WHAT IF IT IS! I'M TOO TIRED TO TAKE THINGS SLOW.
WE ALL KNEW WHERE IT WAS GOING. THE POINT'S SIMPLE! GILES WOULDN'T STAND A CHANCE!
OH, COME ON!
AS IF I WERE JUST BRITISH, OR SIMPLY OLD! AS IF OLD, ENGLISH, GILES COULDN'T PROVE A CHALLENGE!
OH, SURE...AND HOW DO YOU THINK YOU EVEN HAVE A CHANCE AGAINST THIS GROUP OF YOUNG AND STRONG WARRIORS?
WELL, BUT WAIT! IN MY VERSION, YOU TOTALLY ALMOST--
OH YES, I APPRECIATED THAT! QUITE REALISTIC, WILLOW. AND YET...EVEN THAT WAS TOO LINEAR, TRIVIAL EVEN.
TRIVIAL...?
THERE IS, HOWEVER, ONE THING UPON WHICH YOUNG XANDER AND I AGREE.

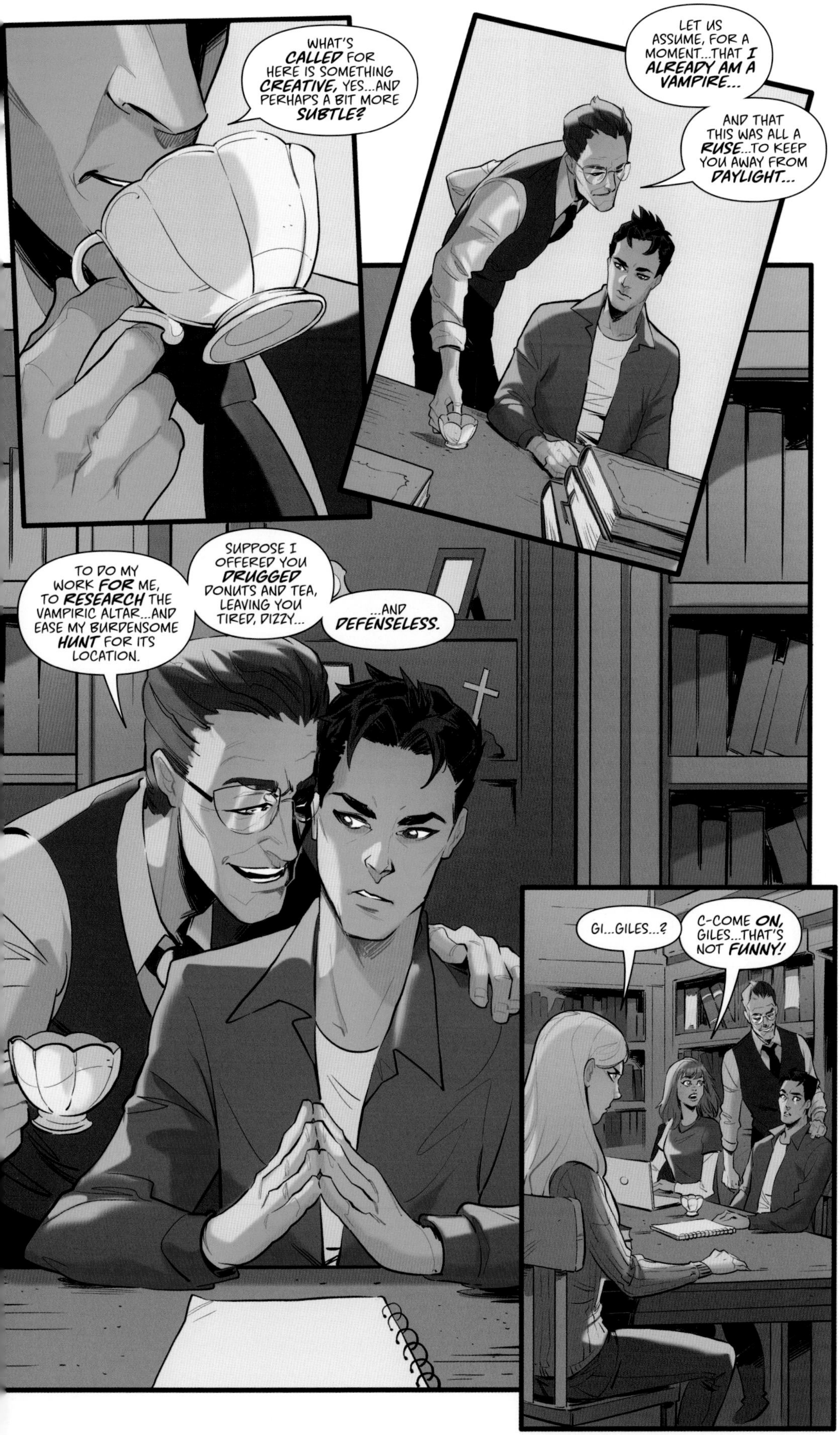
WHAT'S CALLED FOR HERE IS SOMETHING CREATIVE, YES...AND PERHAPS A BIT MORE SUBTLE?
LET US ASSUME, FOR A MOMENT...THAT I ALREADY AM A VAMPIRE...
AND THAT THIS WAS ALL A RUSE...TO KEEP YOU AWAY FROM DAYLIGHT...
TO DO MY WORK FOR ME, TO RESEARCH THE VAMPIRIC ALTAR...AND EASE MY BURDENSOME HUNT FOR ITS LOCATION.
SUPPOSE I OFFERED YOU DRUGGED DONUTS AND TEA, LEAVING YOU TIRED, DIZZY...
...AND DEFENSELESS.
GI...GILES...?
C-COME ON, GILES...THAT'S NOT FUNNY!

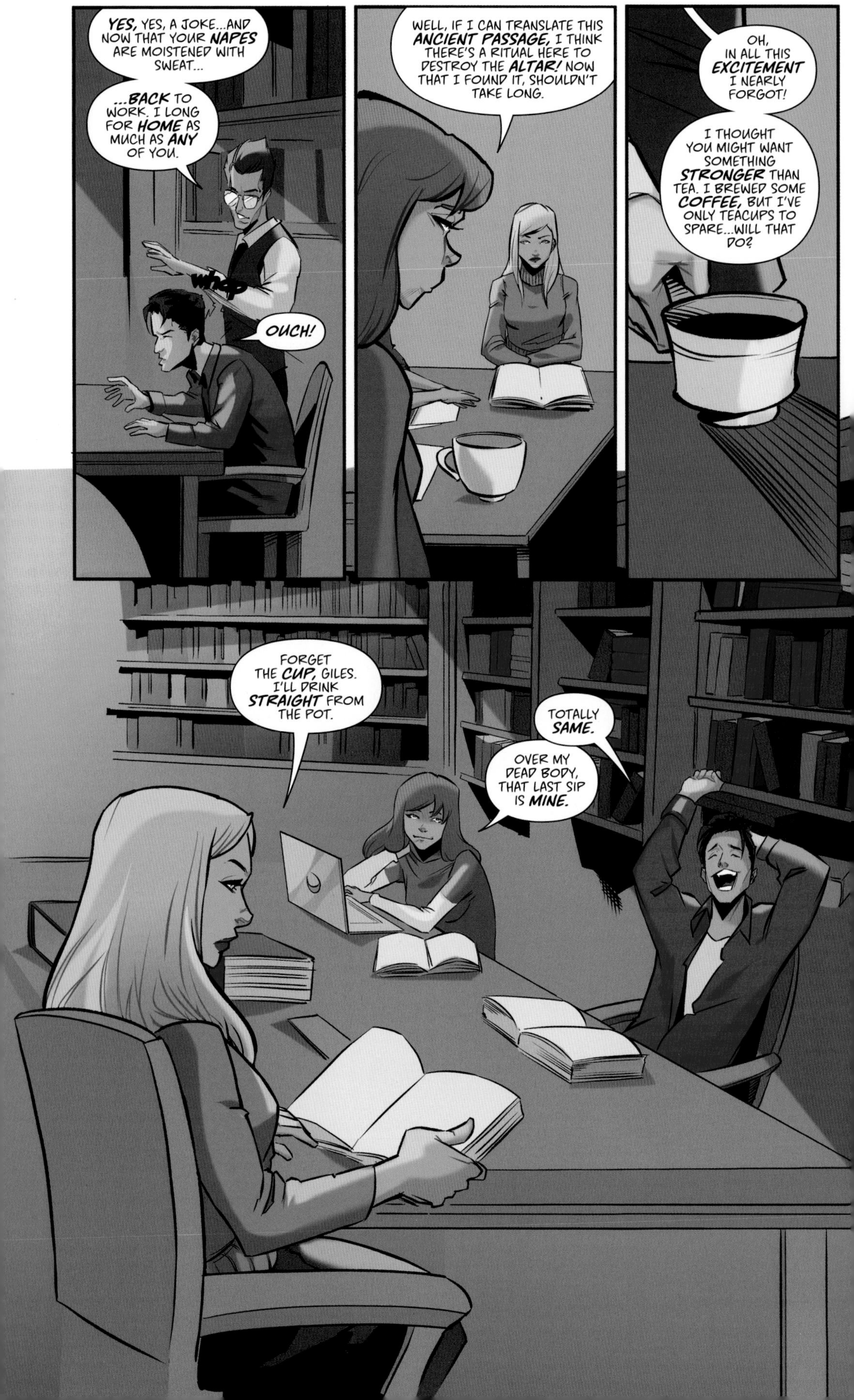

YES, YES, A JOKE...AND NOW THAT YOUR NAPES ARE MOISTENED WITH SWEAT...
...BACK TO WORK. I LONG FOR HOME AS MUCH AS ANY OF YOU.
whap
OUCH!
WELL, IF I CAN TRANSLATE THIS ANCIENT PASSAGE, I THINK THERE'S A RITUAL HERE TO DESTROY THE ALTAR! NOW THAT I FOUND IT, SHOULDN'T TAKE LONG.
OH, IN ALL THIS EXCITEMENT I NEARLY FORGOT!
I THOUGHT YOU MIGHT WANT SOMETHING STRONGER THAN TEA. I BREWED SOME COFFEE, BUT I'VE ONLY TEACUPS TO SPARE...WILL THAT DO?
FORGET THE CUP, GILES. I'LL DRINK STRAIGHT FROM THE POT.
TOTALLY SAME.
OVER MY DEAD BODY, THAT LAST SIP IS MINE.

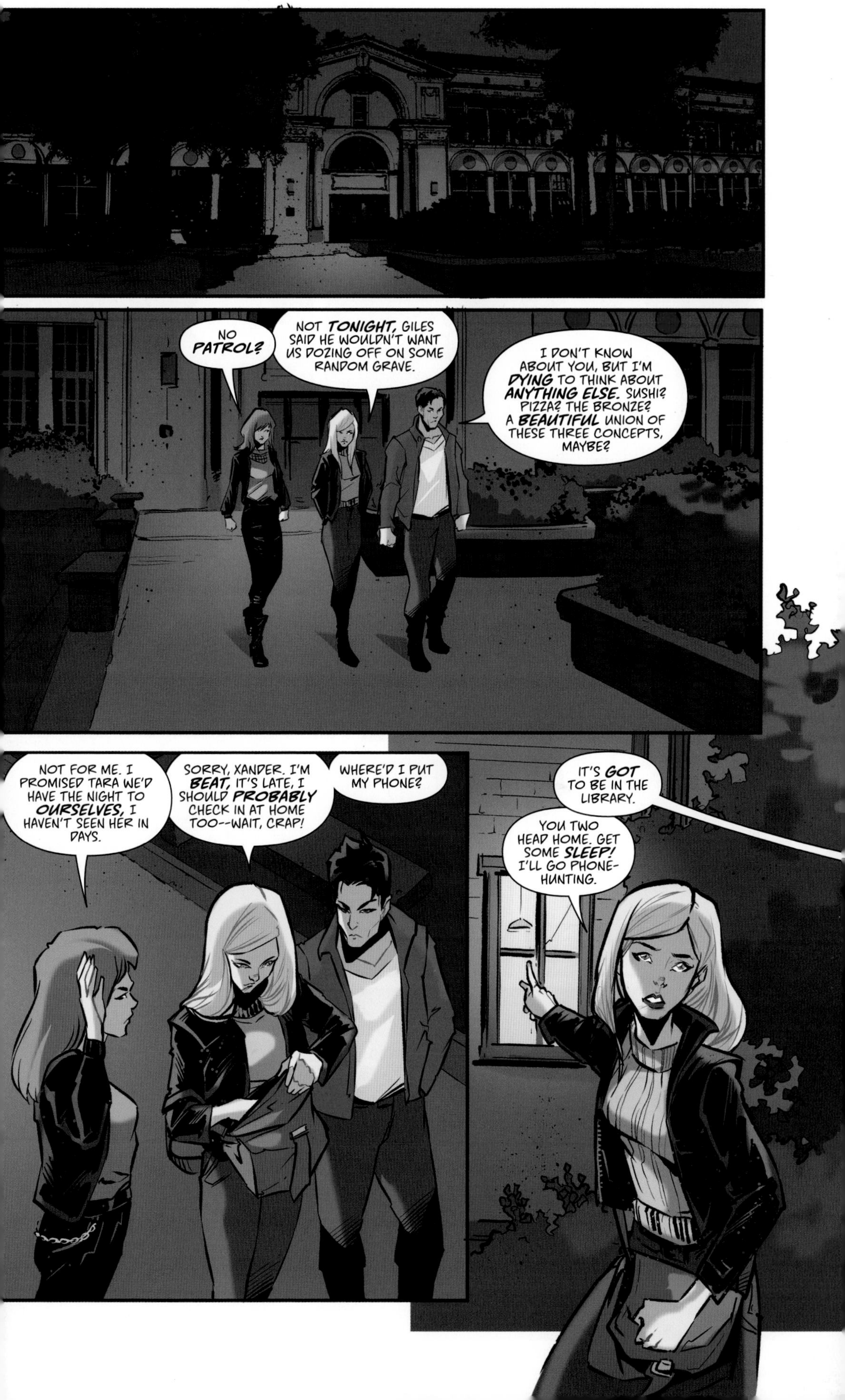
NO PATROL?
NOT TONIGHT, GILES SAID HE WOULDN'T WANT US DOZING OFF ON SOME RANDOM GRAVE.
I DON'T KNOW ABOUT YOU, BUT I'M DYING TO THINK ABOUT ANYTHING ELSE. SUSHI? PIZZA? THE BRONZE? A BEAUTIFUL UNION OF THESE THREE CONCEPTS, MAYBE?
NOT FOR ME. I PROMISED TARA WE'D HAVE THE NIGHT TO OURSELVES, I HAVEN'T SEEN HER IN DAYS.
SORRY, XANDER. I'M BEAT, IT'S LATE, I SHOULD PROBABLY CHECK IN AT HOME TOO--WAIT, CRAP!
WHERE'D I PUT MY PHONE?
IT'S GOT TO BE IN THE LIBRARY.
YOU TWO HEAD HOME. GET SOME SLEEP! I'LL GO PHONE-HUNTING.

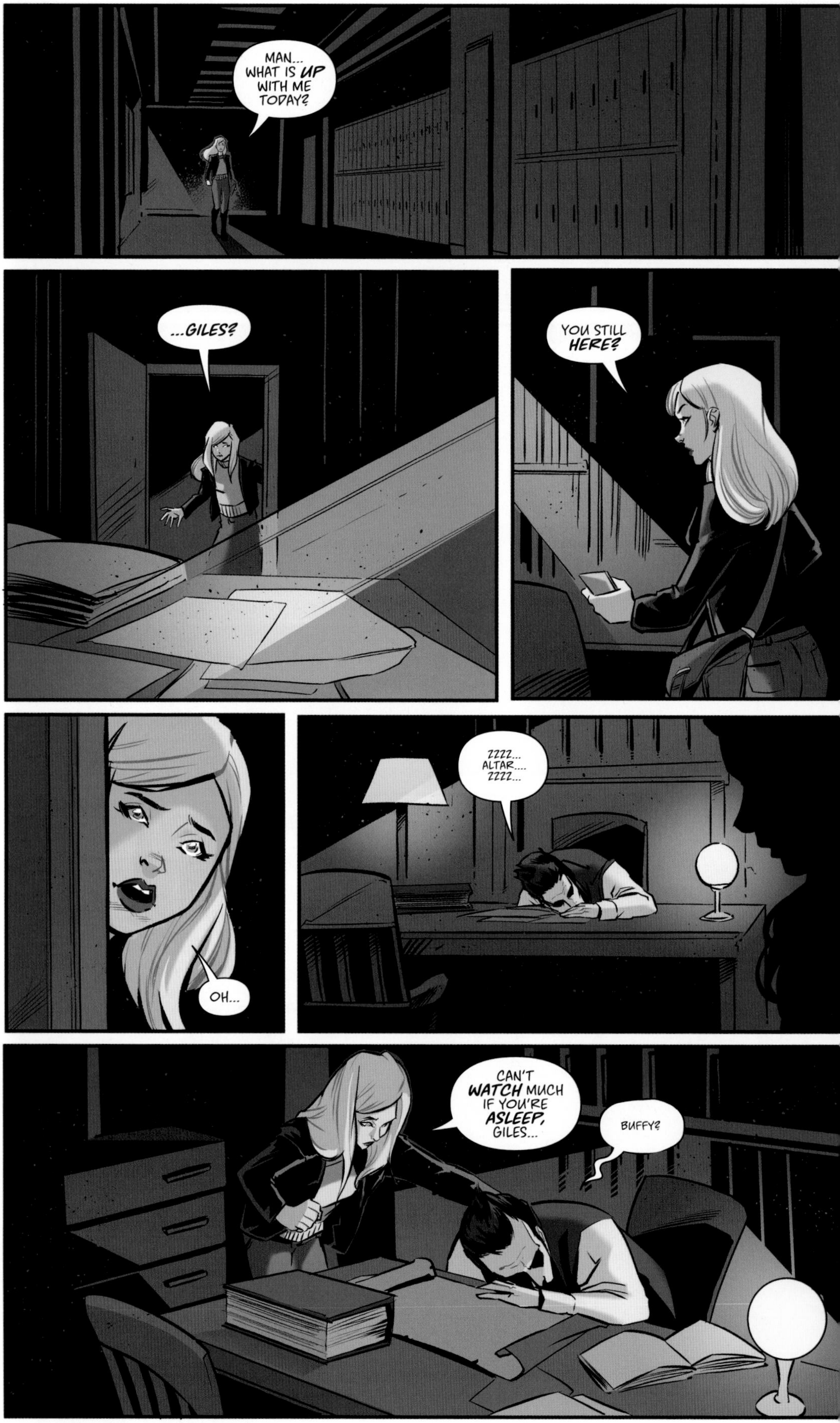

MAN... WHAT IS UP WITH ME TODAY?
...GILES?
YOU STILL HERE?
OH...
ZZZZ... ALTAR.... ZZZZ...
CAN'T WATCH MUCH IF YOU'RE ASLEEP, GILES...
BUFFY?

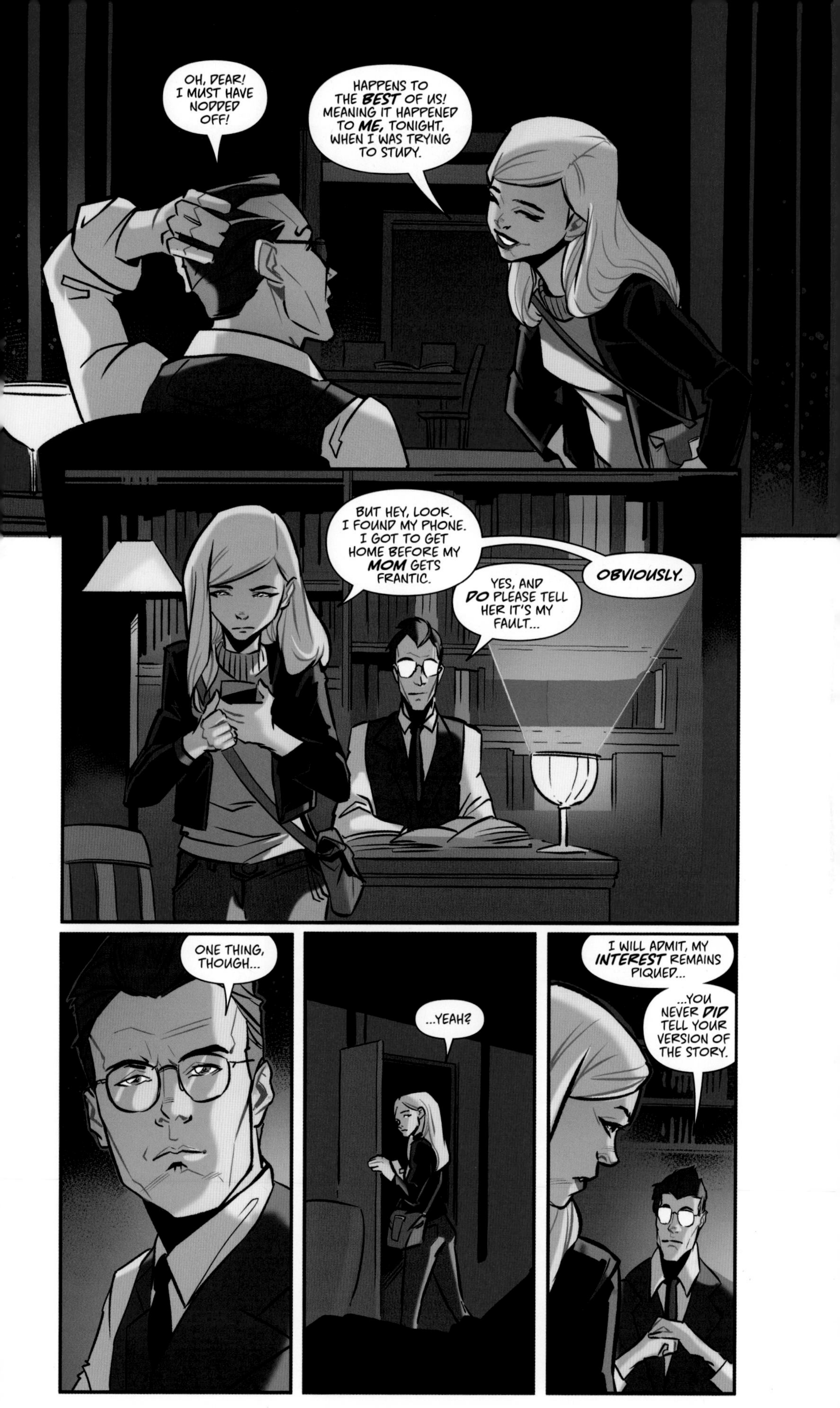
OH, DEAR! I MUST HAVE NODDED OFF!
HAPPENS TO THE BEST OF US! MEANING IT HAPPENED TO ME, TONIGHT, WHEN I WAS TRYING TO STUDY.
BUT HEY, LOOK. I FOUND MY PHONE. I GOT TO GET HOME BEFORE MY MOM GETS FRANTIC.
YES, AND DO PLEASE TELL HER IT'S MY FAULT...
OBVIOUSLY.
ONE THING, THOUGH...
...YEAH?
I WILL ADMIT, MY INTEREST REMAINS PIQUED...
...YOU NEVER DID TELL YOUR VERSION OF THE STORY.

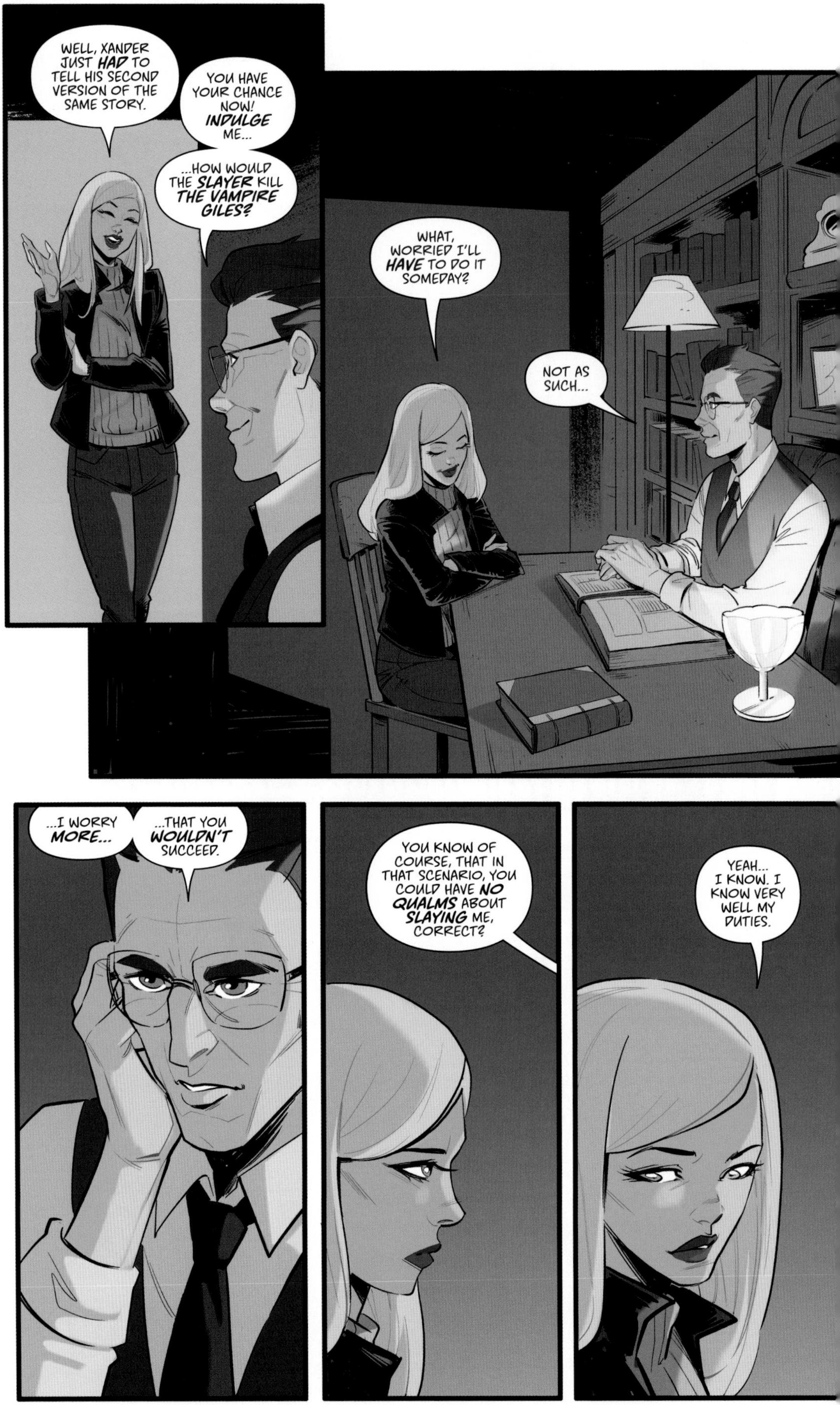
WELL, XANDER JUST **HAD** TO TELL HIS SECOND VERSION OF THE SAME STORY.
YOU HAVE YOUR CHANCE NOW! **INDULGE** ME...
...HOW WOULD THE **SLAYER** KILL **THE VAMPIRE GILES?**
WHAT, WORRIED I'LL **HAVE** TO DO IT SOMEDAY?
NOT AS SUCH...
...I WORRY **MORE...**
...THAT YOU **WOULDN'T** SUCCEED.
YOU KNOW OF COURSE, THAT IN THAT SCENARIO, YOU COULD HAVE **NO QUALMS** ABOUT **SLAYING** ME, CORRECT?
YEAH... I KNOW. I KNOW VERY WELL MY DUTIES.

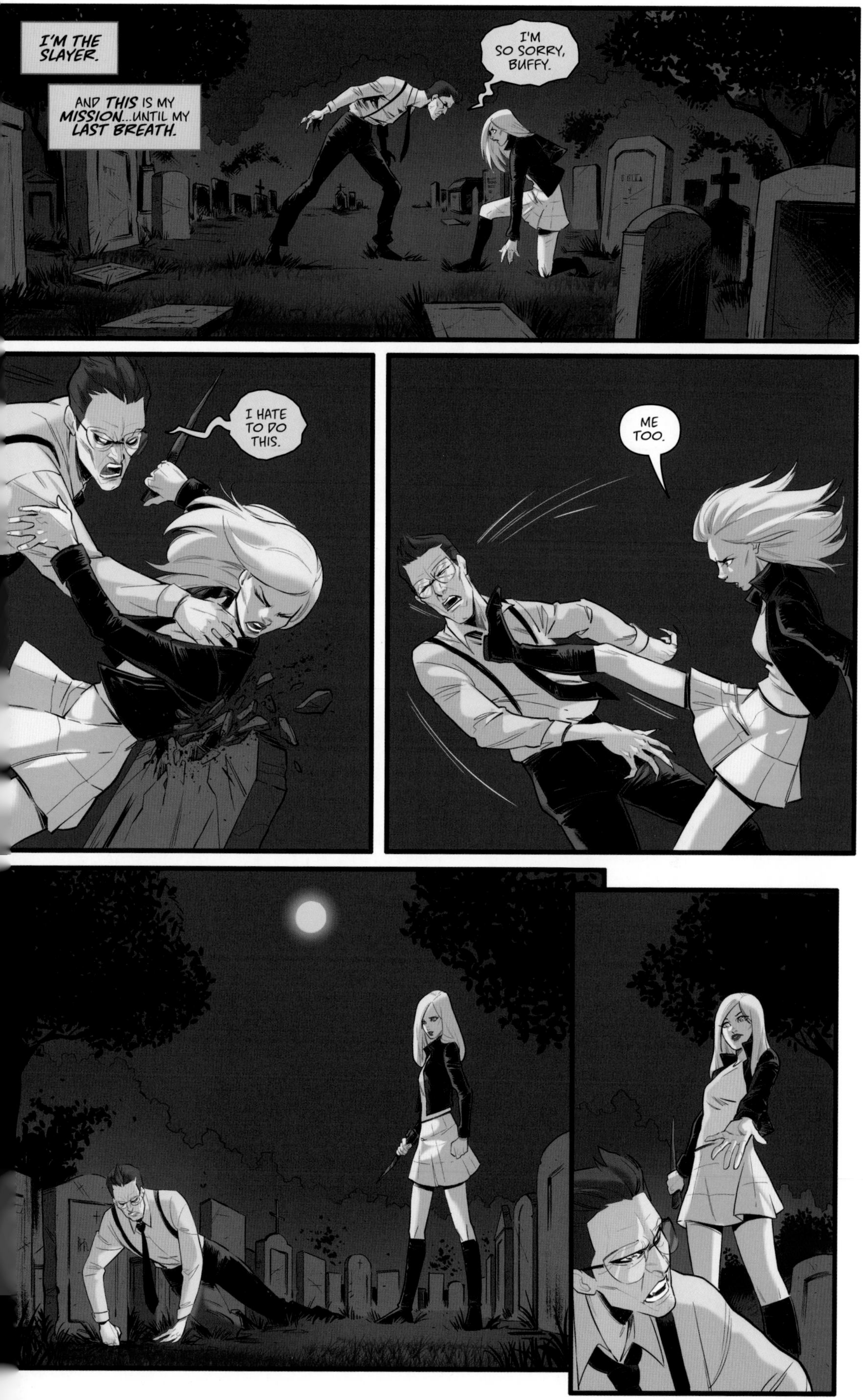
I'M THE SLAYER.
AND THIS IS MY MISSION...UNTIL MY LAST BREATH.
I'M SO SORRY, BUFFY.
I HATE TO DO THIS.
ME TOO.

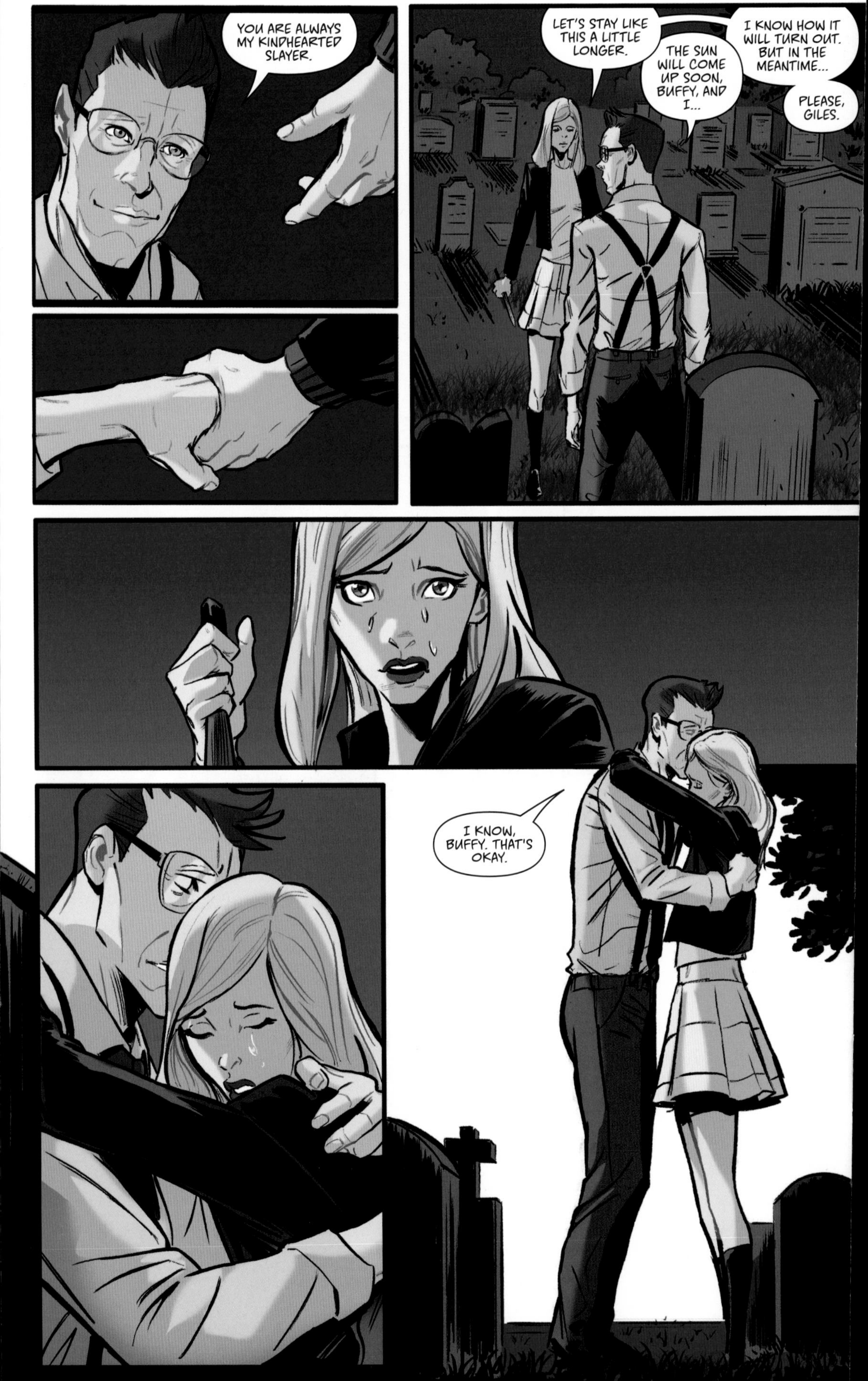
YOU ARE ALWAYS MY KINDHEARTED SLAYER.
LET'S STAY LIKE THIS A LITTLE LONGER.
THE SUN WILL COME UP SOON, BUFFY, AND I...
I KNOW HOW IT WILL TURN OUT. BUT IN THE MEANTIME...
PLEASE, GILES.
I KNOW, BUFFY. THAT'S OKAY.

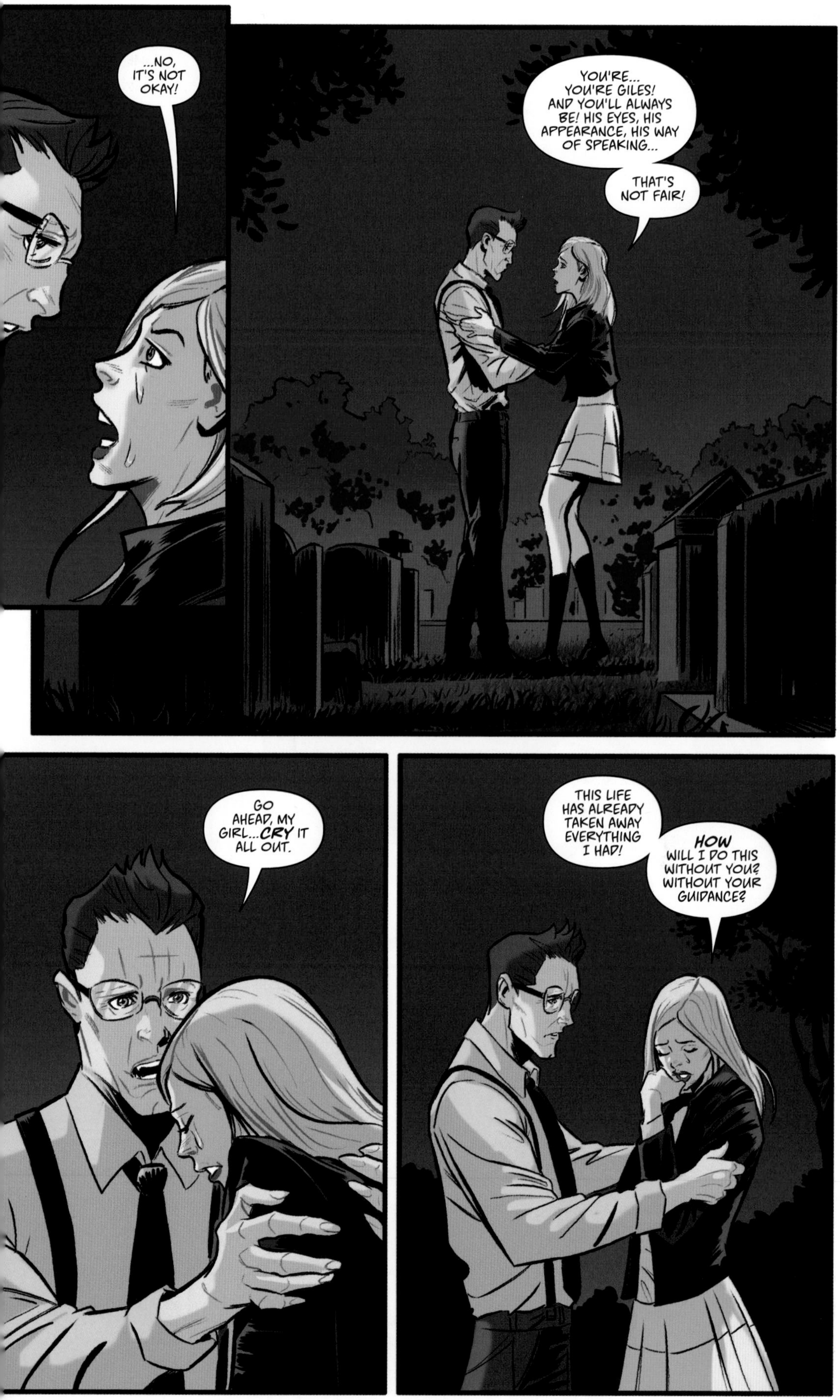
...NO, IT'S NOT OKAY!
YOU'RE... YOU'RE GILES! AND YOU'LL ALWAYS BE! HIS EYES, HIS APPEARANCE, HIS WAY OF SPEAKING...
THAT'S NOT FAIR!
GO AHEAD, MY GIRL...CRY IT ALL OUT.
THIS LIFE HAS ALREADY TAKEN AWAY EVERYTHING I HAD!
HOW WILL I DO THIS WITHOUT YOU? WITHOUT YOUR GUIDANCE?

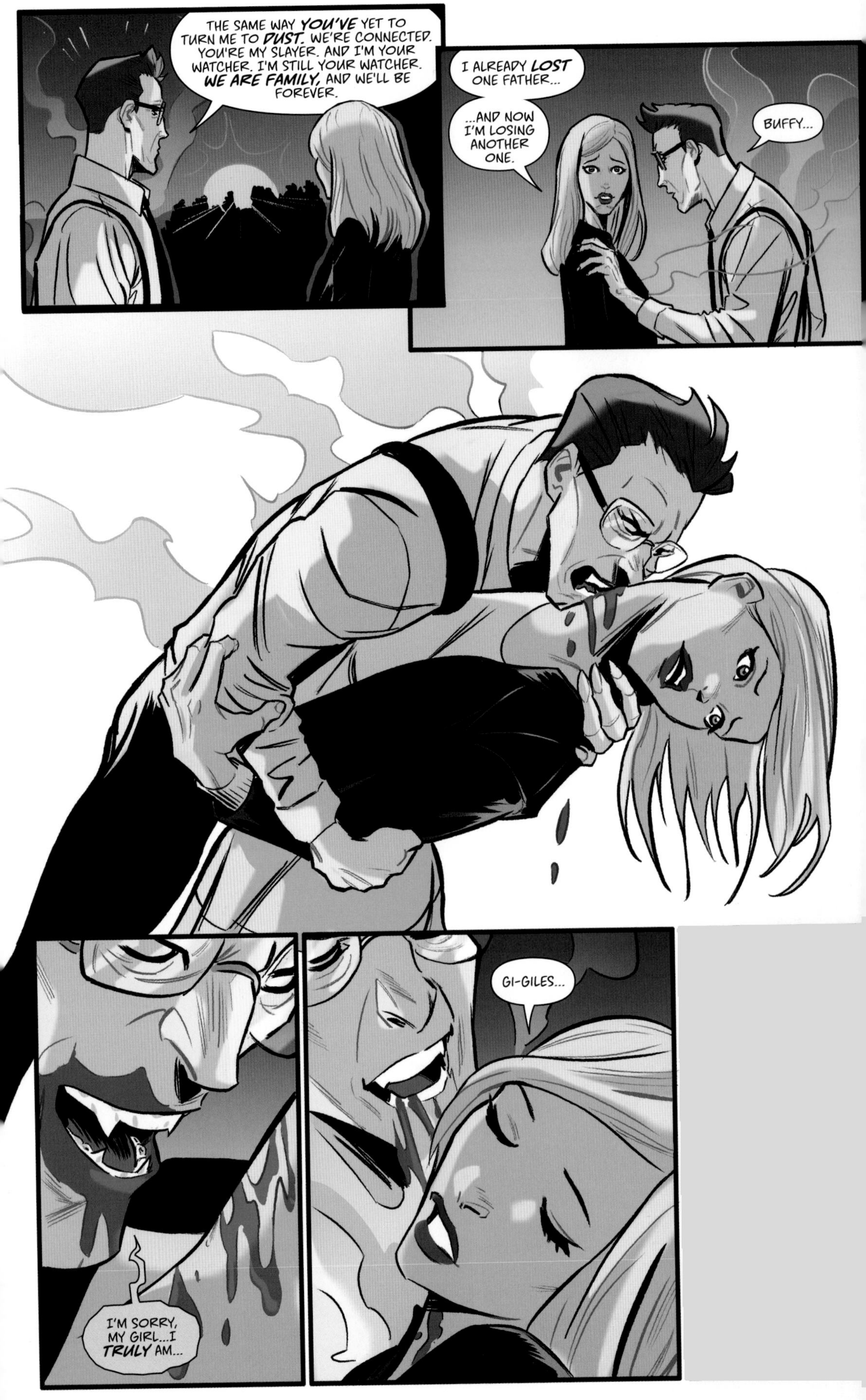
THE SAME WAY *YOU'VE* YET TO TURN ME TO *DUST.* WE'RE CONNECTED. YOU'RE MY SLAYER. AND I'M YOUR WATCHER. I'M STILL YOUR WATCHER. *WE ARE FAMILY,* AND WE'LL BE FOREVER.
I ALREADY *LOST* ONE FATHER...
...AND NOW I'M LOSING ANOTHER ONE.
BUFFY...
GI-GILES...
I'M SORRY, MY GIRL...I *TRULY* AM...

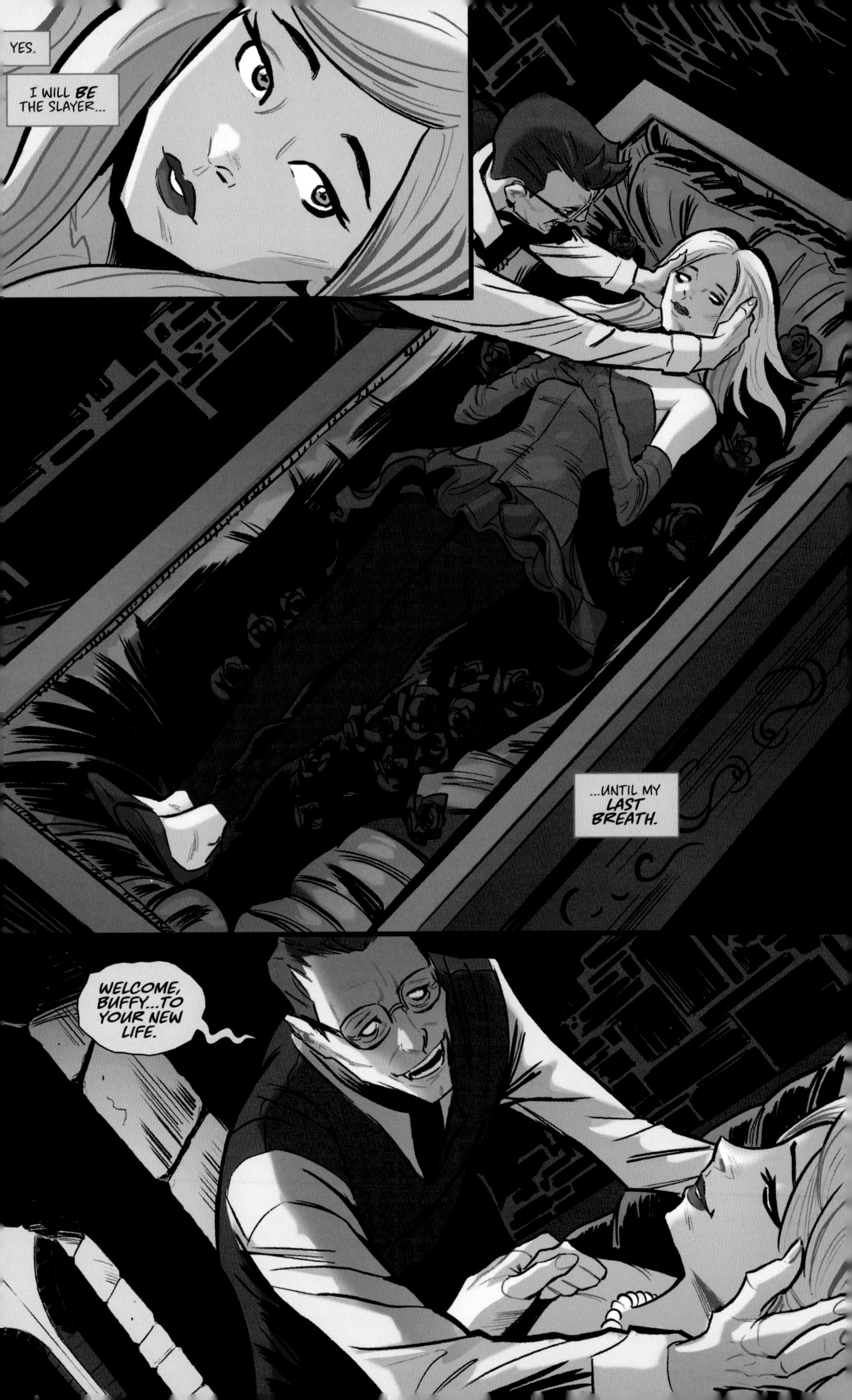
YES.
I WILL BE THE SLAYER...
...UNTIL MY LAST BREATH.
WELCOME, BUFFY...TO YOUR NEW LIFE.

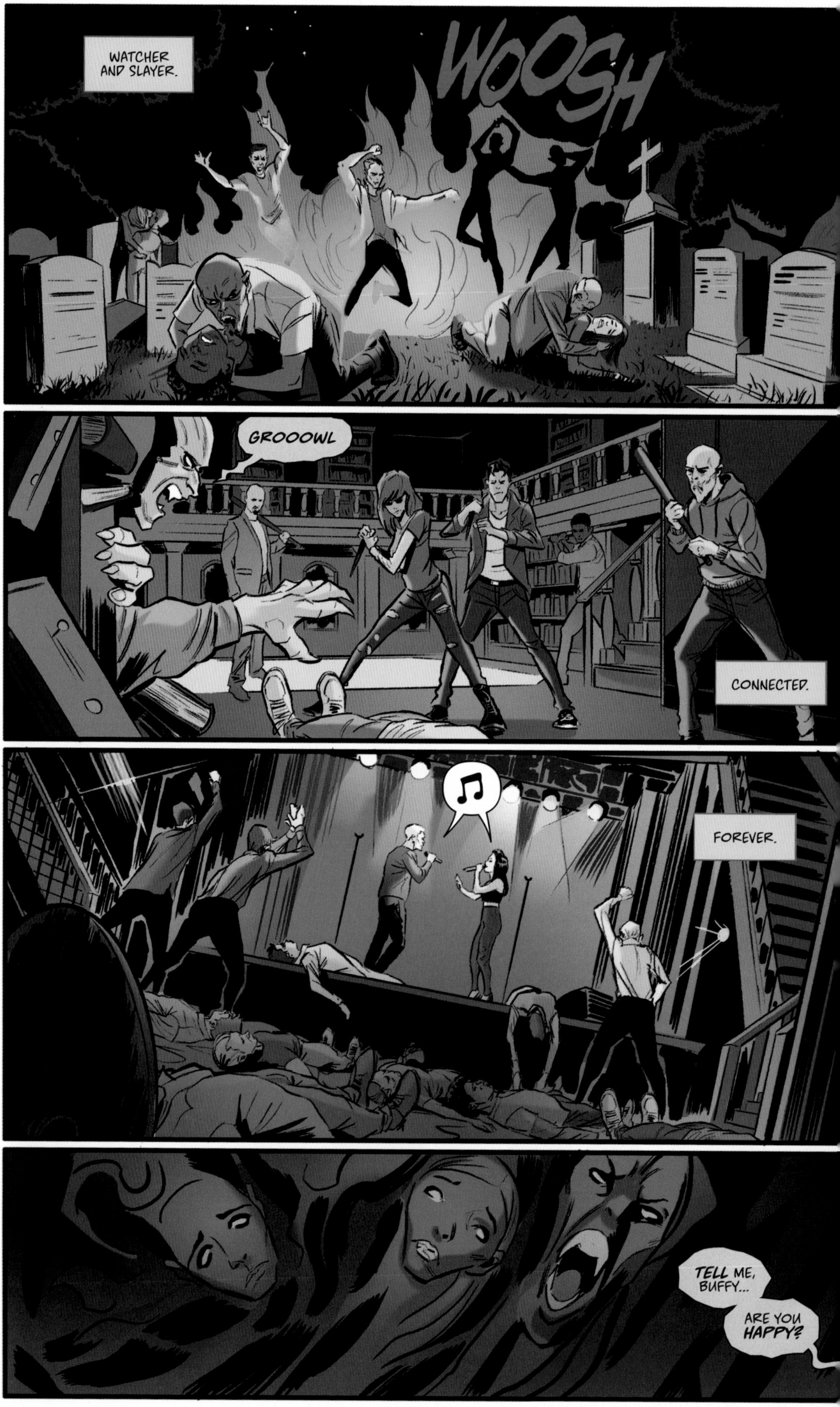
WATCHER AND SLAYER.
WOOSH
GROOOWL
CONNECTED.
♫
FOREVER.
TELL ME, BUFFY...
ARE YOU HAPPY?

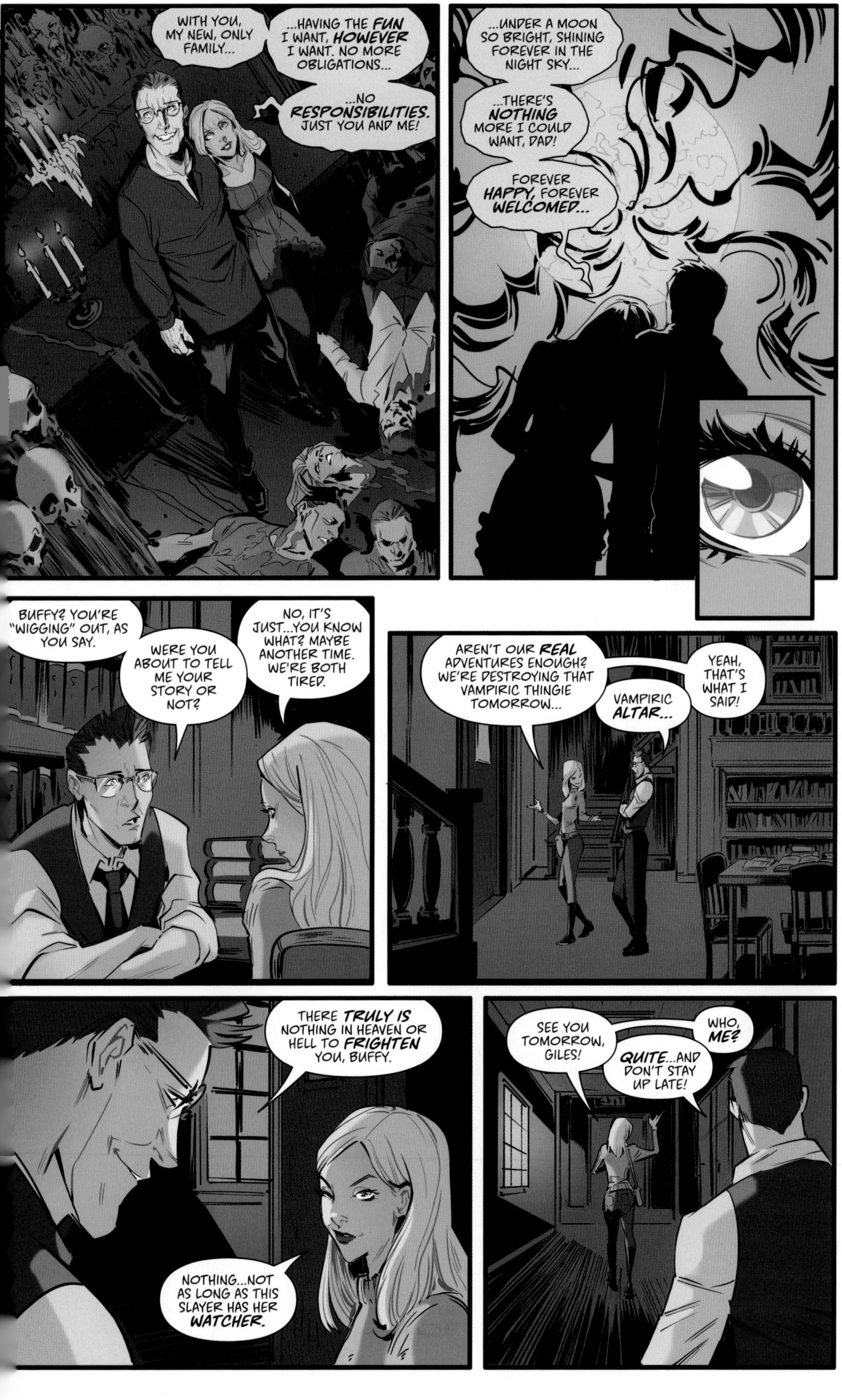
WITH YOU, MY NEW, ONLY FAMILY...
...HAVING THE **FUN** I WANT, **HOWEVER** I WANT. NO MORE OBLIGATIONS...
...NO **RESPONSIBILITIES.** JUST YOU AND ME!
...UNDER A MOON SO BRIGHT, SHINING FOREVER IN THE NIGHT SKY...
...THERE'S **NOTHING** MORE I COULD WANT, DAD!
FOREVER **HAPPY,** FOREVER **WELCOMED...**
BUFFY? YOU'RE "WIGGING" OUT, AS YOU SAY.
WERE YOU ABOUT TO TELL ME YOUR STORY OR NOT?
NO, IT'S JUST...YOU KNOW WHAT? MAYBE ANOTHER TIME. WE'RE BOTH TIRED.
AREN'T OUR **REAL** ADVENTURES ENOUGH? WE'RE DESTROYING THAT VAMPIRIC THINGIE TOMORROW...
VAMPIRIC **ALTAR...**
YEAH, THAT'S WHAT I SAID!
THERE **TRULY IS** NOTHING IN HEAVEN OR HELL TO **FRIGHTEN** YOU, BUFFY.
NOTHING...NOT AS LONG AS THIS SLAYER HAS HER **WATCHER.**
SEE YOU TOMORROW, GILES!
WHO, **ME?**
QUITE...AND DON'T STAY UP LATE!

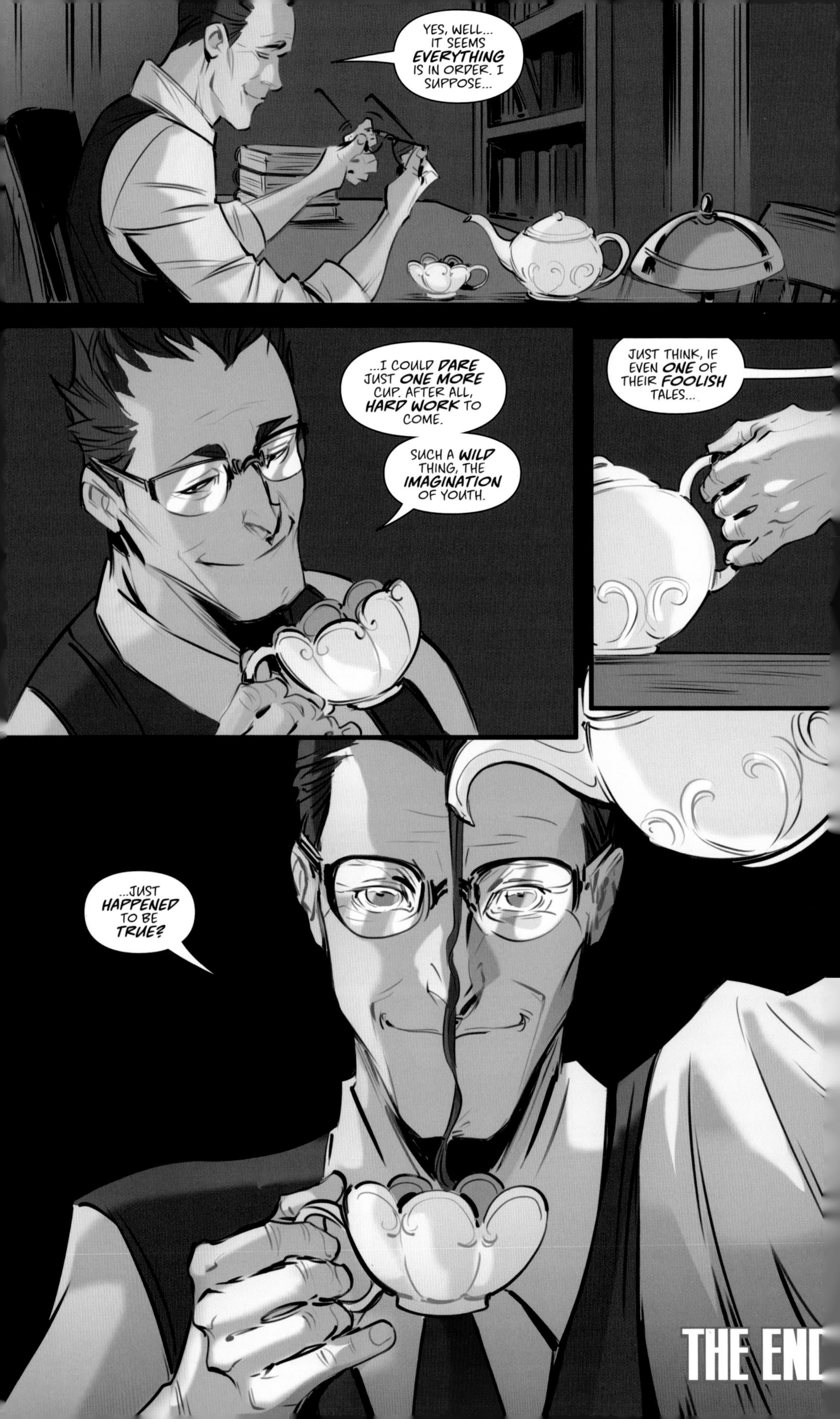
YES, WELL... IT SEEMS EVERYTHING IS IN ORDER. I SUPPOSE...
...I COULD DARE JUST ONE MORE CUP. AFTER ALL, HARD WORK TO COME.
SUCH A WILD THING, THE IMAGINATION OF YOUTH.
JUST THINK, IF EVEN ONE OF THEIR FOOLISH TALES...
...JUST HAPPENED TO BE TRUE?
THE END

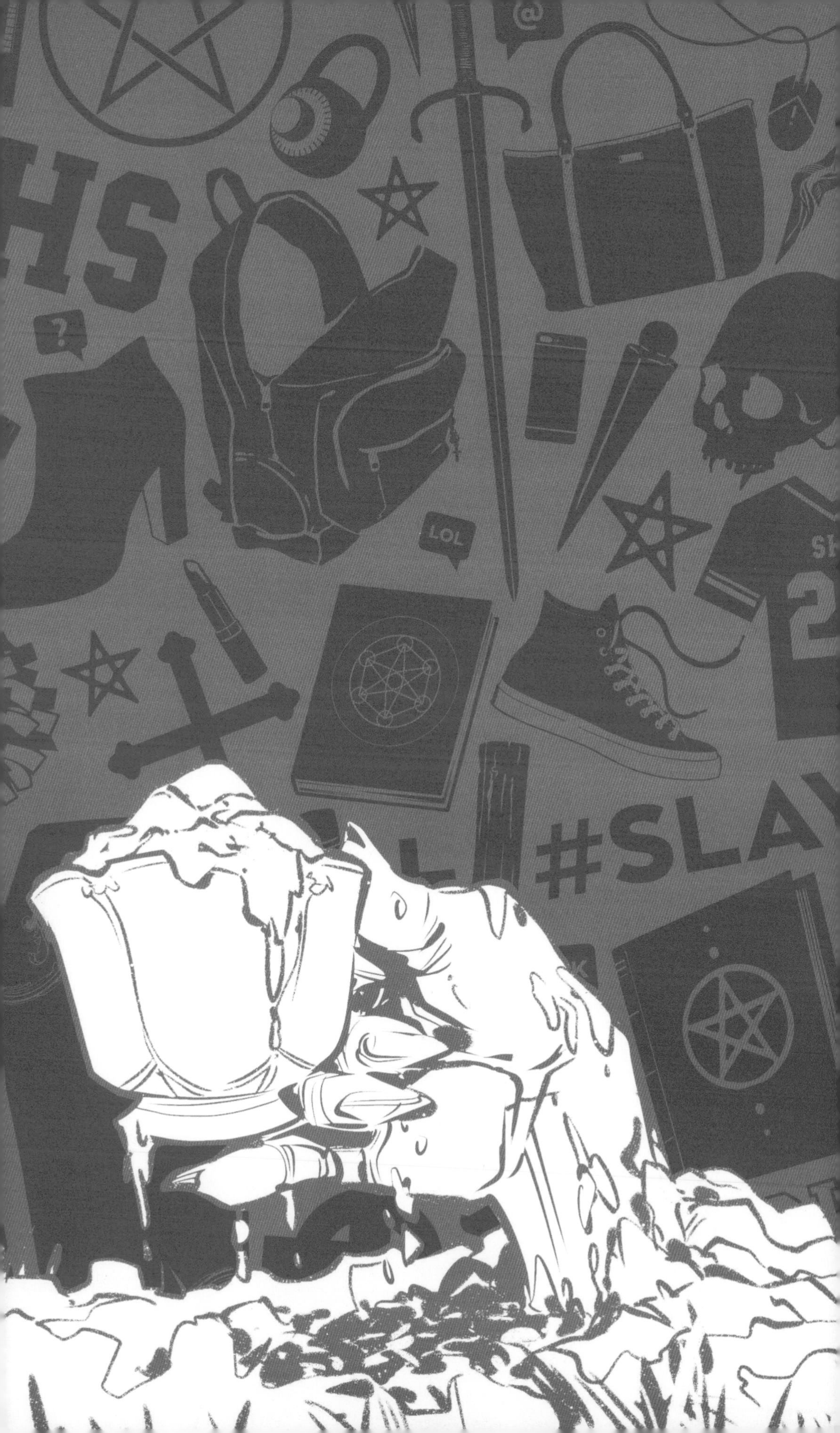
LOL

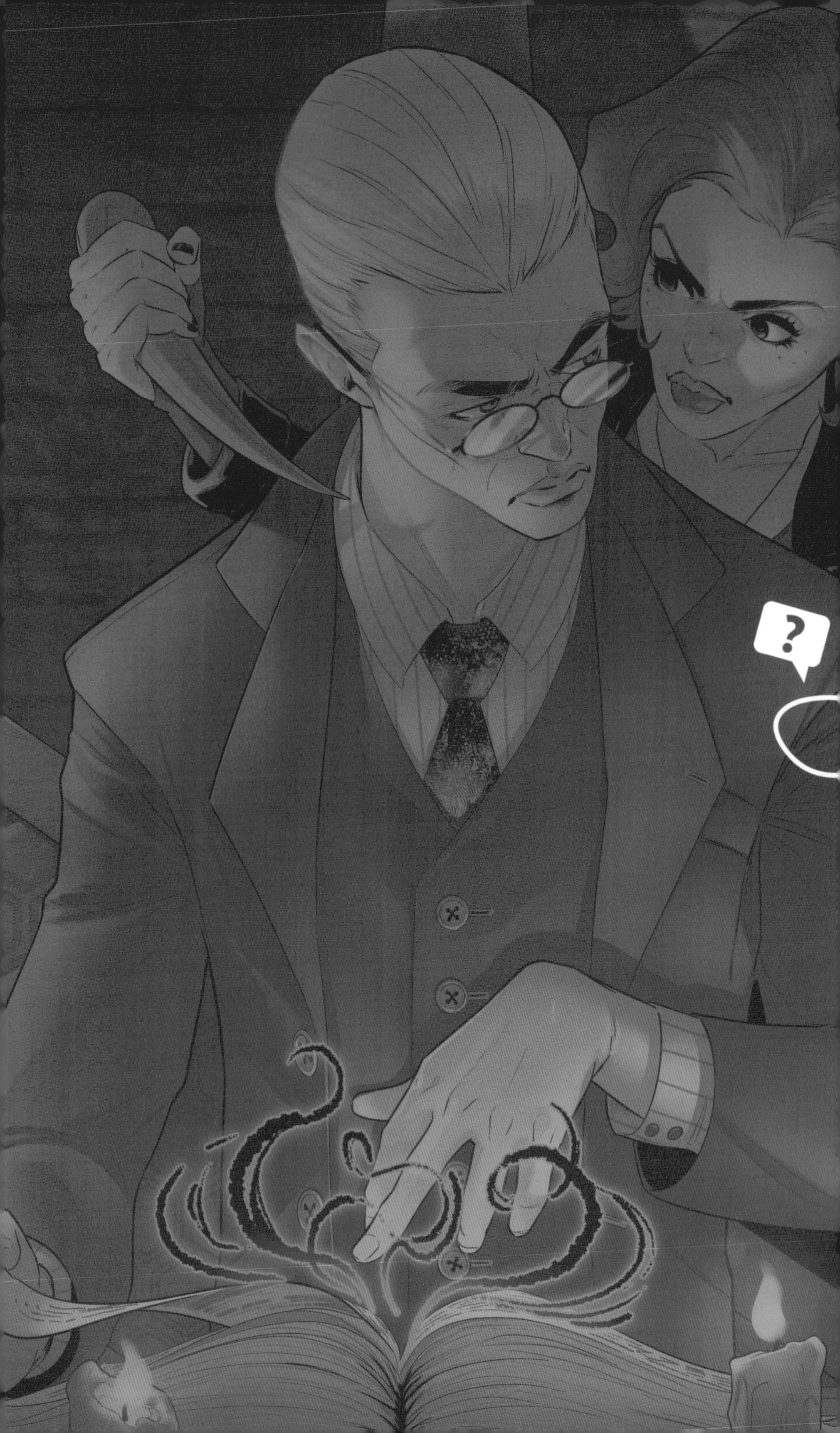
?

COVER GALLERY

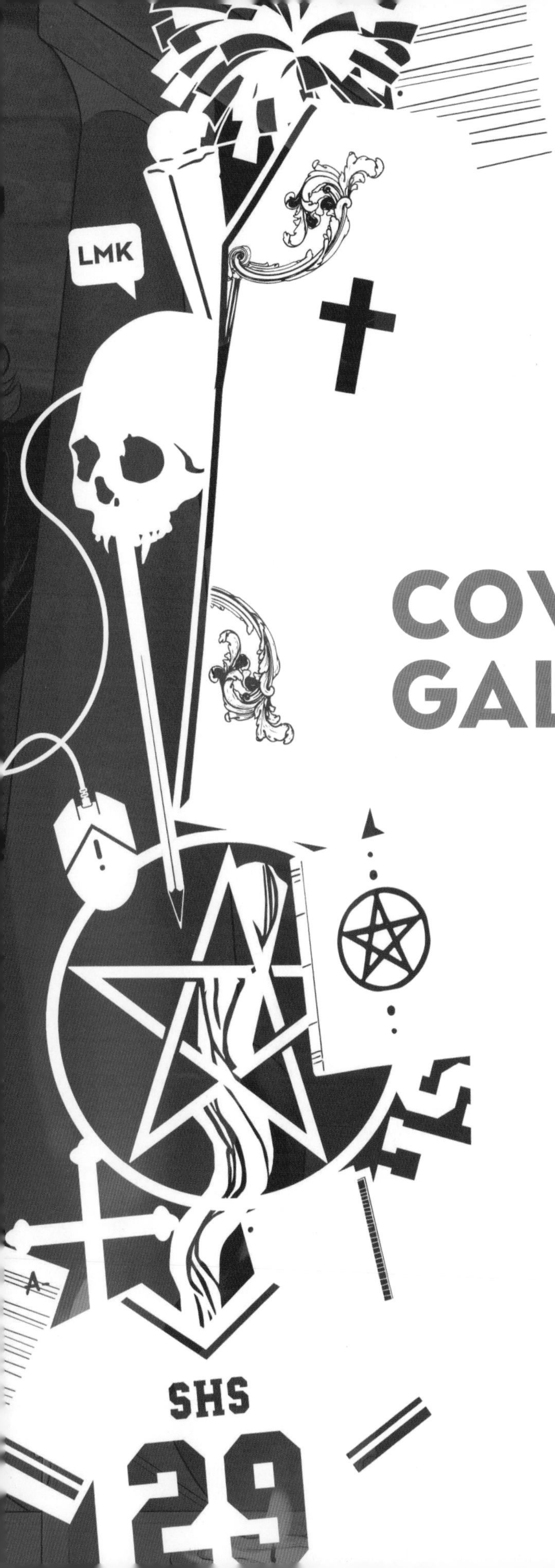
LMK
SHS
29

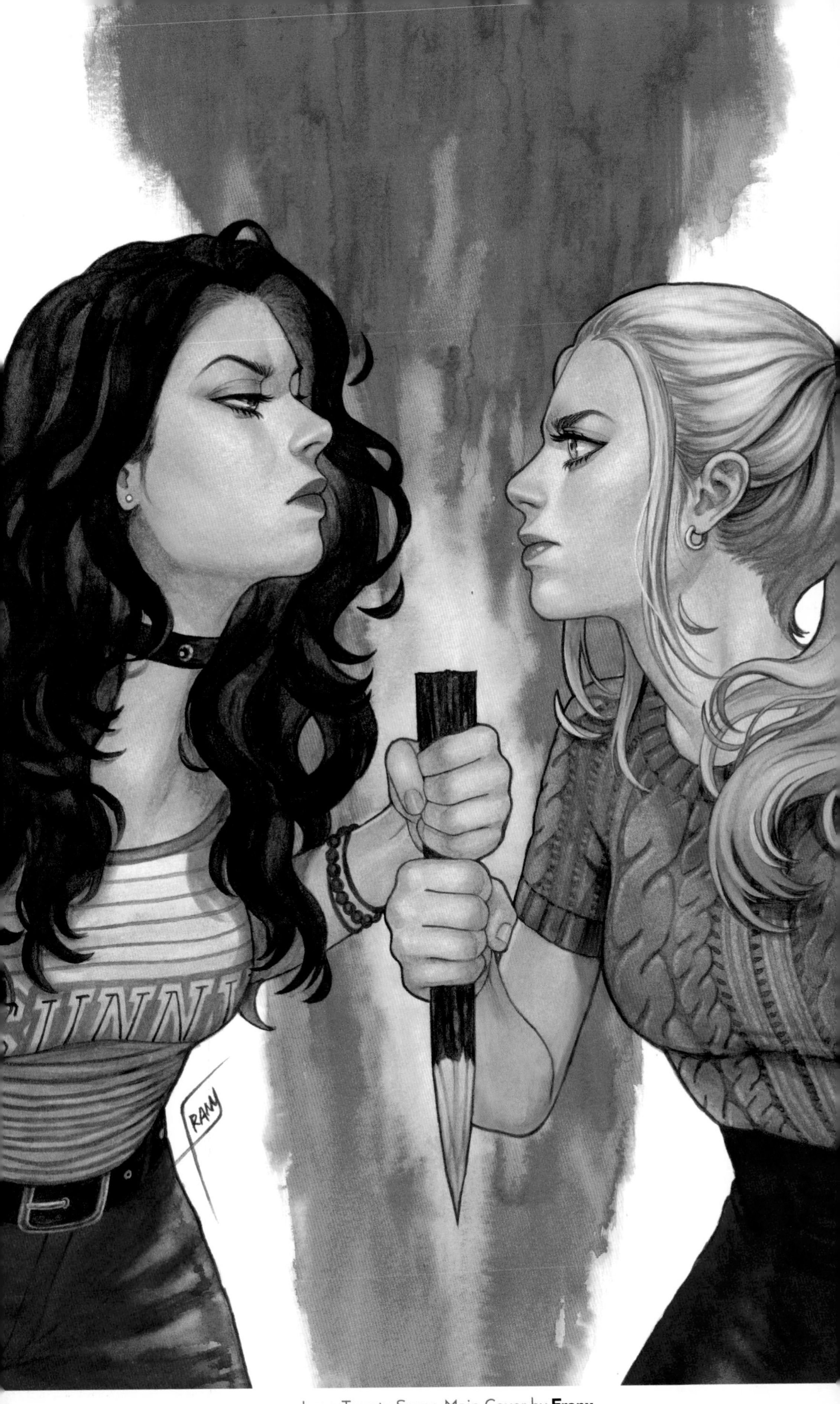

Issue Twenty Seven Main Cover by **Frany**

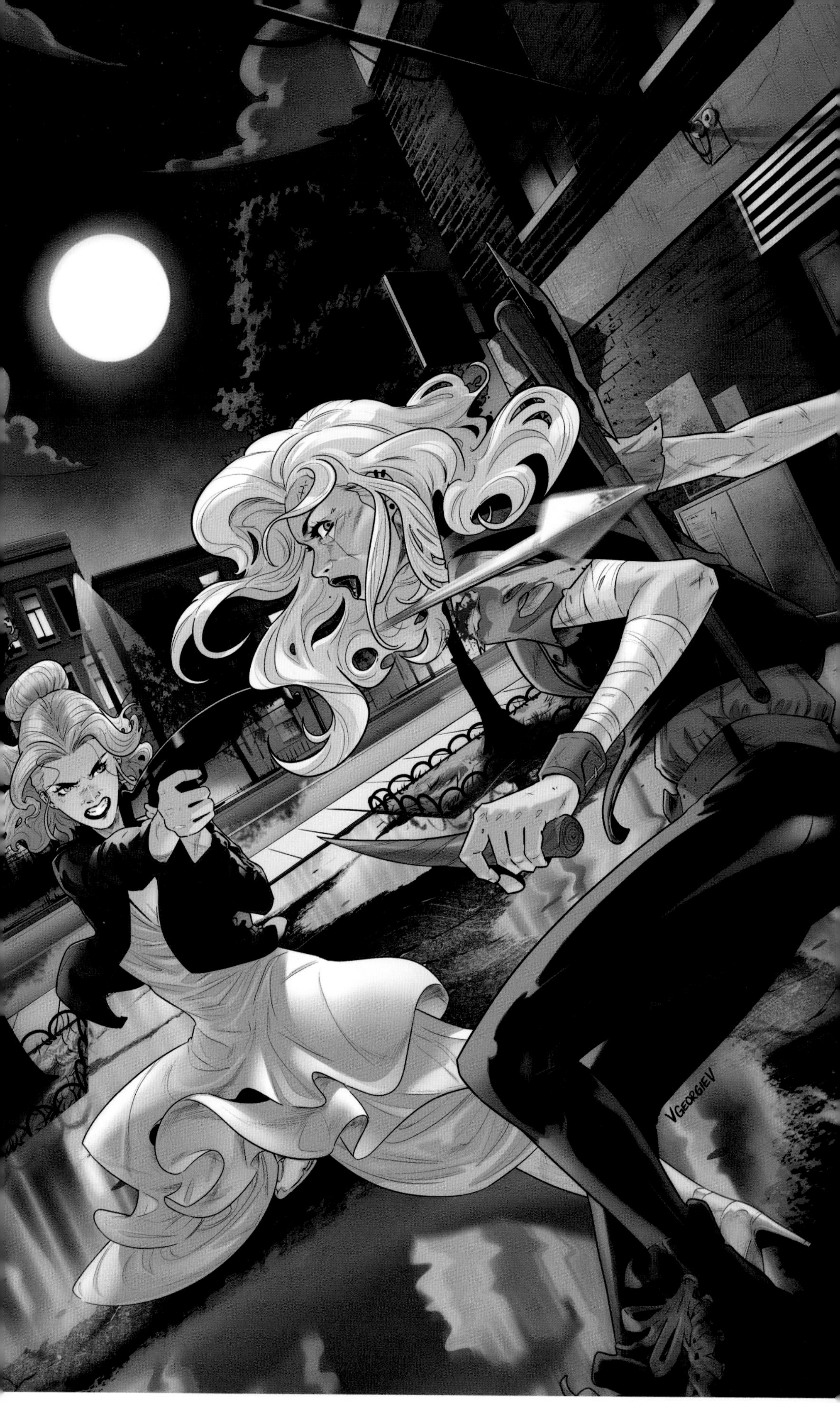
VGEORGIEV

Issue Twenty Seven Multiversus Cover by **Vasco Georgiev**

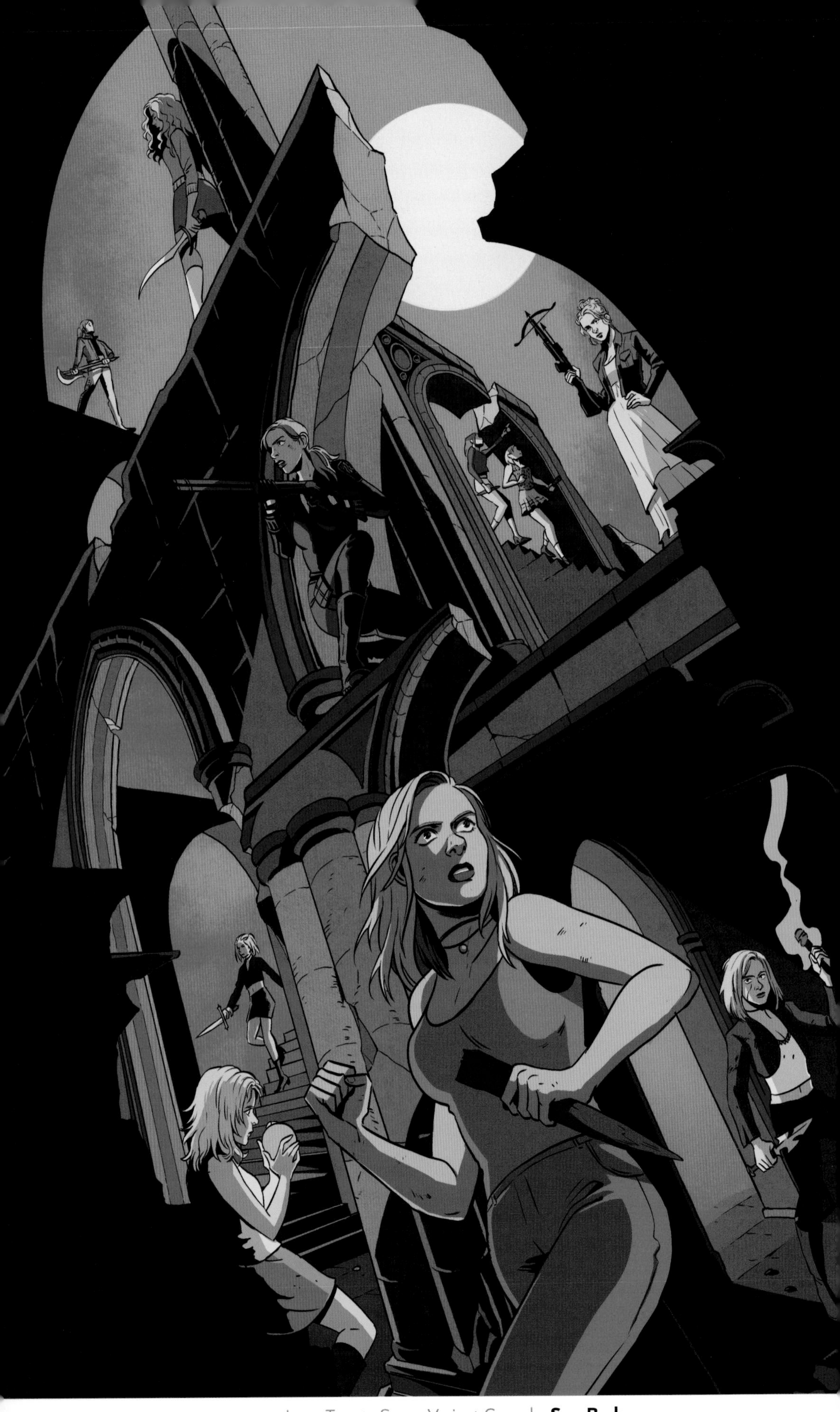

Issue Twenty Seven Variant Cover by **Sam Beck**

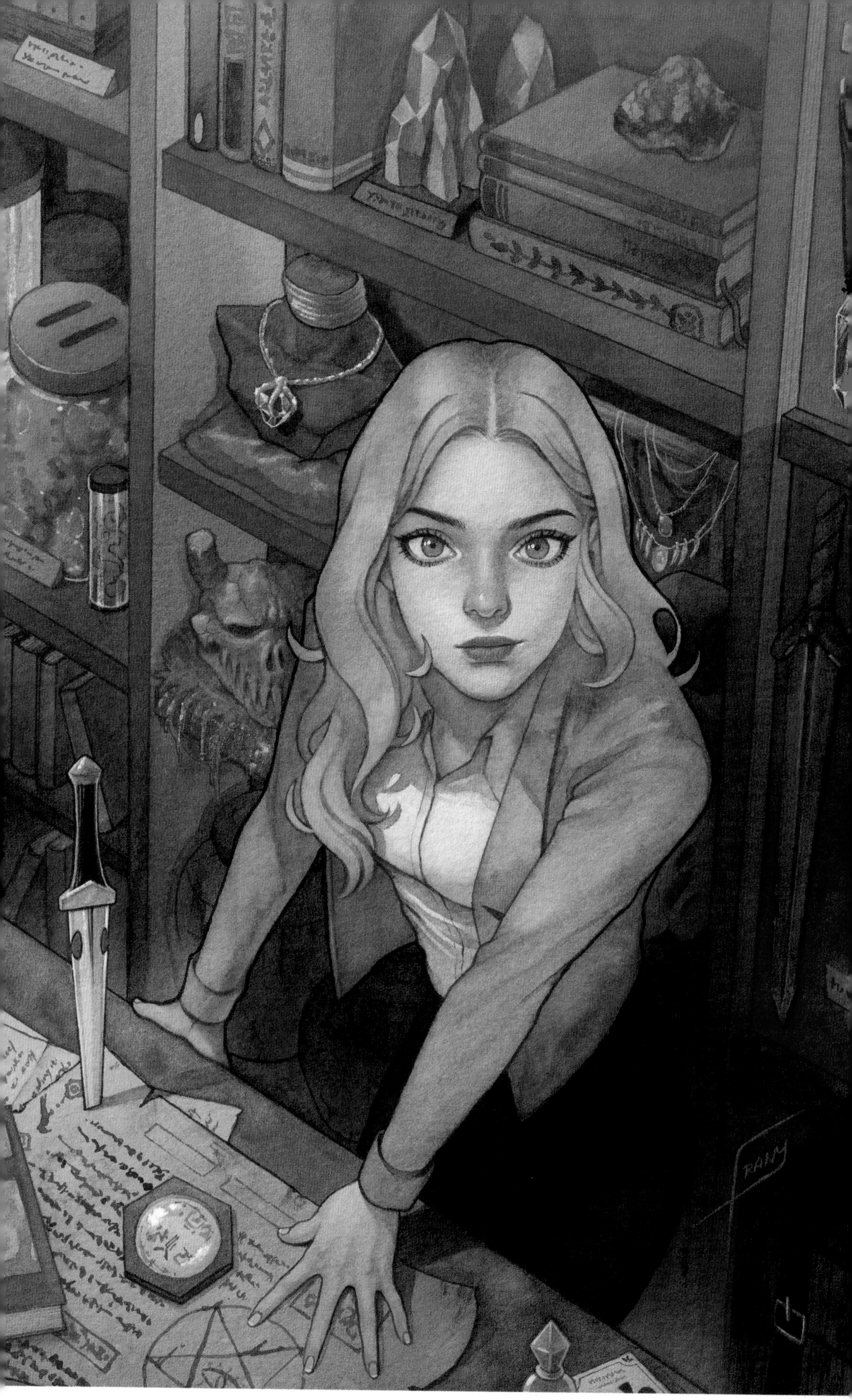
FRANY

Issue Twenty Eight Main Cover by **Frany**

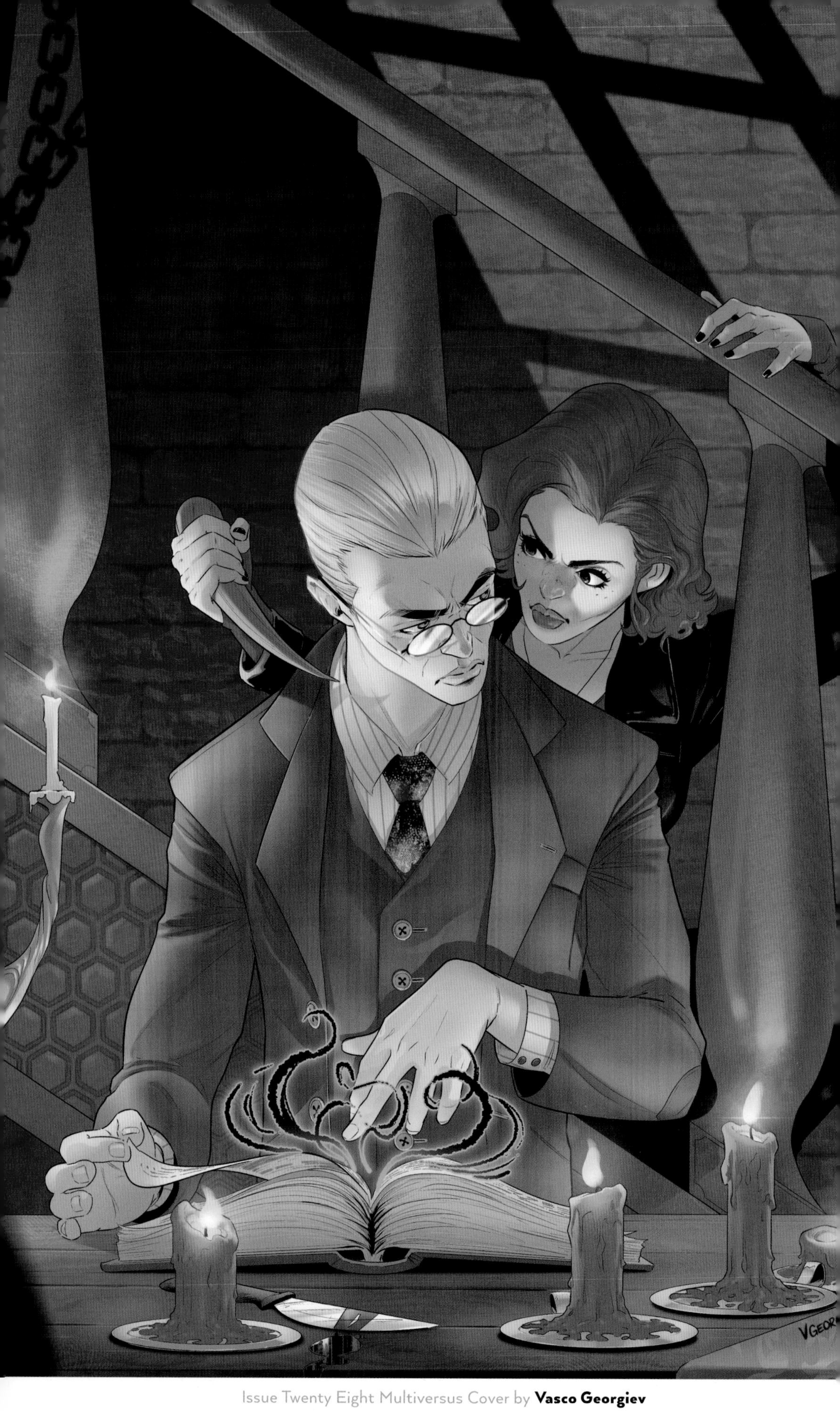

Issue Twenty Eight Multiversus Cover by **Vasco Georgiev**

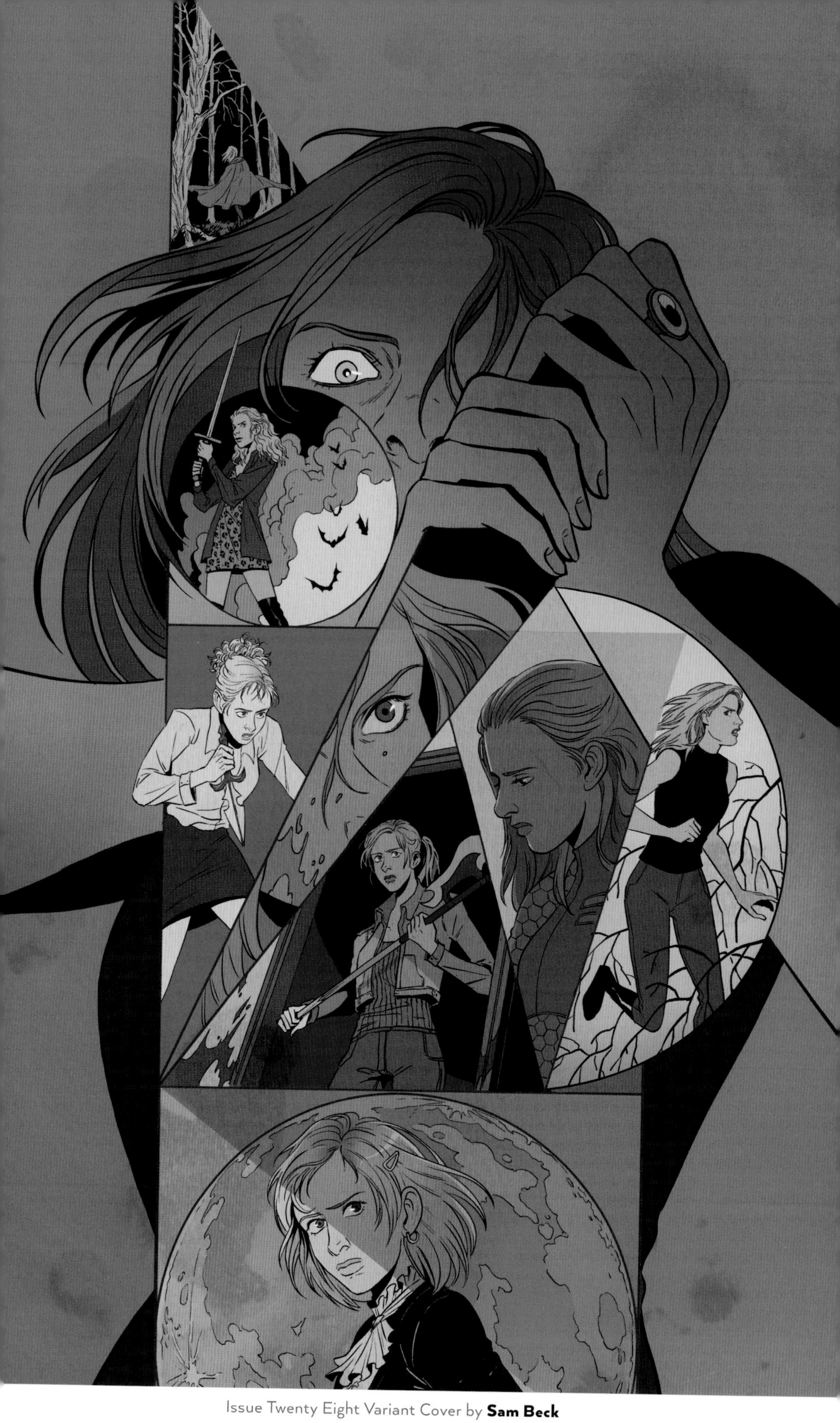

Issue Twenty Eight Variant Cover by **Sam Beck**

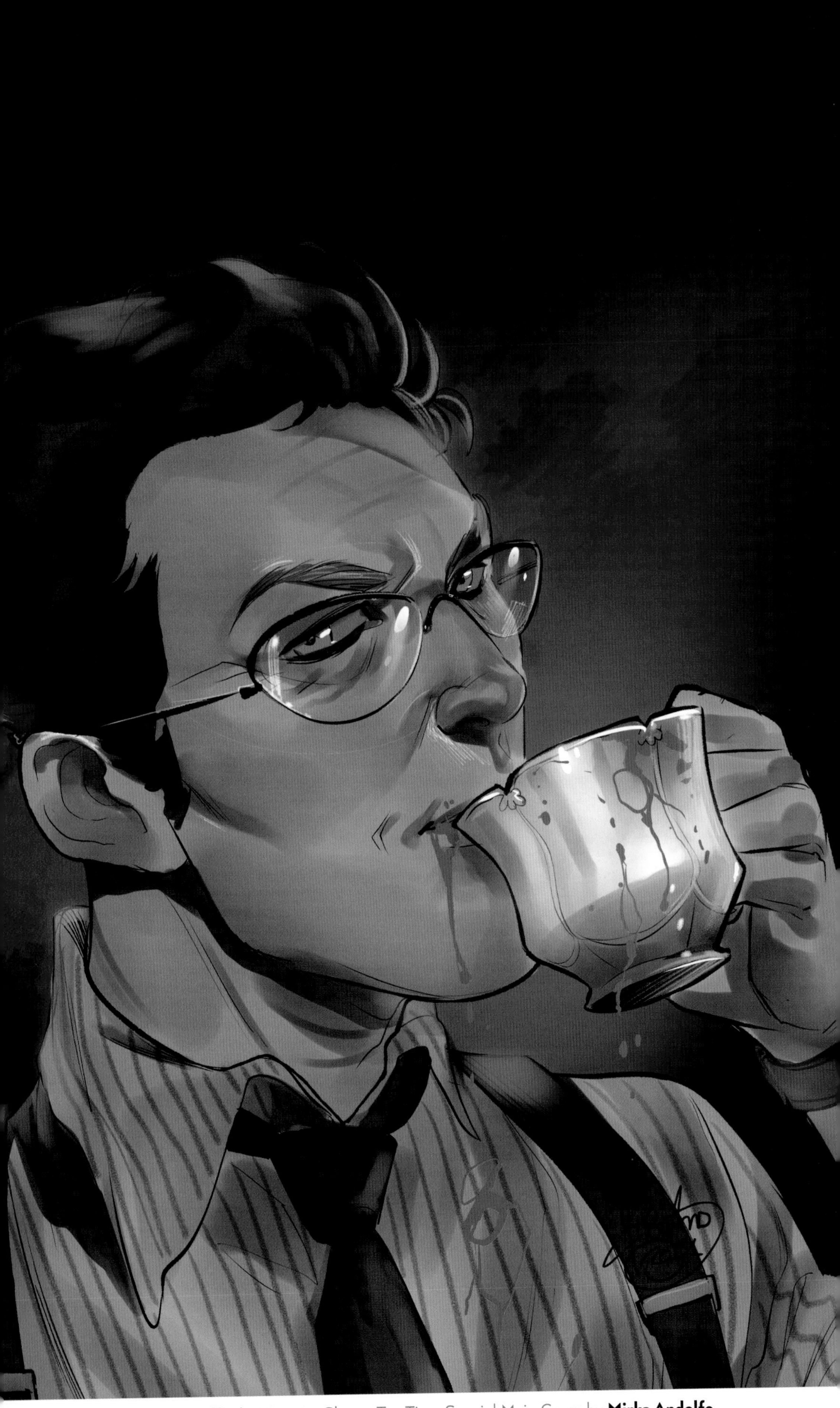

Buffy the Vampire Slayer: Tea Time Special Main Cover by **Mirka Andolfo**

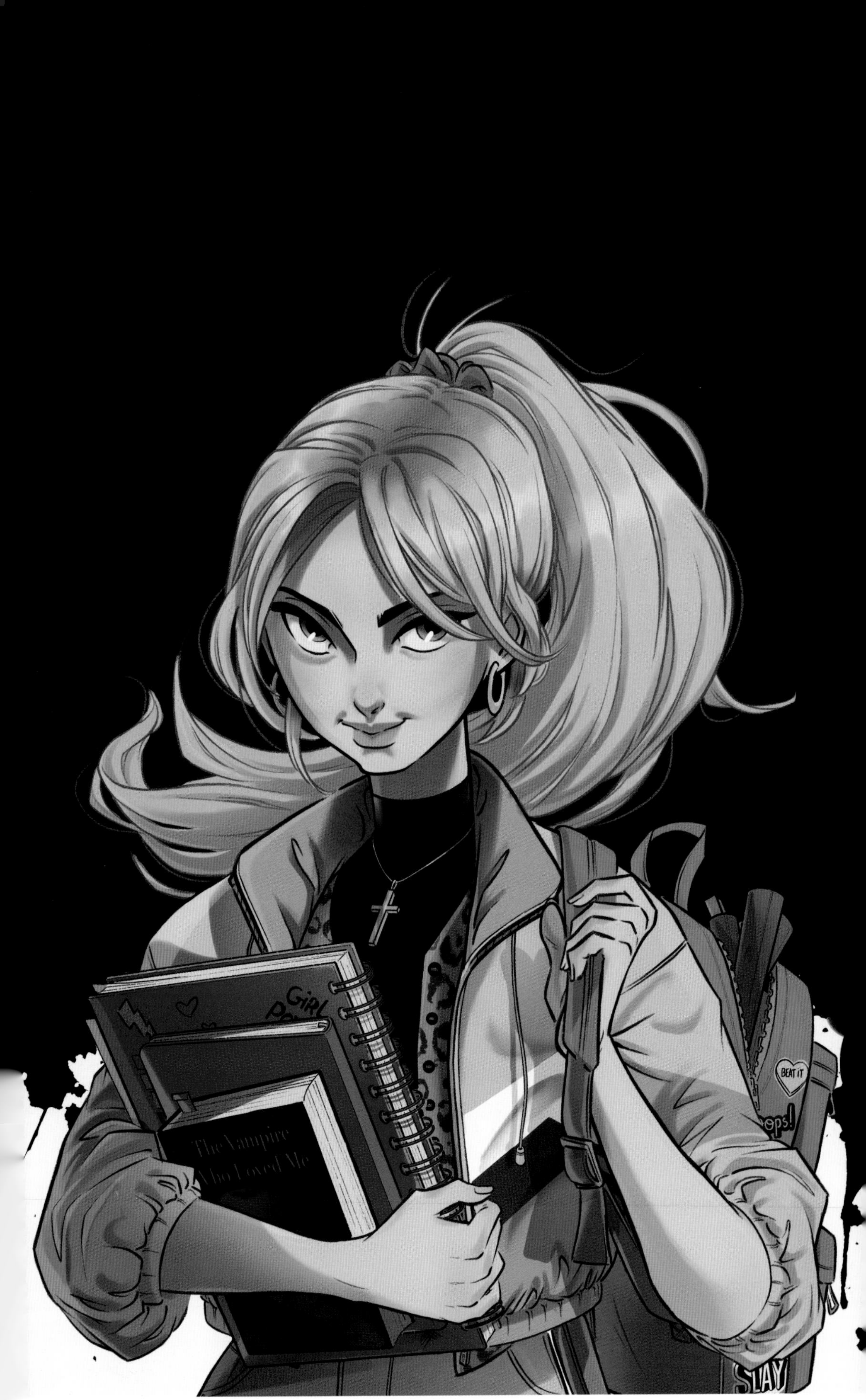
GIRL
The Vampire
Who Loved Me
BEAT IT
SLAY

Buffy the Vampire Slayer: Tea Time Special Variant Cover by **Sweeney Boo**

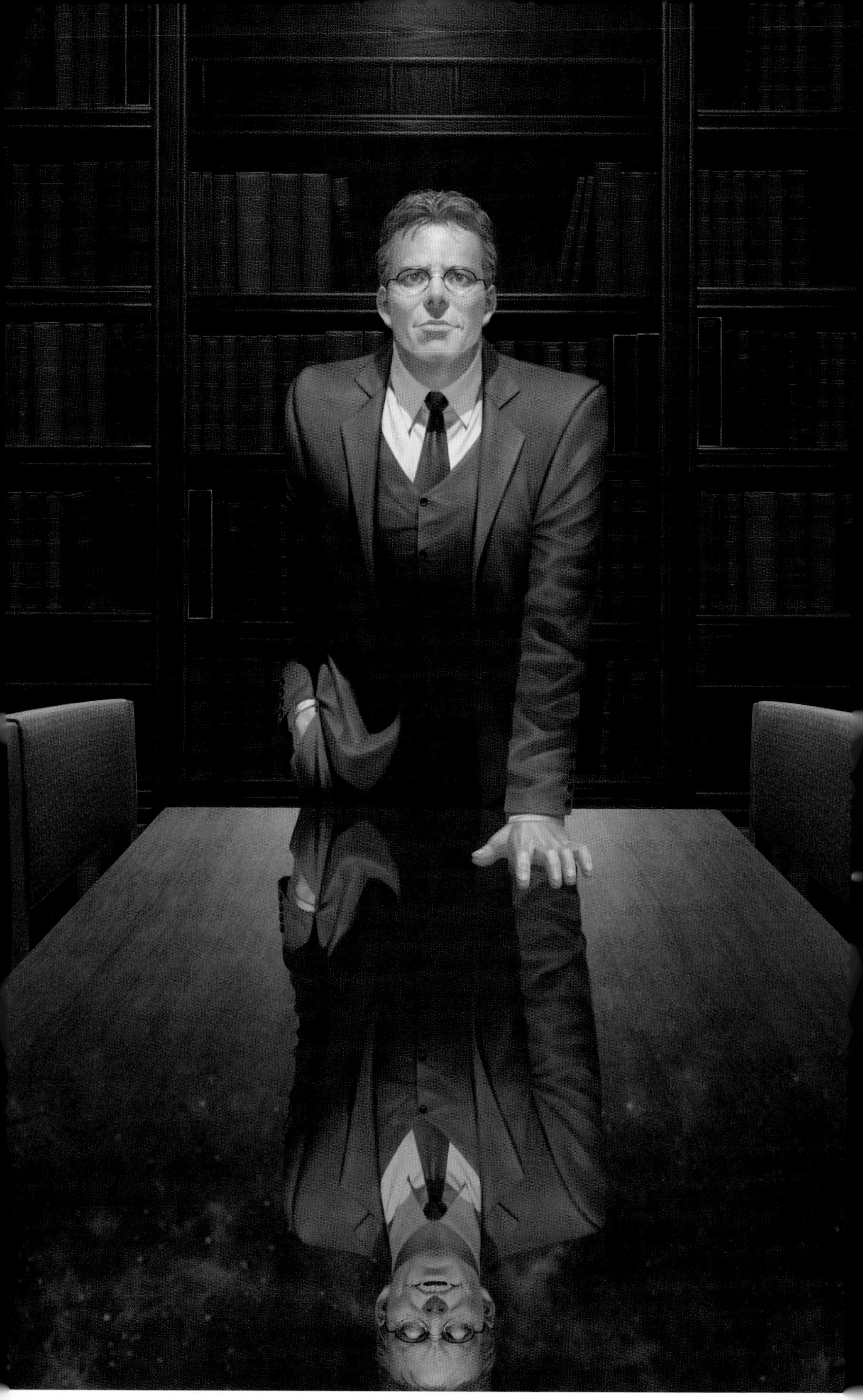

Buffy the Vampire Slayer: Tea Time Special Variant Cover by **Junggeun Yoon**

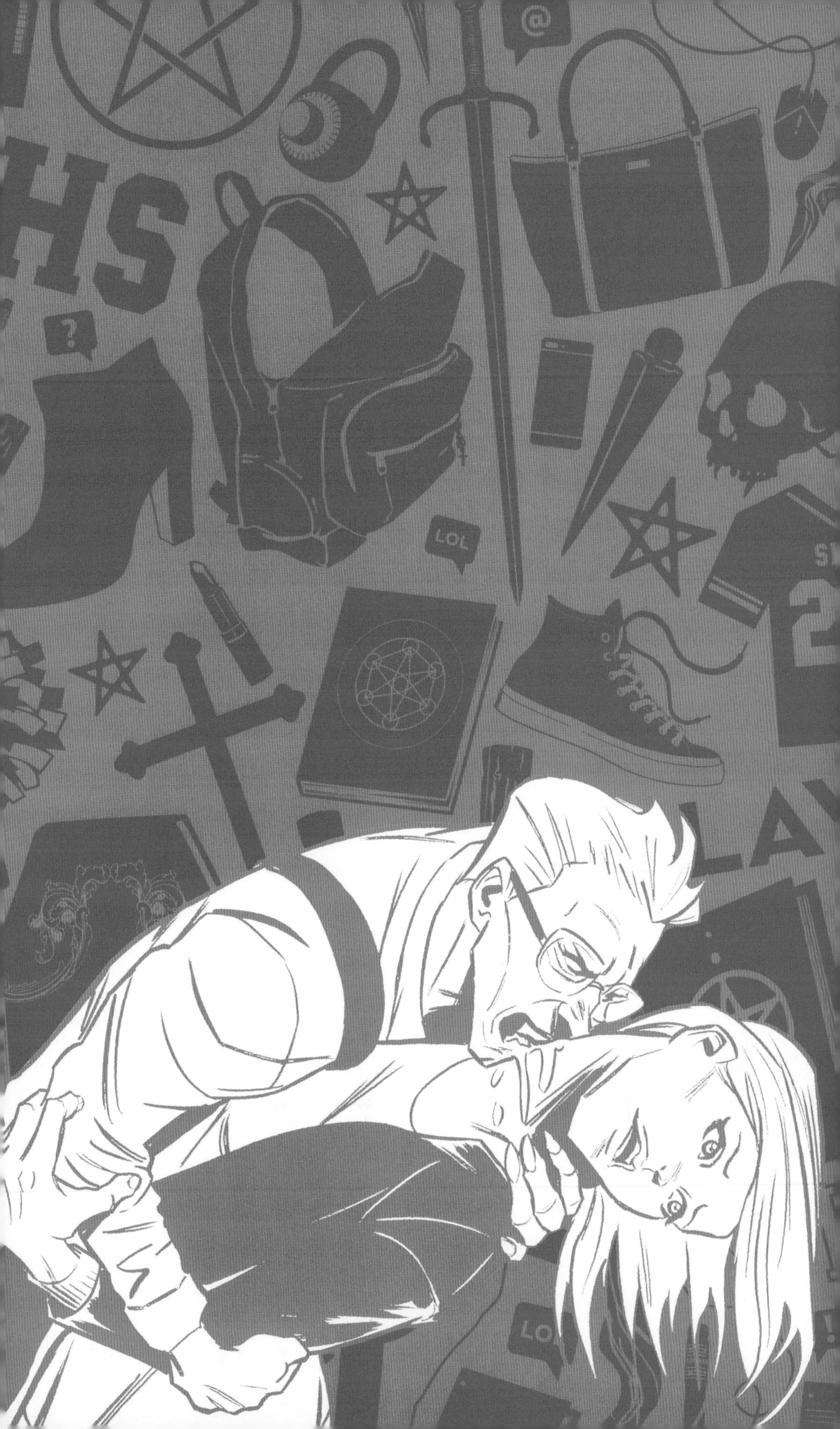
LOL
LOL

NEXT ON BUFFY

BUFFY #29

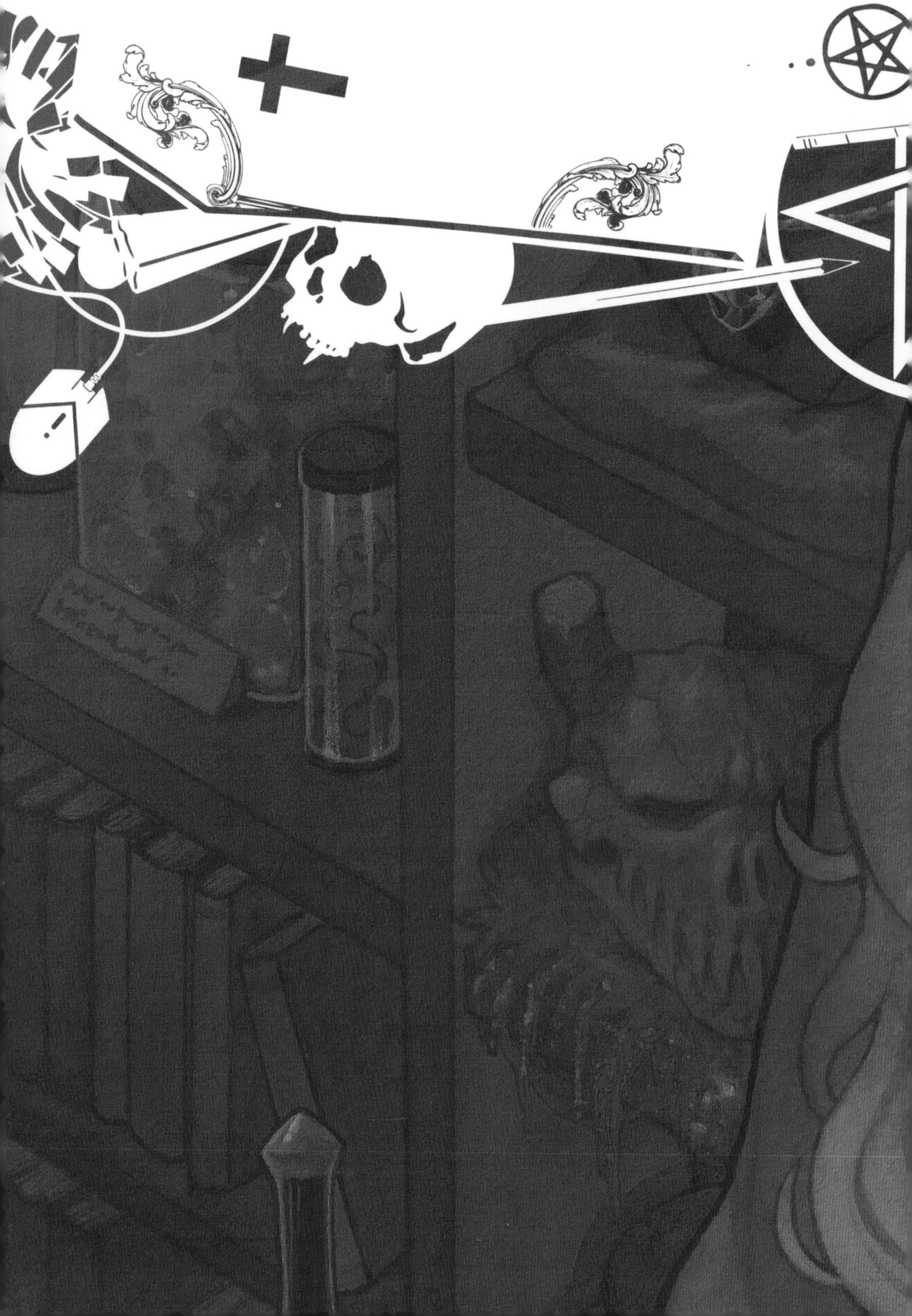

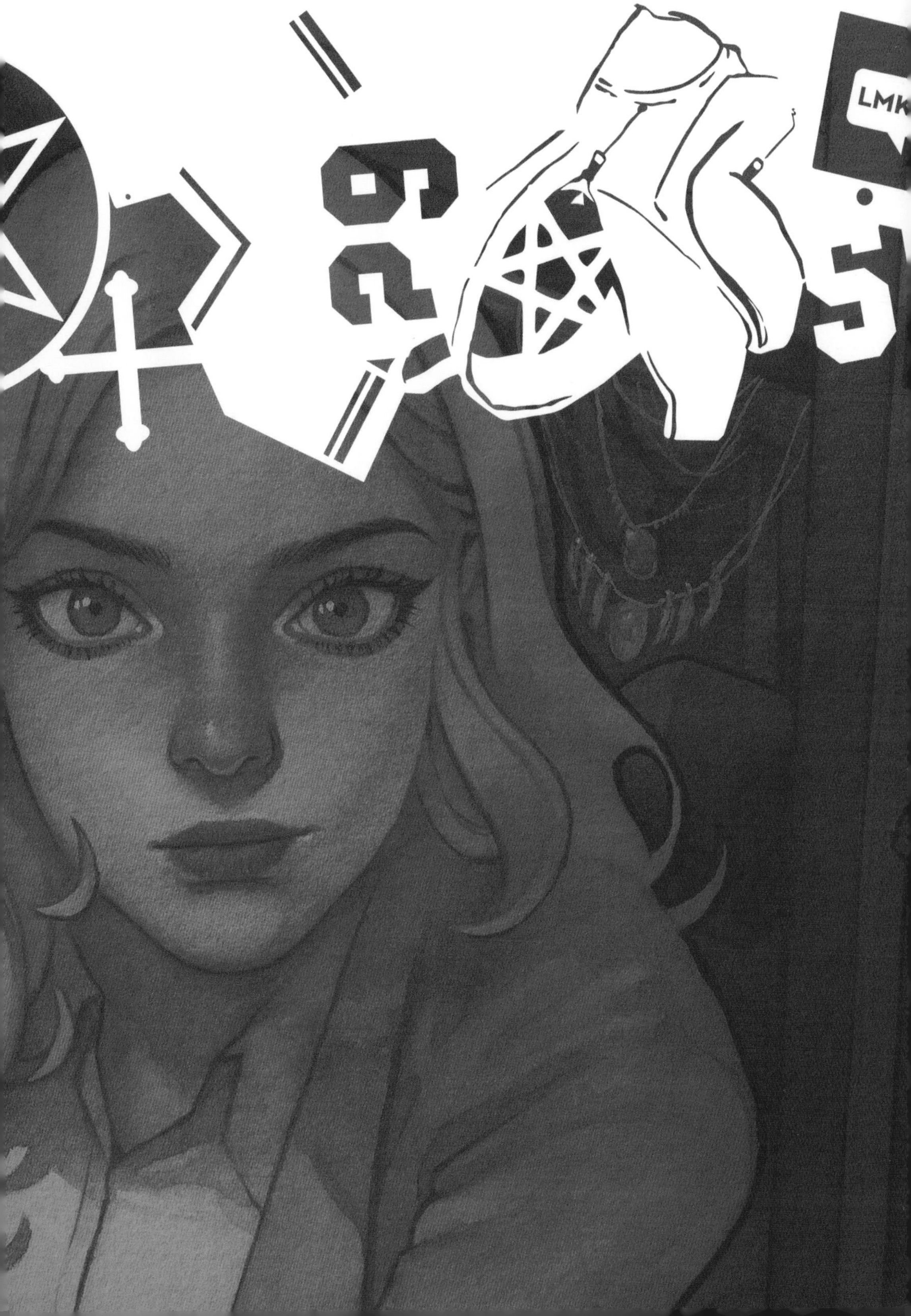
LMK

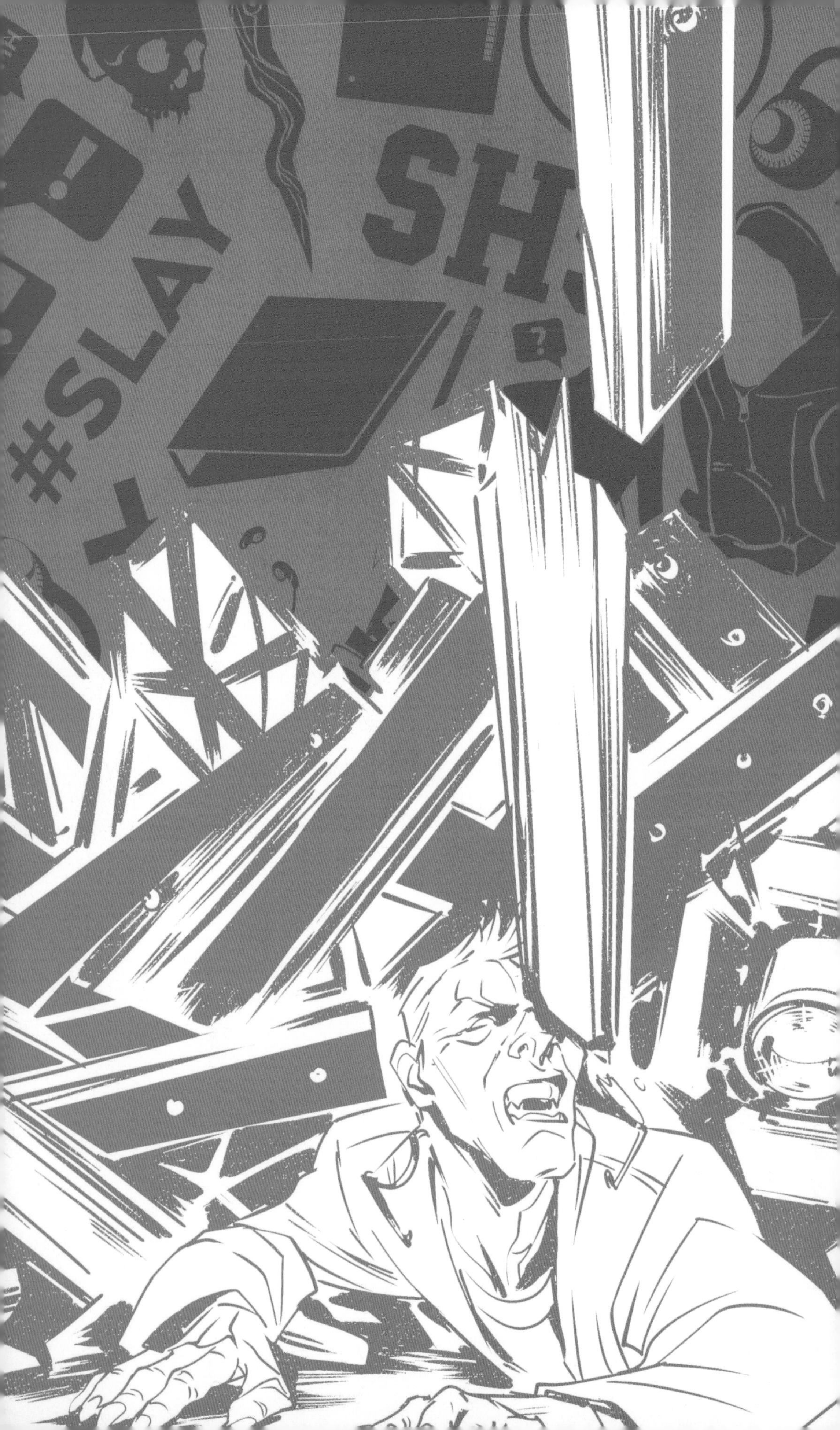
#SLAY

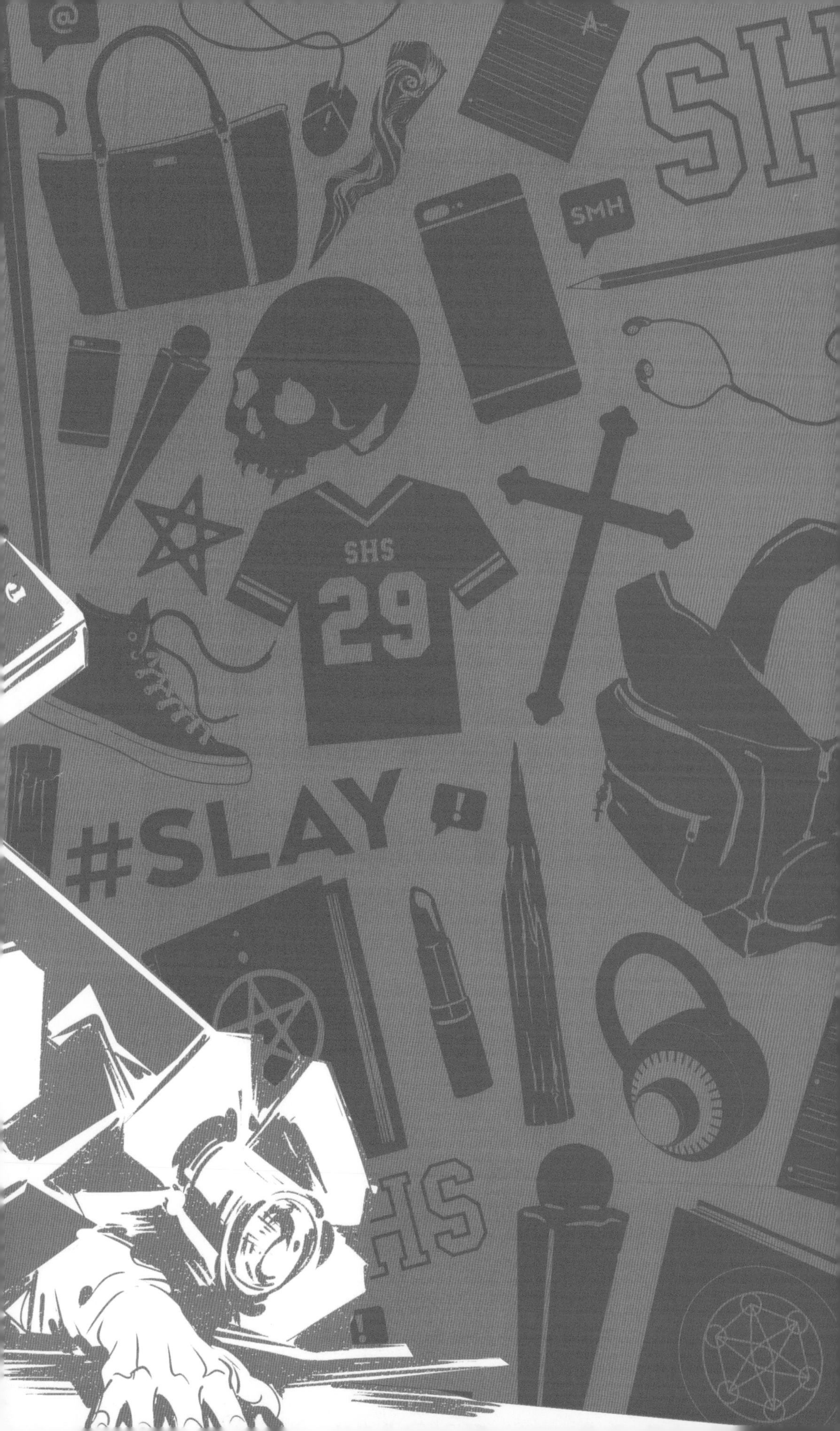
SMH
SHS
29
#SLAY
SHS

DISCOVER
VISIONARY CREATORS

Once & Future
Kieron Gillen, Dan Mora
Volume 1
ISBN: 978-1-68415-491-3 | $16.99 US

Something is Killing the Children
James Tynion IV, Werther Dell'Edera
Volume 1
ISBN: 978-1-68415-558-3 | $14.99 US

Faithless
Brian Azzarello, Maria Llovet
ISBN: 978-1-68415-432-6 | $17.99 US

Klaus
Grant Morrison, Dan Mora
Klaus: How Santa Claus Began SC
ISBN: 978-1-68415-393-0 | $15.99 US
Klaus: The New Adventures of Santa Claus HC
ISBN: 978-1-68415-666-5 | $17.99 US

Coda
Simon Spurrier, Matias Bergara
Volume 1
ISBN: 978-1-68415-321-3 | $14.99 US
Volume 2
ISBN: 978-1-68415-369-5 | $14.99 US
Volume 3
ISBN: 978-1-68415-429-6 | $14.99 US

Grass Kings
Matt Kindt, Tyler Jenkins
Volume 1
ISBN: 978-1-64144-362-3 | $17.99 US
Volume 2
ISBN: 978-1-64144-557-3 | $17.99 US
Volume 3
ISBN: 978-1-64144-650-1 | $17.99 US

Bone Parish
Cullen Bunn, Jonas Scharf
Volume 1
ISBN: 978-1-64144-337-1 | $14.99 US
Volume 2
ISBN: 978-1-64144-542-9 | $14.99 US
Volume 3
ISBN: 978-1-64144-543-6 | $14.99 US

Ronin Island
Greg Pak, Giannis Milonogiannis
Volume 1
ISBN: 978-1-64144-576-4 | $14.99 US
Volume 2
ISBN: 978-1-64144-723-2 | $14.99 US
Volume 3
ISBN: 978-1-64668-035-1 | $14.99 US

Victor LaValle's Destroyer
Victor LaValle, Dietrich Smith
ISBN: 978-1-61398-732-2 | $19.99 US